The Baby Boom Generation and the Economy

Studies in Social Economics

TITLES PUBLISHED

STUDIES IN SOCIAL ECONOMICS

Louise B. Russell

The Baby Boom Generation and the Economy

THE BROOKINGS INSTITUTION
Washington, D.C.

Library of Congress Cataloging in Publication Data:
Russell, Louise B.
    The baby boom generation and the economy.
    (Studies in social economics)
    Includes index.
    1. United States—Population—Economic
aspects.   2. Fertility, Human—Economic aspects
—United States.   3. Age distribution
(Demography)—Economic aspects—United States.
4. United States—Economic conditions—1945–
I. Title.
HB3505.R87   1982   330.973′092   82-70890
ISBN 0-8157-7628-4
ISBN 0-8157-7627-6 (pbk.)

9 8 7 6 5 4 3 2 1

THE BROOKINGS INSTITUTION is an independent organization devoted to nonpartisan research, education, and publication in economics, government, foreign policy, and the social sciences generally. Its principal purposes are to aid in the development of sound public policies and to promote public understanding of issues of national importance.

The Institution was founded on December 8, 1927, to merge the activities of the Institute for Government Research, founded in 1916, the Institute of Economics, founded in 1922, and the Robert Brookings Graduate School of Economics and Government, founded in 1924.

The Board of Trustees is responsible for the general administration of the Institution, while the immediate direction of the policies, program, and staff is vested in the President, assisted by an advisory committee of the officers and staff. The by-laws of the Institution state: "It is the function of the Trustees to make possible the conduct of scientific research, and publication, under the most favorable conditions, and to safeguard the independence of the research staff in the pursuit of their studies and in the publication of the results of such studies. It is not a part of their function to determine, control, or influence the conduct of particular investigations or the conclusions reached."

The President bears final responsibility for the decision to publish a manuscript as a Brookings book. In reaching his judgment on the competence, accuracy, and objectivity of each study, the President is advised by the director of the appropriate research program and weighs the views of a panel of expert outside readers who report to him in confidence on the quality of the work. Publication of a work signifies that it is deemed a competent treatment worthy of public consideration but does not imply endorsement of conclusions or recommendations.

The Institution maintains its position of neutrality on issues of public policy in order to safeguard the intellectual freedom of the staff. Hence interpretations or conclusions in Brookings publications should be understood to be solely those of the authors and should not be attributed to the Institution, to its trustees, officers, or other staff members, or to the organizations that support its research.

Foreword

Probably no one born during the baby boom that extended from just after World War II to the early 1960s is unaware of belonging to a special generation. Many parents and teachers remember the challenge of educating what was to be the brightest and best-educated generation ever—and what was certainly the largest. That shining promise did not last into the 1970s. Indeed, as economic difficulties persisted through the decade, some observers suggested that the baby boom generation was in large part to blame, arguing that as its members crowded into the labor and housing markets, they pushed unemployment up, slowed the growth in real wages, and sent house prices spiraling.

This study examines the economic record, from the educational system to the labor market, the housing market, and the social security system, to determine whether the baby boom generation has been a major driving force behind the economy. The author concludes that it has not been. In some areas—saving, for example—the generation appears to have had little or no effect. In others, such as housing, careful investigation shows that the baby boom generation has been only one of several forces tending in the same direction, and that it has not dominated the outcome. Thus the existence of the baby boom generation tells us very little about the future course of the economy. By the same token, it is clear that the generation does not create its own bad times wherever it goes. The nation's economic problems largely stem from other causes.

The author is grateful to Michael S. McPherson, Alicia H. Munnell, Harvey S. Rosen, and Walter S. Salant, who read the entire manuscript and provided detailed comments. Comments on parts of the manuscript were provided by Henry J. Aaron, David W. Breneman, Edward F. Denison, Anthony Downs, Paul O. Flaim, Richard Goode, Clifford S. Russell, and Wayne Vroman. Ørjar Øyen and V. Jeffery Evans offered helpful suggestions in conversations with the author.

Richard J. Rosen provided the major part of the research assistance for the study, including programming the calculations for the lifetime rates of return under social security reported in chapter 6. J. Elizabeth Callison, Matthew Gelfand, Amy Raths, and Julie A. Carr also assisted with parts of the study. Christine C. de Fontenay and Eric V. Armen programmed the tabulation of homeownership rates by age for 1976 and 1980, presented in chapter 5. Charlotte Kaiser typed the manuscript. Caroline Lalire edited the manuscript for publication, and Ellen W. Smith verified its factual content. Diana Regenthal prepared the index.

The study relied heavily on data from many federal statistical agencies, and members of their staffs tracked down and explained a wide range of statistics. It is impossible to list all the individuals who helped, but the study could not have been done without the services of the Census Bureau, the Bureau of Labor Statistics, the National Center for Education Statistics, the National Center for Health Statistics, and the Social Security Administration.

The study was financed by a grant from the National Institute of Child Health and Human Development, Department of Health and Human Services. The views expressed are the author's alone and should not be ascribed to the officers, trustees, or other staff members of the Brookings Institution, to the National Institute, or to any of those who were consulted or who commented on the manuscript.

BRUCE K. MACLAURY
President

Washington, D.C.
July 1982

Contents

Contents

Appendix Table

Figures

chapter one Introduction

The postwar baby boom has been blamed for many of the economy's troubles during the 1970s, the decade when the older members of the generation grew to adulthood and its youngest members to adolescence. Since young adults and teenagers have higher rates of unemployment than older adults, the huge numbers of young people contributed to a stubbornly high overall rate of unemployment. Since young adults leave their parents' households and set up their own, their large numbers could explain the buoyant housing market, and spiraling housing prices. An unprecedented effort was made to educate the baby boom generation during the 1950s, 1960s, and even the 1970s. And another unprecedented effort may be required to support them in old age. A few moments' thought about the possibilities is enough to show that the baby boom generation is a pervasive phenomenon, and quite possibly a major influence on its own and the economy's fortunes.

The purpose of this book is to examine the importance of the baby boom generation for the economy. This large generation represents a discontinuity in the age structure of the population, one unique in the history of the United States. Whatever its effects, they are here now and will continue to shape events for the next fifty or sixty years at least. It is thus of immediate and continuing interest to know what those effects are and how important they are. The book will try to identify them, weigh the strength of the evidence for and against them, and, whenever possible, quantify them.

The baby boom generation encompasses the people born in the years 1946 through l964. During World War II the annual number of births was already above the low point reached in the Great Depression, but after the war, in 1946 and again in 1947, it hit new peaks—3.4 million and 3.8 million, respectively (figure 1-1). The number fell back slightly in the late 1940s and then began to rise during the 1950s. Between 1956 and

1

Figure 1-1. Live Births in the United States, 1909–80[a]

Millions

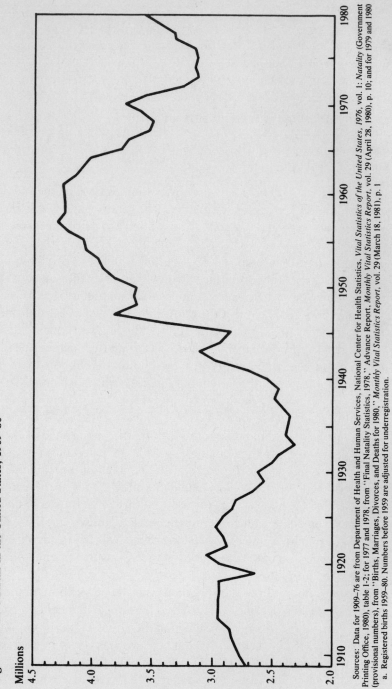

Sources: Data for 1909–76 are from Department of Health and Human Services, National Center for Health Statistics, *Vital Statistics of the United States, 1976*, vol. 1: *Natality* (Government Printing Office, 1980), table 1-2; for 1977 and 1978, from "Final Natality Statistics, 1978," *Advance Report, Monthly Vital Statistics Report*, vol. 29 (April 28, 1980), p. 10; and for 1979 and 1980 (provisional numbers), from "Births, Marriages, Divorces, and Deaths for 1980," *Monthly Vital Statistics Report*, vol. 29 (March 18, 1981), p. 1

a. Registered births 1959–80. Numbers before 1959 are adjusted for underregistration.

1961 more than 4.2 million babies were born every year. Thereafter births declined, but did not fall below 4 million until 1965. As they declined further and then remained low during the rest of the 1960s and the 1970s, the baby boom generation was conclusively defined—a large generation preceded and followed by smaller generations.

This study investigates the potential effects of the baby boom generation over its entire life span. It is impossible to examine every facet of the economy that might be influenced, but most of the more obvious possibilities are considered. Chapter 2 begins by describing the baby boom and the trends in marriage and birth rates that produced it. Chapter 3 turns to its experience in the schools, chapter 4 to its experience in the job market. Chapter 5 examines consumption patterns, including the housing market, and chapter 6 speculates about future effects on medical care and the social security system when the generation grows old.

The study thus looks for a series of consequences that develop in chronological order. If the baby boom generation is important to the economy, it is likely to be important throughout its lifetime, not just at one or two points. The search for a sequence of effects is particularly valuable because the baby boom is only one large generation, even though it spans almost twenty years. It is difficult, sometimes impossible, to disentangle the effects of a single generation from the effects of other unique historical events occurring at the same time. But if a series of outcomes can be identified, each related to the baby boom generation, the case for its significance is strengthened.

In its simplest form, the idea that changes in age structure may have predictable, recognizable effects on economic activity depends on the fact that important differences in behavior are closely linked to age, and on the assumption that these differences are stable across generations. For example, the notion that the baby boom generation is the major force behind the housing market of the 1970s rests on the knowledge that people first establish separate households when they are young adults, and on the assumption that today's young adults are leaving their parents, marrying, and buying houses on schedules much like those of yesterday's adults. A variant of this idea, associated with Richard Easterlin, states that patterns of behavior may differ across generations, but that the differences can be explained in large part by age structure, so that they too are predictable.[1]

1. Richard A. Easterlin, *Birth and Fortune: The Impact of Numbers on Personal Welfare* (Basic Books, 1980).

The stability (or predictability) of age-related behavior is crucial. If the behavior of people at given ages changes—and the change is not itself a consequence of age structure—the effects of age structure may be swamped. Some effects may never appear, having been completely offset by unrelated changes in behavior. Others, attributed to age structure, may in fact be primarily due to changes in behavior that occurred at the same time and worked in the same direction.

Thus a study of the economic effects of the baby boom generation must consider the stability of the behavior through which the effects operate. The succeeding chapters stress this point repeatedly. Age-related behavior has changed rapidly since World War II, and often these changes have been as important as age structure, or even more important, although their joint consequences have sometimes been attributed to age structure alone.

As a natural by-product, the investigation of behavior shows the experience of the baby boom generation—school attendance and educational attainment, employment and unemployment, patterns of household formation, and so on—and compares it with the experience of earlier generations. This history stands on its own as a record of the baby boom's formative years. And as a comparative record, it establishes benchmarks that show how well or badly the generation has fared, quite apart from whether age structure has played a major part in events.

Three principal questions run through the study and are used to organize its conclusions in chapter 7:

1. Has the baby boom generation had a harder time economically than earlier generations? And a subtler, but related, issue: has it had a harder time than a smaller generation would have had in the same circumstances?

2. What effects has the baby boom generation had on the economy and how large are they?

3. How much can the age structure of the population help in predicting the future?

chapter two A Statistical Portrait

Two aspects of the age structure of the population help to indicate how the baby boom generation might affect the economy. The first is the changes over time in the numbers of people in each age group. As the number at a particular age grows or declines, institutions associated with that age must expand or contract, and may change character in the process. The second is the age structure at any particular moment, which is shown by the proportions of the population at different ages, or by a closely related concept, the ratios between the numbers in one age group and those in another. When these proportions are stable over long periods, as they are whenever the population is growing fairly smoothly, society becomes accustomed to operating with the same relative numbers of people at different, complementary stages of life—school age and working age, for example, or younger and older workers. When the proportions change a great deal, institutions may have to change.

In the early years of the century, growth was standard for every age group (table 2-1), and this had been true for many decades before 1900 as well.[1] The exact rates of change fluctuated considerably, but the direction was always up—each age group was larger at the next census than it had been at the previous one. This situation came to an end in 1930, when the number of children under 5 declined for the first time. The decline continued during the next decade; in 1940 there were even fewer children under 5 than in 1930.

1. The population includes immigrants, who were a more important component in the early years of the century than they are now, as well as native-born citizens. For example, between 1900 and 1909, more than 8 million people emigrated to the United States. The immigrants altered the age structure somewhat, since most of them, consistently more than 80 percent before 1915, were between 14 and 44. Bureau of the Census, *Historical Statistics of the United States: Colonial Times to 1957* (Government Printing Office, 1960), ser. C 133–38, p. 62.

Table 2-1. Population by Age, Selected Years, 1900–2000[a]

Thousands

Age group	1900	1910	1920	1930	1940	1950	1960	1970	1980	1990	2000
Under 5	9,171	10,631	11,573	11,444	10,542	16,164	20,321	17,154	16,344	...	...
5–9	8,874	9,761	11,398	12,608	10,685	13,200	18,692	19,956	16,697	...	...
10–14	8,080	9,107	10,641	12,005	11,746	11,119	16,773	20,789	18,241	...	...
15–19	7,556	9,064	9,431	11,552	12,334	10,617	13,219	19,070	21,162	16,777	...
20–24	7,335	9,057	9,277	10,870	11,588	11,482	10,801	16,371	21,313	17,953	...
25–29	6,529	8,180	9,086	9,834	11,097	12,242	10,869	13,477	19,518	20,169	16,469
30–34	5,556	6,972	8,071	9,120	10,242	11,517	11,949	11,430	17,558	20,917	17,981
35–39	4,965	6,396	7,775	9,209	9,545	11,246	12,481	11,107	13,963	19,261	20,435
40–44	4,247	5,262	6,346	7,990	8,788	10,204	11,600	11,981	11,668	17,331	20,909
45–49	3,455	4,469	5,764	7,042	8,255	9,070	10,879	12,116	11,088	13,889	18,990
50–54	2,943	3,901	4,735	5,976	7,257	8,272	9,606	11,104	11,709	11,442	16,885
55–59	2,211	2,787	3,549	4,646	5,844	7,235	8,430	9,973	11,614	10,416	13,106
60–64	1,791	2,267	2,983	3,751	4,728	6,059	7,142	8,617	10,086	10,360	10,151
65 and over	3,080	3,950	4,933	6,634	9,019	12,270	16,560	20,066	25,544	29,824	31,822
Total	75,995	91,972	105,711	122,775	131,669	150,697	179,323	203,212	226,505	...	...

Sources: Data for 1900–70 are from Bureau of the Census, *Historical Statistics of the United States: Colonial Times to 1970* (Government Printing Office, 1975), pt. 1, ser. A 119–34, p. 15: for 1980, from Bureau of the Census, *Census of Population, 1980*, Supplementary Report PC80-S1-1, "Age, Sex, Race, and Spanish Origin of the Population by Regions, Divisions, and States: 1980" (GPO, 1981), p. 3; and for 1990–2000, from Bureau of the Census, *Current Population Reports*, series P-25, no. 704, "Projections of the Population of the United States: 1977 to 2050" (GPO, 1977), pp. 50, 60. The projections assume 2.1 births per woman over her lifetime.

a. Data for 1900–80 are most likely resident population. Projections for 1990–2000, made several years before the 1980 census, are for total population. Only projections for age groups whose members were already born in 1975 have been included in the table.

The table shows the rapid rates of growth as births turned up after the middle 1930s. Even before the baby boom officially began in 1946 there were substantial gains. The number of 5- through 9-year-olds grew 24 percent between 1940 and 1950; children in this age group in 1950 were born during World War II. The first wave of the baby boom proper shows up in the huge increase—53 percent—in the under-5 group between 1940 and 1950. The continuation of the baby boom appears as a further increase in the two youngest age groups: in 1960 the number of children aged 5 through 9 was 42 percent greater than in 1950, and the number under 5 was 26 percent greater. With the decline in births during the 1960s, the number of children under 5 was down in 1970, and down again in 1980.

This roller-coaster pattern will mark the population for years to come. The new pattern not only shows frequent reversals of direction—decline followed by growth followed by decline again—but also involves rates of change that are often considerably larger than those in earlier years. Compare, for example, the growth in the under-5 group between 1940 and 1950, or 1950 and 1960, with the growth in this group early in the century.

As the baby boom generation ages, the pattern will appear in increasingly older age groups. Table 2-1 includes projections through the year 2000 for those age groups whose members had been born by 1975, and whose future numbers can therefore be predicted fairly reliably. With the help of the projections it is possible to follow the course of the baby boom generation through the end of the century, when its oldest members will be over 50. In 2000 the age groups 55 through 59 and 50 through 54 show the effects of the war babies and the first wave of the baby boom, swelling 26 percent and 48 percent, respectively, over the numbers in 1990. Between 1980 and 1990 these same age groups decline as the small cohorts of the 1920s and the 1930s move into them.

The new pattern points to a more difficult series of adjustments than the old one. Constant growth means that the direction of adjustment is always the same and mistakes are temporary. New resources may be brought in too early if the size of the change is misjudged, but they will eventually prove useful. The more recent up-and-down pattern means that even if the future is forecast perfectly, there is no way to avoid having too many or too few resources in a particular institutional form, say schools, at least some of the time. It takes too long to train new teachers, and school buildings do not fall apart fast enough. The more

Table 2-2. Percent Distribution of Population by Age, Selected Years, 1900-80ᵃ

Age group	1900	1910	1920	1930	1940	1950	1960	1970	1980
Under 5	12.1	11.6	11.0	9.3	8.0	10.7	11.3	8.4	7.2
5–9	11.7	10.6	10.8	10.3	8.1	8.8	10.4	9.8	7.4
10–14	10.6	9.9	10.1	9.8	8.9	7.4	9.4	10.2	8.1
15–19	9.9	9.9	8.9	9.4	9.4	7.1	7.4	9.4	9.3
20–24	9.7	9.9	8.8	8.9	8.8	7.6	6.0	8.1	9.4
25–29	8.6	8.9	8.6	8.0	8.4	8.1	6.1	6.6	8.6
30–34	7.3	7.6	7.6	7.4	7.8	7.6	6.7	5.6	7.8
35–39	6.5	6.7	7.4	7.5	7.3	7.5	7.0	5.5	6.2
40–44	5.6	5.7	6.0	6.5	6.7	6.8	6.5	5.9	5.2
45–49	4.6	4.9	5.5	5.7	6.3	6.0	6.1	6.0	4.9
50–54	3.9	4.2	4.5	4.9	5.5	5.5	5.4	5.5	5.2
55–59	2.9	3.0	3.4	3.8	4.4	4.8	4.7	4.9	5.1
60–64	2.4	2.5	2.8	3.1	3.6	4.0	4.0	4.2	4.5
65 and over	4.1	4.3	4.7	5.4	6.9	8.1	9.2	9.9	11.3
Total	100.0	100.0	100.0	100.0	100.0	100.0	100.0	100.0	100.0
5–14	22.3	20.5	20.9	20.1	17.0	16.1	19.8	20.1	15.4
25–59	39.3	41.3	42.9	43.8	46.3	46.3	42.3	40.0	42.9
50 and over	13.2	14.0	15.3	17.1	20.4	22.5	23.3	24.5	26.0

Source: Table 2-1. Figures are rounded.
a. See note a, table 2-1.

durable the investment, or the more time required for its completion, the greater the difficulties. When the problem is compounded by the impossibility of forecasting perfectly, the mismatches can be serious.

A steadily growing population has a smooth and stable age structure. In one with alternate declines and increases in births, the proportions in a given age group will fluctuate. The distribution of the population by age in the early years of the century was much like the distribution produced by steady growth (table 2-2). The proportions at each age changed gradually between censuses. The age structure was strongly hierarchical—the older the group, the smaller its share of the population, and the shares dropped off rather quickly with age. For example, 4.6 percent of the population was between the ages of 45 and 49 in 1900, but only 2.4 percent was between 60 and 64. The newer, irregular pattern first appeared in 1930. The under-5 group dropped sharply, and for the first time its share was smaller than that of the next older group—indeed, than the shares of the next three older groups.

The last three lines of table 2-2 summarize some of the characteristics of the new pattern by aggregating across several age groups. Children aged 5 through 14 dropped from 22 percent of the population in 1900 to 16 percent in 1950, rose to 20 percent in 1970, and fell again to a new low, 15 percent, by 1980. This age group made up a slightly smaller share of the population in 1970, when it included the children born during the peak years of the baby boom, than in 1900, a fact which shows that the baby boom generation is unusual less for its size than because it is preceded and followed by two small generations. Over the same years adults 25 through 59 rose to 46 percent of the population in 1940 and 1950, fell to 40 percent in 1970, and then began to rise again. The ratio of working-age adults to dependent young was lower in 1970 than at any time since the early 1900s. (It must be remembered, however, that age groups correspond only roughly to the numbers of people at different stages of life—young people attend school longer and adults retire earlier than they used to.)

Since 1930 the age structure has grown increasingly irregular. Older groups are often larger than younger ones, a feature that will move up through the age distribution as the baby boom generation grows older. The change in age structure has been reinforced by a second factor, separate from the baby boom but equally powerful—the decline in mortality and the consequent lengthening of life span among older people. The number of people 50 and older grew steadily from 13 percent of the population in 1900 to 26 percent in 1980, even though the small cohorts of the 1920s moderated the trend somewhat in the later year. In contrast to 1900, the four age groups between 40 and 60 in 1980 each accounted for approximately the same proportion of the population, about 5 percent.

The Fertility Patterns That Produced the Baby Boom[2]

In a country that accepts few immigrants, the age structure of the population depends on the number of children born each year. This depends in turn on the number of women of childbearing age and the rate at which they have children. That rate, not numbers of women, has been the crucial determinant of the current age structure. In fact, the number of women 15 through 44 grew most slowly during the 1950s, when births were at their highest levels, and fastest during the 1960s and 1970s, when the number of births began to drop.

The number of births per 1,000 total population—the crude birth rate—is not the best measure of the rate at which women have children,

2. This section describes events in the United States. For a brief review of the trends in other countries, see appendix A.

Figure 2-1. Births per 1,000 Total Population and per 1,000 Women Aged 15 through 44, Selected Years, 1820–1980

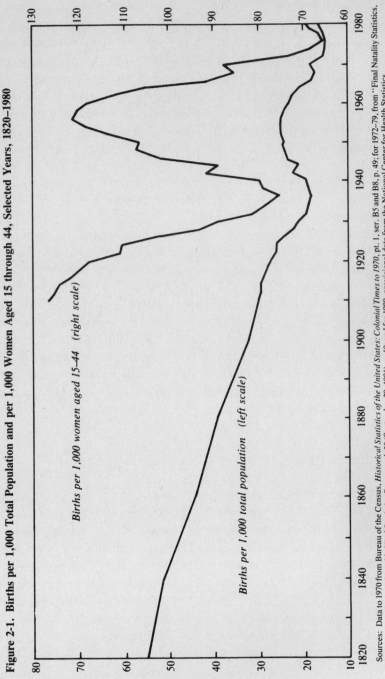

Births per 1,000 women aged 15–44 *(right scale)*

Births per 1,000 total population *(left scale)*

Sources: Data to 1970 from Bureau of the Census, *Historical Statistics of the United States: Colonial Times to 1970,* pt. 1, ser. B5 and B8, p. 49; for 1972–79, from "Final Natality Statistics, 1979," Advance Report, *Monthly Vital Statistics Report,* vol. 30 (September 29, 1981), p. 10; and for 1980, provisional data from the National Center for Health Statistics.

but it parallels that rate reasonably well and is available for a much longer period. The crude birth rate in the United States declined steadily from the early 1800s to the 1930s, from an estimated 55 births per 1,000 population in 1820 to about 18 or 19 per 1,000 in the 1930s (figure 2-1). In the 1940s, to the complete surprise of demographers, it began to move back up. By the late 1940s it was almost 25 per 1,000, close to the peak achieved in the 1950s. Since then, births have declined again, and by the mid-1970s the rate was about 15 per 1,000, below even the record lows of the 1930s. Over the years for which both measures are available, the turning points in the crude birth rate match those in the more precise measure, births per 1,000 women aged 15 through 44 (the general fertility rate), but as the figure makes clear, the movements in the latter measure are more extreme.

Four demographic factors caused the baby boom. More women married than ever before. More women who married had children. They had their children earlier. And some had more children. The women primarily involved were those born during the later 1920s and the 1930s. And since the difference in age between husband and wife averaged about 2.5 years, their husbands were also born during approximately the same span of years.[3]

The proportion of women marrying at some point during their lives had been increasing for several decades before the cohorts of the 1920s and 1930s reached adulthood.[4] The proportions were 91 percent for women born during the 1880s and 1890s, 92 percent for those born during the 1900s, 94 percent for the cohorts of the 1910s, and almost 95 percent for those of the 1920s. Women born during the 1930s set the record, with 96 percent marrying. These women also married earlier than their predecessors: more than 54 percent of the women born between 1935 and 1939 had married before they were 21, compared with 51 percent of those born in the early 1930s and 44 percent of those born in the late 1920s.[5]

Once married, more of these women had children. For married women

3. Paul C. Glick, "Updating the Life Cycle of the Family," *Journal of Marriage and the Family,* vol. 39 (February 1977), pp. 5–13.

4. Ibid, p. 8.

5. Maurice J. Moore and Martin O'Connell, "Perspectives on American Fertility," Bureau of the Census, *Current Population Reports,* Special Studies, series P-23, no. 70 (GPO, 1978), p. 17.

born between 1880 and 1910, the proportion remaining childless was 14 percent or higher. This proportion dropped precipitously for more recent cohorts—to 9 percent for those born in the 1920s and 7 percent for those born in the 1930s.[6] In fact, when Norman Ryder examined the pattern of childbearing before and during the baby boom, he concluded that the boom could be explained in large part by the sharp decline in the numbers of married women who had no children or only one.[7] Given that not all women marry and that not all women can have children, he found that the 1931–35 cohort had close to the maximum number of first, second, and even third children that they could possibly have produced.

The women who produced the baby boom had their children at younger ages than the preceding generations of women had done. In doing so, they fit in with a longer-term trend toward concentrating childbearing in the years between 20 and 30.[8] Here the cohort born between 1935 and 1939 set the record: before they were 22, they had produced 692 children per 1,000 women, compared with 610 per 1,000 for the 1930–34 cohort, 467 for the 1925–29 cohort, 397 for the 1920–24 cohort, and somewhat lower rates for the cohorts of women born during the 1910s.[9] Part of the baby boom was thus due to a timing overlap— younger women began to have babies before older women, working according to a different schedule, had finished having theirs. A period of overlap like this produces a bulge in births even if the younger generations ultimately have families no larger than those of the older generations.

And finally, of course, more women than in the generations just preceding went on to have four, five, or six children. Over one-third of the women born during the early 1930s had had four or more children by the time they were 35 (table 2-3). Only about one-fifth of the women born during the early years of the century had such large families. The table also shows the decreases, noted earlier, in the percentages of women having no children or one child, and the increases in those having two or three.

6. Glick, "Updating the Life Cycle of the Family," p. 8.

7. Norman B. Ryder, "The Emergence of a Modern Fertility Pattern: United States, 1917–66," in S. J. Behrman, Leslie Corsa, Jr., and Ronald Freedman, eds., *Fertility and Family Planning: A World View* (University of Michigan Press, 1970), pp. 99–123.

8. Moore and O'Connell, "Perspectives on American Fertility"; and Conrad Taeuber and Irene B. Taeuber, *The Changing Population of the United States*, Census Monograph Series (John Wiley for the Social Science Research Council, 1958), p. 254.

9. Bureau of the Census, *Current Population Reports*, series P-20, no. 315, "Trends in Childspacing: June 1975" (GPO, 1978), p. 17. These statistics understate the number of children somewhat, since they assume that all single women are childless.

Table 2-3. Percent Distribution of Women by Size of Family at Age 35 through 39, by Year of Birth[a]

	Number of children					
Year of birth	0	1	2	3	4 or more	Total
1901–05	22.0	23.4	20.7	12.7	21.3	100.0
1906–10	24.0	23.6	21.8	12.4	18.1	100.0
1911–15	21.0	22.2	24.4	14.4	18.0	100.0
1916–20	16.4	19.3	26.4	17.3	20.6	100.0
1921–25	12.0	16.1	26.2	20.0	25.7	100.0
1926–30	11.4	11.9	23.5	21.3	32.0	100.0
1931–35	9.4	10.0	22.3	22.6	35.8	100.0
1936–40	9.6	11.1	24.7	23.6	31.1	100.0

Source: Department of Health and Human Services, National Center for Health Statistics, *Vital Statistics of the United States, 1976*, vol. 1: *Natality* (GPO, 1980), table 1-13. Figures are rounded.

a. Based on all women, married and unmarried. Births are cumulative totals as of thirty-five years after the last year in the interval (for example, as of 1975 for the 1936–40 interval).

Interestingly, the baby boom cannot be explained in terms of growth in groups with traditionally high birth rates. Virtually every subgroup in the population—whether defined by income, education, race, or some other characteristic—contributed to the rising birth rate in surprisingly equal measure. With differences between groups remaining fairly stable, the trend in each group was rising during the baby boom and declining after the boom ended. The changes in both directions were led by younger, better-educated women, which, as Rindfuss and Sweet point out "reinforce[s] the perspective that the baby boom was essentially voluntary and that its explanations are necessarily social."[10]

It is not yet possible to tell the full story of the decline in births that followed the baby boom. Most of the women involved in that decline are still in their childbearing years, and until they are older it will not be clear how much of the decline is due to intentionally smaller families and how much to delays in marriage and childbearing. The facts so far are these.

Women currently in their twenties are marrying later than their predecessors and more of them have yet to marry. As mentioned earlier, of the cohort born between 1935 and 1939, 54 percent had married before they were 21. This proportion dropped to 50 percent for the 1940–44 cohort and to 45 percent for the 1945–49 and 1950–54 cohorts.[11] Between 1965 and 1979 the proportion of women 20 through 24 who had never

10. Ronald R. Rindfuss and James A. Sweet, *Postwar Fertility Trends and Differentials in the United States* (Academic Press, 1977), p. 41.

11. Moore and O'Connell, "Perspectives on American Fertility," p. 17.

married rose from 33 percent to 49 percent; the proportion for women 25 through 29 rose from 8 to 20 percent.[12] It is too early to tell whether what is clearly a postponement of marriage will eventually mean that a smaller proportion of women born during the 1940s and 1950s ever marry.

In part because they are marrying later, young women today are having children later than the women who produced the baby boom. Again, the cohort of 1935–39 had 692 children per 1,000 women before they were 22. The number dropped to 663 for the 1940–44 cohort and to 513 for the cohort of the late 1940s, and was projected to be less than 400 for the cohort of the early 1950s.[13] Some of the decline was due not simply to later marriage but to a delay in childbearing after marriage as well. The proportion of women having children during the first three years of marriage has declined sharply in recent years—from a high of 78 percent for women married in the late 1950s, to 68 percent for those married in the late 1960s and 58 percent for those married in the early 1970s.[14] Surveys indicate only a slight increase in the number of married women planning not to have children—4 percent in 1960, 5.4 percent in 1976.[15] But many of the young married women who are currently postponing children may eventually decide not to have them, and those who are not yet married may choose to remain childless when they do marry. It will be some years yet before it becomes clear how much of the current postponement is truly postponement and how much will evolve into decisions not to have children at all.

Later marriage and childbearing have played a part in the recent decline in births, but the main factor is simply that couples who married in the late 1960s and in the 1970s have so far had fewer children than those who married earlier.[16] And if their current plans are a good predictor, they will continue to have fewer. Surveys show a sharp drop

12. Ibid., p. 18; and Bureau of the Census, *Current Population Reports,* series P-20, no. 349, "Marital Status and Living Arrangements: March 1979" (GPO, 1980), p. 2.

13. Moore and O'Connell, "Perspectives on American Fertility," p. 17.

14. Campbell Gibson, "The U.S. Fertility Decline, 1961–1975: The Contribution of Changes in Marital Status and Marital Fertility," *Family Planning Perspectives,* vol. 8 (September–October 1976), p. 251.

15. Moore and O'Connell, "Perspectives on American Fertility," p. 25. These percentages are based on married women aged 18 through 39. Data for married women aged 18 through 34 in 1979 show that 5.7 percent of them expected to have no children. Bureau of the Census, *Current Population Reports,* series P-20, no. 358, "Fertility of American Women: June 1979" (GPO, 1980), p. 22.

16. Gibson, "U.S. Fertility Decline, 1961–1975."

since the middle 1960s in the number of children married women expect to have. In 1960 married women aged 18 through 24 reported that they planned to have an average of 3.1 children, and those 25 through 29 planned to have 3.4 children. By 1979 married women in these age groups were planning to have only slightly more than two children, on average, and expectations had been steady at this low level since the mid-1970s.[17]

The Future: Theories of the Birth Rate

Whether the birth rate remains low will depend in part on the resolution of the preliminary patterns set by couples now in their twenties and thirties, and in part on the childbearing behavior of the cohorts who will reach adulthood in the coming years. Not surprisingly, there is more agreement on what is likely to happen during the next several years than on the prospects for the longer run.

For the very short run, the general consensus is that birth rates will remain low. The numbers of births planned by young married women are at least as low in the most recent surveys as they were in the early and middle 1970s, and with the use of contraceptives nearly universal— the overwhelming majority of married couples use some method of contraception, and three out of four of these rely on the pill, the intrauterine device (IUD), or sterilization—most couples are quite able to limit births to the number they want.[18] The increase since 1975 in the birth rate for women 30 through 34 gives some support for the speculation that couples who have been postponing births will begin to make them up over the next few years (table 2-4). But if they stick to their currently planned quota of two children, birth rates will not rise much.[19]

Because modern contraceptives give couples a high degree of control

17. Moore and O'Connell, "Perspectives on American Fertility," p. 24; and Bureau of the Census, "Fertility of American Women: June 1979," p. 7.
18. Bureau of the Census, "Fertility of American Women: June 1979," p. 7; Moore and O'Connell, "Perspectives on American Fertility," p. 55; and prepared statement of Peter A. Morrison, "Overview of Demographic Trends Shaping the Nation's Future," in *Special Study on Economic Change,* Hearings before the Joint Economic Committee, 95 Cong. 2 sess., pt. 1 (GPO, 1978), pp. 68–83.
19. Campbell Gibson, "The Elusive Rise in the American Birthrate," *Science,* April 29, 1977, pp. 500–03. *Total* births have, of course, risen moderately in recent years. This has happened not because the rate at which women are having children has risen but because the rate has been stable for several years while the number of women of childbearing age has continued to grow.

Table 2-4. Live Births per 1,000 Women, by Age, 1970–79

Year	15–19	20–24	25–29	30–34	35–39	40–44
1970	68.3	167.8	145.1	73.3	31.7	8.1
1971	64.7	150.6	134.8	67.6	28.7	7.1
1972	62.0	131.0	118.7	60.2	24.8	6.2
1973	59.7	120.7	113.6	56.1	22.0	5.4
1974	58.1	119.0	113.3	54.4	20.2	4.8
1975	56.3	114.7	110.3	53.1	19.4	4.6
1976	53.5	112.1	108.8	54.5	19.0	4.3
1977	53.7	115.2	114.2	57.5	19.2	4.2
1978	52.4	112.3	112.0	59.1	18.9	3.9
1979	53.4	115.7	115.6	61.8	19.4	3.9

Source: "Final Natality Statistics, 1979," Advance Report, *Monthly Vital Statistics Report*, vol. 30 (September 29, 1981), p. 13.

over the timing as well as the number of births, many demographers believe that short-run fluctuations will be a more important source of variation in births in the future than in the past.[20] These fluctuations may very well occur in response to economic conditions. Indeed, birth rates have traditionally risen during the boom phase of the business cycle and fallen during recessions. But William Butz and Michael Ward find that birth rates have followed a countercyclical pattern in recent years, falling during boom periods and staying level during recessions; their analysis indicates that women have been scheduling their babies during periods of economic slack because the cost in terms of their lost wages is lower.[21] More generally, the possibility of fluctuations around a stable, and fairly low, birth rate is supported by experience in Western Europe, where birth rates have fluctuated around replacement level for most of this century in such countries as West Germany, France, Sweden, and England and Wales.[22]

There will clearly be future short-term fluctuations in births, and thus future fluctuations of at least modest size in the age structure of the population. But what are the prospects for larger, longer-run swings—a repeat of the baby boom perhaps? The question has been debated at

20. Morrison, "Overview of Demographic Trends"; Ryder, "Emergence of a Modern Fertility Pattern"; and Charles F. Westoff, "Some Speculations on the Future of Marriage and Fertility," *Family Planning Perspectives*, vol. 10 (March–April 1978), pp. 79–83.

21. William P. Butz and Michael P. Ward, "The Emergence of Countercyclical U.S. Fertility," *American Economic Review*, vol. 69 (June 1979), pp. 318–28.

22. Hilde Wander, "Zero Population Growth Now: The Lessons from Europe," in Thomas J. Espenshade and William J. Serow, eds., *The Economic Consequences of Slowing Population Growth* (Academic Press, 1978), pp. 42–43, 51–52.

length by social scientists, and several interesting theories have been proposed.

The theory of longest standing—the theory of the demographic "echo"—has suffered at the hands of events during the last several decades. This theory states that a large generation will produce another large generation, a small generation another small one; the rate at which women have children is assumed to be stable (or to follow a smooth rising or falling trend), and the primary determinant of large fluctuations in total births is thus the number of women of childbearing age. On this basis demographers predicted that the baby boom generation would create a second baby boom—perhaps not as large in relative terms as the first, but still a baby boom. This did not happen, of course. Instead the baby boom generation has so far produced an unusually small number of children. And it was itself produced by an unusually small generation— the people born during the late 1920s and the 1930s.

Charles Westoff has proposed a variant of the theory of the demographic echo.[23] He argues that the baby boom of the 1950s was an aberration, one that cannot be entirely explained, and that the decline in birth rates during the 1960s and 1970s represents a return to (and possibly the culmination of) the lengthy historical decline interrupted by the baby boom. Indeed, as described earlier in this chapter, the baby boom was due in great part to earlier marriage and childbearing, and less childlessness, rather than to larger families. It was thus less out of line with current preferences for small families than might appear at first. Drawing on this longer historical perspective, on European experience, and on recent trends in contraception, marriage, and women's work, Westoff concludes that "low fertility at one level or another seems here to stay."[24]

Richard Easterlin insists that a credible theory must explain the baby boom as well as the more recent decline in the birth rate, and has offered a theory that does so.[25] According to his theory, now that immigration is no longer available to fill in when native-born labor is scarce, the members of a small generation will, by virtue of their fewness, face good

23. Westoff, "Some Speculations on the Future of Marriage and Fertility"; and Charles F. Westoff, "The Decline of Fertility," *American Demographics*, vol. 1 (February 1979), pp. 16–19.

24. Westoff, "Decline of Fertility," p. 19.

25. He has presented the theory in a number of books and articles—most recently, Richard A. Easterlin, *Birth and Fortune: The Impact of Numbers on Personal Welfare* (Basic Books, 1980).

Figure 2-2. Population Aged 5 through 14, 1900–77, and Projections to 2050[a]

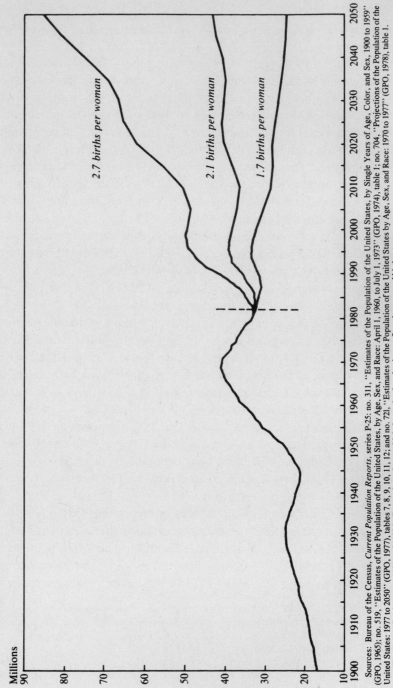

Millions

2.7 births per woman

2.1 births per woman

1.7 births per woman

Sources: Bureau of the Census, *Current Population Reports*, series P-25: no. 311, "Estimates of the Population of the United States, by Single Years of Age, Color, and Sex, 1900 to 1959" (GPO, 1965); no. 519, "Estimates of the Population of the United States, by Age, Sex, and Race: April 1, 1960, to July 1, 1973" (GPO, 1974), table 1; no. 704, "Projections of the Population of the United States: 1977 to 2050" (GPO, 1977), tables 7, 8, 9, 10, 11, 12; and no. 721, "Estimates of the Population of the United States by Age, Sex, and Race: 1970 to 1977" (GPO, 1978), table 1.
a. The dashed line between 1981 and 1982 indicates the point at which the projections begin to reflect the assumed birth rates.

labor market conditions and earn better incomes than they aspired to. In response to their affluence they will have larger families. Conversely, members of a large generation will not do as well as they hoped and will respond to their economic circumstances by having smaller families. The emphasis is on aspirations—the members of a large generation may actually earn more at each age than members of a preceding smaller generation, but if their incomes are not enough to support their aspirations, they will consider themselves badly off, and have fewer children as a result. Easterlin hypothesizes that the members of each generation build their aspirations on the basis of their parents' incomes.

It is difficult to measure aspirations or relative incomes, but the theory is clearly consistent with the course of births over the last several decades—the baby boom *was* produced by a small generation, and the baby bust by a large one. Further, the theory has one correct prediction to its credit. In a book published in 1968, Easterlin predicted, very cautiously, but, as it turned out, correctly, that birth rates would decline further and then probably level off.[26] Westoff notes, however, that even in this country the evidence in support of the theory is quite limited— one complete cycle—and that the pattern has not been shown to exist in many other countries.[27]

Butz and Ward have proposed an alternative theory that, like Easterlin's, successfully explains the baby boom and the baby bust, though it has very different implications for the future.[28] They argue that a couple will have more children when the husband's income is high, but that decisions about the number and timing of births will also be affected by the wife's earnings. If the wife's earnings are high, the cost of dropping out of the labor market to have and raise children is correspondingly high, and the couple will choose to have fewer children. In the affluent 1950s, when relatively few women held jobs, the effect of husbands' incomes dominated, and couples had larger families and had them sooner. But as rising real wages drew more and more women into the labor market, women's earnings became more important and began to outweigh the effect of husbands' incomes. The birth rate dropped.

26. Richard A. Easterlin, *Population, Labor Force, and Long Swings in Economic Growth: The American Experience* (Columbia University Press for the National Bureau of Economic Research, 1968), pp. 134–35.

27. Westoff, "Some Speculations on the Future of Marriage and Fertility," p. 79.

28. Butz and Ward, "Emergence of Countercyclical U.S. Fertility"; and William P. Butz and Michael P. Ward, "Baby Boom and Baby Bust: A New View," *American Demographics*, vol. 1 (September 1979), pp. 11–17.

This explanation has been subjected to careful statistical tests and has stood up well. One of its most impressive successes is its ability to "predict" the decline in the birth rate during the 1960s and 1970s from an equation based only on data for the years 1947 through 1956, when birth rates were rising. Further, as noted earlier, it explains the recent pattern of birth rates over the business cycle. It has not yet, however, had the chance to show whether it can correctly predict the future.

None of these theories has been sufficiently tested by events to be considered a reliable guide to the future. To date, the Bureau of the Census continues to use the principle of the demographic echo for projecting births, although in recent years it has published projections based on several different assumed birth rates in the hope of bracketing the true rate. It makes no attempt to project short-run fluctuations due to timing. Figure 2-2 charts the bureau's projections of the population aged 5 through 14 until the year 2050. Starting from the rates of the late 1970s, the projections gradually approach constant birth rates consistent with average lifetime births per woman of 2.7, 2.1, and 1.7. The results are a series of wavelike movements, reflecting alternating larger and smaller generations of parents, which grow less extreme with the passage of time.

The various theories face a crucial test during the 1980s. Easterlin predicts that birth rates will rise over the decade as the smaller cohorts born in the 1960s and 1970s reach adulthood, and that there will be a second baby boom, although it may not be as large as the first. Westoff, and Butz and Ward, predict that birth rates will remain low, or perhaps decline somewhat further, and therefore that total births will fall as the smaller cohorts become parents.[29]

The resulting age structure of the population will be irregular regardless of which theory is right, but the pattern of that irregularity will differ considerably, and with it the size and timing of its effects on the economy and on society in general. The remaining chapters examine the economic effects of the existing age structure, both to explain the past and to suggest the outlines of the future.

---

29. The prediction by Butz and Ward is conditional on their prediction that women's labor force participation will remain high.

chapter three **The Schools**

The baby boom led to a period of unprecedented growth in school enrollment. The children born in 1946 entered first grade in 1952, and enrollment grew rapidly through the 1950s. Growth continued during the 1960s but at a slower pace. Between 1950 and 1960 enrollment in elementary and secondary schools rose from 28 million students to 42 million (table 3-1). Between 1960 and 1970 almost 10 million more students were added, bringing the total to 51 million.

Steady growth had also characterized the school system during the early decades of the century. Not only were numbers of school-age children increasing, but the proportion attending school rose with every census as education became truly universal. In 1900 half the children between the ages of 5 and 19 were in school.[1] By 1930 the proportion had risen to 70 percent, and it continued upward in the years that followed. But rising enrollment rates were not enough to offset the decline in births that began in the late 1920s. By the mid-1930s total enrollment had reached its peak and started down again. It continued to decline through the rest of the 1930s and the war years.

Declining enrollments together with the depression, and then the restrictions on the civilian economy during World War II, meant that few new schools were built, and even the care of existing schools was often neglected.[2] Some teachers were drafted, and others left teaching

1. Bureau of the Census, *Historical Statistics of the United States: Colonial Times to 1970* (Government Printing Office, 1975), pt. 1, ser. H 433, pp. 369–70.
2. Capital outlays plus interest payments fell to only 6 percent of total expenditures by public school systems during the war. Bureau of the Census, *Historical Statistics . . . to 1970*, pt. 1, ser. H 492, H 499, and H 500, pp. 373–74. References to the effects of the depression and the war on school construction are made in Ray L. Hamon, "School and College Building Crisis," *School Life*, vol. 31 (October 1948), p. 12; George J. Hecht, "'War Babies' Will Increasingly Swamp the Schools," *School Management*, vol. 18 (September 1948), p. 4; and "You Can Expect a Bigger Crop of America's Most Valuable Product—Children," *Michigan Education Journal*, vol. 27 (February 1950), p. 349.

Table 3-1. Elementary and Secondary School Enrollment, Selected Years, 1900–80[a]
Thousands

Year	All grades Total[b]	All grades Public school	Elementary grades[c]	Secondary grades
1900	16,885	15,503	16,168	699
1910	19,372	17,814	18,410	1,115
1920	23,278	21,578	20,933	2,500
1930	28,329	25,678	23,677	4,811
1940	28,045	25,434	21,061	7,130
1942	27,179	24,562	20,260	6,924
1944	25,758	23,267	19,735	6,021
1946	26,124	23,300	19,891	6,227
1948	26,998	23,945	20,642	6,304
1950	28,492	25,111	22,067	6,453
1952	30,372	26,563	23,715	6,597
1954	33,175	28,836	25,952	7,108
1956	35,872	31,163	28,058	7,775
1958	38,756	33,529	29,764	8,870
1960[d]	41,762	36,087	32,042	9,600
1962	44,285	38,269	33,403	10,769
1964	46,674	40,187	34,280	12,255
1966	48,479	42,174	35,527	13,021
1968	50,742	44,742	37,044	13,984
1970	51,319	45,619	36,892	14,519
1972	51,594	46,081	36,380	15,214
1974	50,562	45,409	35,135	15,427
1976	50,086	44,791	34,282	15,804
1978	49,031	43,971	33,231	15,800
1980	46,940	41,780	31,605	15,335

Sources: Data to 1970 are from Bureau of the Census, *Historical Statistics of the United States: Colonial Times to 1970* (Government Printing Office, 1975), pt. 1, ser. H 418–32; for 1970–76, from Bureau of the Census, *Statistical Abstract of the United States, 1979* (GPO, 1979), p. 136; for 1978, from W. Vance Grant and C. George Lind, *Digest of Education Statistics, 1979*, Department of Health, Education, and Welfare, National Center for Education Statistics (GPO, 1979), p. 6; and for 1980, from W. Vance Grant and Leo J. Eiden, *Digest of Education Statistics, 1980*, Department of Education, National Center for Education Statistics (GPO, 1980), p. 6.

a. Enrollment for the school year ending in the year specified. Data after 1960 are for the fall of the preceding calendar year.

b. Partially estimated.

c. Kindergarten through grade 8.

d. Alaska and Hawaii included for the first time.

for war work, which offered plenty of jobs and better pay.[3] As the war went on, it became more and more difficult to get trained teachers; the states were frequently reduced to issuing temporary emergency certificates to people whose training did not meet the usual standards. More

3. See, for example, W. Earl Armstrong, "Teacher Situation Critical—What Can Be Done?" *School Life*, vol. 33 (January 1951), pp. 49–50.

Table 3-2. Percentage of Population Enrolled in School as of October, by Age, Selected Years, 1940–80[a]

Age group	1940[b]	1945	1950	1955	1960	1965	1970	1975	1980
3–4	n.a.	n.a.	n.a.	n.a.	n.a.	10.6	20.5	31.5	36.7
5–6	43.0	60.4	74.4	78.1	80.7	84.9	89.5	94.7	95.7
7–13	95.0	98.1	98.7	99.2	99.5	99.4	99.2	99.3	99.3
14–17	79.3	78.4	83.3	86.9	90.3	93.2	94.1	93.6	93.4
18–19	28.9	20.7	29.4	31.5	38.4	46.3	47.7	46.9	46.4
20–21	} 6.6	} 3.9	} 9.0	} 11.1	{ 19.4	27.6	31.9	31.2	31.0
22–24					{ 8.7	13.2	14.9	16.2	16.3
25–29	n.a.	n.a.	3.0	4.2	4.9	6.1	7.5	10.1	9.3
30–34	n.a.	n.a.	n.a.	1.6	2.4	3.2	4.2	6.6	6.4

Sources: Bureau of the Census, *Current Population Reports,* series P-20: no. 24, "School Enrollment of the Population: October 1948" (GPO, 1949), p. 8; no. 54, "School Enrollment: October 1954" (GPO, 1955); no. 80, "School Enrollment: October 1957" (GPO, 1958), p. 8; no. 110, "School Enrollment, and Education of Young Adults and Their Fathers: October 1960" (GPO, 1961), p. 10; no. 278, "School Enrollment—Social and Economic Characteristics of Students: October 1974" (GPO, 1975), p. 4; and no. 362, "School Enrollment—Social and Economic Characteristics of Students: October 1980," Advance Report (GPO, 1981), p. 5.

n.a. Not available.

a. Civilian noninstitutional population.

b. As of April.

than a year after the war ended, the *New York Times* reported that one out of every seven teachers still held an emergency certificate.[4]

The Deluge

The baby boom proper was only beginning in the years after World War II, but the school system was faced with rising enrollments almost immediately because of the large numbers of births during the war. By 1942 births totaled 3 million a year, the level of the early 1920s, and continued at nearly that rate through the war years. As these children reached the ages of 5 and 6, enrollment in the elementary grades began to grow.

The growth in numbers was complicated by several factors. One was that enrollment rates continued to rise at the same time (table 3-2). By the mid-1940s the enrollment rate for children of elementary school age was almost as high as it could go—over 98 percent of children between the ages of 7 and 13 were in school. But the decline in the population of children of high school age, which might have been expected to help ease the absorption of so many students in the lower grades, was more

4. Benjamin Fine, "Teacher Shortage Imperils Our Public School System: Survey by The Times Shows Millions of Children Receive Impaired Education as Instructors Quit for Better Jobs," *New York Times,* February 10, 1947.

than offset by the increase in enrollment rates in this age group. The proportion of young people 14 through 17 enrolled in school rose from 78 percent in 1945 to 83 percent in 1950 and 90 percent in 1960. As kindergarten became an accepted part of every child's education, enrollment rates for children aged 5 and 6 jumped from 60 percent in 1945 to 75 percent in 1948 and edged up to 81 percent by 1960. The jump in the late 1940s was particularly important because it coincided with the larger numbers of young children, reinforcing their effect on school enrollment.

But a more important complication was the major movements of population that began during the war as workers and their families moved to new military bases and centers of war production, and that continued after the war as these centers were abandoned.[5] It was during these years that the population moved to the suburbs. Some states faced declines in their school-age populations at the same time that other states were overwhelmed by students, and within the same state some districts lost enrollment while others gained.[6] Between 1940 and 1950, for example, when the national population of 5- through 14-year-olds grew about 8 percent, this age group increased by more than 50 percent in California and Oregon and declined by 14 percent in Oklahoma. As the baby boom generation entered school between 1950 and 1960 the population aged 5 through 14 grew 46 percent nationally and doubled in Alaska, Arizona, California, Florida, and Nevada. Only Arkansas lost school-age population during that period.[7]

The school system faced two particular difficulties in responding to the onslaught of children—one peculiar to the time, the other inherent in the situation. The peculiar difficulty was that the schools had been starved during World War II and later suffered from further restrictions on materials, and from competition for teachers, during the Korean

5. The importance of migration is stressed in "Growing Pressure on Schools: Increase in Grade Pupils as Building Lags," *U.S. News and World Report*, September 3, 1948, pp. 36–37; Hamon, "School and College Building Crisis"; Newton P. Edwards, "Educational Implications of Population Change in the United States," *Journal of Teacher Education*, vol. 1 (March 1950), pp. 3–13; and "The Outlook for School Enrollments," *Journal of Teacher Education*, vol. 4 (March 1953), pp. 46–52.

6. For example, growth rates by school district for Utah, 1939–54, are presented in Utah Foundation, *Facts, Figures, and Charts on Utah Schools* (Salt Lake City: Utah Foundation, 1955).

7. Growth rates for the states were calculated from Bureau of the Census, *Historical Statistics . . . to 1970*, pt. 1, ser. A 195–209, pp. 24–37. National growth rates are from table 2-1.

War.[8] Offsetting these initial handicaps was the unparalleled prosperity of the postwar period.

The inherent difficulty was in predicting how long the baby boom would last and how big it would be. The time between the publication of birth statistics and the enrollment of those children in elementary school is quite short, and has been made shorter as kindergarten and then nursery school have become commonplace. Thus, in order to have time to plan, the school system must guess at future births—which have been notoriously difficult to predict in the postwar period, as shown in chapter 2—and if it guesses seriously wrong, its plans will be seriously wrong. Further, in a highly mobile society it is necessary to guess not only how many children there will be but where they will be.

In the late 1940s no one expected the baby boom to last long. Birth rates in the United States had dropped steadily for a century before World War II, and most observers expected the trend to reassert itself quickly.[9] Projections of school enrollment at first showed elementary school enrollment peaking in the mid-1950s, and then, as births remained high, later in the decade.[10] It was not until the 1950s were well under way that forecasters decided that births would remain high for the foreseeable future and projected rising enrollments through the end of the decade.[11] By the late 1950s some observers were convinced that the boom would never stop.[12]

Regardless of the longer-term projections, however, the immediate future was always the same during the fifteen or twenty years after World War II—numbers of students were rising, and more classrooms and teachers were needed to accommodate them. The obvious response was to try to add new classrooms and teachers as fast as possible, preferably

8. The problems of the Korean War period are discussed in Earl James McGrath, "Report on Education—1951," *School Life,* vol. 34 (May 1952), pp. 118–23; and in *New York Times,* March 19, 1951, September 10, 1951, January 14, 1952, January 16, 1952, and January 17, 1952.

9. Frank W. Notestein, "The Facts of Life," *Atlantic Monthly,* June 1946, pp. 75–83; and Edwards, "Educational Implications of Population Change."

10. See the projections presented in Hecht, "'War Babies' Will Increasingly Swamp the Schools"; Hamon, "School and College Building Crisis,"; and Emery M. Foster, "Magnitude of the Nation's Educational Task Today and in the Years Ahead," *School Life,* vol. 32 (March 1950), pp. 88–89.

11. "Outlook for School Enrollments"; and Milton S. Eisenhower, "Not Enough Teachers or Schools," *Pennsylvania School Journal,* vol. 100 (January 1952), pp. 178–79.

12. Samuel Everett, "Our Population Growth: Are We Planning for It?" *School Executive,* vol. 77 (October 1957), pp. 21–23.

fast enough to maintain existing standards, or, since conditions had deteriorated during the war, to return to prewar standards. Considering the size of the job, it would not have been surprising if school districts had found themselves unable to maintain standards and had absorbed the growing numbers of students at the cost of larger classes, more poorly trained teachers, and even the reversal of trends toward universal enrollment in certain age groups. These strains did appear, particularly in some places and for short periods of time in many places. But in general, all the signs indicate that standards and resources did better than keep pace with enrollments—both improved substantially.

Some school districts postponed the onslaught briefly by raising the minimum age for enrollment.[13] Statistics on enrollment rates suggest that this response was of measurable importance only for a year or two in the early 1950s. As noted earlier, the enrollment rate for 5- and 6-year-olds shot up after the war. The rate was reported as 60 percent in 1945 and 74 percent in 1947.[14] It rose slightly higher, to 76 percent, by 1949. But it fell back a point or two between 1950 and 1952 and did not exceed the 1949 figure until 1953. During the rest of the 1950s it was virtually flat, and only during the 1960s did it begin to rise again. Thus some children entered first grade later than they would have otherwise, and, more generally, the expansion of kindergartens and nursery schools took second place to the expansion of the elementary schools. On the other hand, rates of enrollment among teenagers continued to rise slowly throughout the period.

The number of teachers employed by the schools rose rapidly. There were just over 800,000 teachers in the public elementary and secondary schools at the end of World War II.[15] By 1960 the number was 1.4 million. To attract these teachers, school districts had to increase their salary schedules again and again. The available data indicate that teachers' salaries stayed even with inflation during the depression and the war years. But after the war they grew substantially faster than prices, and faster than wages elsewhere in the economy. In the late 1940s teachers were paid about the same amount as the average worker in the private,

13. "Classroom Crowding Gets Worse: Birth Boom to Mean Substandard Education," *U.S. News and World Report,* September 9, 1949, p. 15. The "birth boom" in the title refers to the children born during the war, not the postwar baby boom.

14. It rose sharply during the war as well—it was 43 percent in 1940.

15. Bureau of the Census, *Historical Statistics . . . to 1970,* pt. 1, ser. H 526, p. 375.

nonagricultural sector of the economy. By 1960 teachers' salaries were 20 percent higher, and by 1970 they were more than a third higher.[16]

There was much complaint, especially in the late 1940s and early 1950s, about the number of teachers with substandard certificates. The problem was most acute during and after the war. As noted earlier, shortly after the war one in seven teachers still held a substandard certificate. The situation improved quickly, and by 1950 between 7 and 8 percent of all teachers—about one in twelve or fourteen—held substandard certificates. After that the proportion remained at about 7 percent through the 1950s and declined only a little, to about 5 percent, during the 1960s.[17]

The stubborn persistence of substandard certificates had less to do with the exigencies of dealing with overwhelming numbers of students than with the fact that, at the same time, the minimum standards for teachers were being raised. This was especially true for elementary school teachers. In 1930 only two states required elementary teachers to have a B.A. degree, and in 1940 the number was still only eleven. The trend toward higher requirements continued during the 1940s and 1950s in spite of the growth in enrollment. By 1950 twenty-one states required elementary teachers to have the B.A., and by 1961 forty-four did. The push for stricter educational requirements for high school teachers had

16. No adjustment is made in the salary statistics for changes in the age composition of the teacher pool, teachers' qualifications, or other factors. The average wage in the private, nonagricultural sector is also not adjusted. The statements about teachers' salaries are based on data for elementary and secondary school classroom teachers for the years 1956–78, and for instructional staff for the years 1932–78, from W. Vance Grant and Leo J. Eiden, *Digest of Education Statistics 1980*, National Center for Education Statistics (GPO, 1980), pp. 56–57; and on data for elementary and secondary school teachers in cities of various sizes from Beardsley Ruml and Sidney G. Tickton, *Teaching Salaries, Then and Now: A 50-year Comparison with Other Occupations and Industries*, Bulletin 1 (New York: The Fund for the Advancement of Education, 1955). These salary data were compared with the consumer price index (and a Federal Reserve Board price index given in Ruml and Tickton for the years in the 1920s and 1930s, when the CPI did not exist) and with average weekly earnings in the private, nonagricultural sector of the economy. Both series are from *Economic Report of the President, January 1981*, pp. 275, 289.

17. Data for the 1940s and 1950s are from "Teacher Forecast for the Public Schools," *Journal of Teacher Education*, vol. 4 (March 1953), p. 55; "The Teacher Shortage—Better or Worse?" *Journal of Teacher Education*, vol. 9 (December 1958), p. 341; and *New York Times*, January 15, 1951, January 14, 1952, and February 8, 1953. Data for the 1960s are from Department of Health, Education, and Welfare, Office of Education, *Statistics of Public Elementary and Secondary Schools, Fall 1969* (GPO, 1970), and issues for 1964 and 1967.

started earlier—by 1940 forty states required the B.A.—and was completed during the 1950s.[18]

The proportion of elementary school teachers with a B.A., or even graduate training, grew in line with the new requirements. In the late 1940s fewer than half of all elementary school teachers had completed college. By 1961 three-quarters had B.A.'s.[19] Reporting on the trends in 1957, one source observed that "this vast upgrading movement has gone forward in the face of staggering odds," as indeed it had.[20] Not only were enrollments growing at an unprecedented pace, but the number of young adults—from among whom new teachers would ordinarily be drawn—was unusually small, reflecting the low levels of births during the 1930s.

The states, which were responsible for setting standards for teacher certification, tried to draw people into teaching in a number of ways besides the straightforward inducement of higher salaries. Some states kept tuition charges at their teachers colleges very low in order to attract students. And it was during this period that special intensive programs were developed to train people with B.A.'s in fields other than education to be teachers.[21] In fact, many people holding substandard certificates had B.A.'s but failed to meet other requirements for a standard certificate. In some cases they had not specialized in education; in others they had specialized in high school subjects when the need was for elementary teachers.[22] The state of Ohio reported that it employed many B.A.'s who had not trained for teaching or had trained in the wrong field—in 1953,

18. Lucien B. Kinney, *Certification in Education* (Prentice-Hall, 1964), especially p. 83. Currently all states (and the District of Columbia) require elementary and secondary teachers to have at least a B.A., according to Elizabeth H. Woellner, *Teachers, Counselors, Librarians, Administrators: Requirements for Certification for Elementary Schools, Secondary Schools, Junior Colleges*, 45th ed. (University of Chicago Press, 1980).

19. "The Postwar Struggle to Provide Competent Teachers," *NEA Research Bulletin*, vol. 35 (October 1957), p. 120; and *Education Yearbook, 1972–73* (Macmillan and the Free Press, 1972), p. 536.

20. "Postwar Struggle to Provide Competent Teachers," p. 123.

21. Governors Conference Round Table, "Elementary and Secondary Education," *State Government*, vol. 29 (August 1956), pp. 148–49; and Ohio School Survey Committee, *Report of the Ohio School Survey Committee to the Governor and the General Assembly* (Columbus, 1955).

22. Throughout the late 1940s and the 1950s more education majors prepared for high school than for elementary teaching. "Postwar Struggle to Provide Competent Teachers," pp. 109–10.

for example, these people held the majority of the temporary certificates issued by the state.[23]

Along with the need for more teachers, the growing numbers of students created an equally pressing need for more classrooms—perhaps more pressing, because the mobility of the population meant that new classrooms had to be built even as existing ones were abandoned or underused because they were in the wrong places. A newsmagazine reported in 1948 that, but for the movement of the population, the existing number of classrooms would probably have been adequate for the higher enrollments of that year.[24] After a slow start in the late 1940s, construction expenditures were historically high throughout the 1950s, averaging 20 to 25 percent of total school expenditures.[25]

Here, too, more was attempted than the simple accommodation of numbers.[26] The discussions of the time frequently stressed the goals of replacing obsolete facilities as well as building new ones, and of upgrading school buildings to fit both expanded curricula and more ambitious notions of what schools should offer the community. In 1950 Commissioner McGrath of the federal Office of Education declared that "many of the buildings which are physically sound are antiquated in terms of the functions of modern education" and that activities "now considered essential . . . were unknown only a few years ago."[27] The old buildings did not always have indoor plumbing; the new were to have libraries, cafeterias, gymnasiums, and swimming pools, and to serve not only as schools for the young but also as centers of adult education and community activity.

Not all students were, of course, housed in buildings that met the high standards set by Commissioner McGrath. At some times and in some

23. Ohio School Survey Committee, *Report*.

24. "Growing Pressure on Schools."

25. Bureau of the Census, *Historical Statistics . . . to 1970*, pt. 1, ser. H 492, H 499, and H 500, pp. 373–74. Capital outlays plus interest payments were a similarly high proportion of total expenditures for the public schools in the 1920s.

26. Harry Hewes, "Government's Role in School Building," *Nation's Schools*, vol. 40 (July 1947), pp. 39–40; Hamon, "School and College Building Crisis"; Earl James McGrath, "Education in 1949—Review and Recommendations," *School Life*, vol. 32 (February 1950), p. 72; Foster, "Magnitude of the Nation's Educational Task"; Illinois School Problems Commission, *Illinois School Problems*, Report 3 (Springfield: The Commission, March 1955); and Ohio School Survey Committee, *Report*.

27. McGrath, "Education in 1949," p. 72.

places, school districts could not build fast enough and had to accommodate students in buildings considered to be inadequate, in rooms never intended for regular classes, such as auditoriums, or even in rented lodge halls and church basements. Some of the new construction consisted of temporary rooms set up in the school yard. And sometimes it was impossible to find enough space, so that teachers and students attended school for only half the school day.

The incomplete statistics available indicate that the school system managed to stay even with enrollments in simple numbers of rooms and teachers. Class sizes in public elementary schools were a little higher than they had been during the war but about the same as in the 1930s.[28] The average size remained close to thirty-three students per teacher through the 1950s, consistently above the twenty-five to thirty considered desirable,[29] and began to drop only in the 1960s, when enrollment growth slowed in the elementary grades. The average disguises serious crowding in areas where the student population grew fastest, but there are no data to show, for example, how many students were in classes of forty or more. Statistics on the percentage of students attending half-day sessions are only sporadically available for the crucial period. For example, 7 percent of the schoolchildren in Virginia were on half-day schedules in 1952–53, and a nationwide survey of urban school districts in 1957–58 reported that 2.4 percent of the students attended half-day sessions.[30] National data begin in 1960, at which point just under 2 percent of all public school students were on short sessions.[31] The percentage declined through the 1960s to less than 1 percent.

28. Bureau of the Census, *Historical Statistics . . . to 1970*, pt. 1, ser. H 423, p. 368. High school classes declined in size throughout the late 1940s and the 1950s.

29. Ray L. Hamon, "How Many Classrooms Do We Need? An Estimate for Public Elementary and Secondary Schools," *School Life*, vol. 34 (November 1951), pp. 17, 31; and Stephen J. Carroll, "The Federal Influence on the Production and Employment of Teachers," in Michael Timpane, ed., *The Federal Interest in Financing Schooling*, Rand Educational Policy Study (Ballinger, 1978), pp. 99–117.

30. Hazel F. Gabbard, "Children on Double Shifts—A State Studies the Problems," *School Life*, vol. 36 (November 1953), pp. 19, 27; and National Education Association, Research Division, "Class Size in Elementary Schools of Urban School Districts, 1957–58," Special Memo (Washington, D.C.: NEA, 1958), cited in Myrtle M. Imhoff and Wayne Young, "School Organization," in *Review of Education Research*, vol. 29 (April 1959), pp. 155–64.

31. DHEW, Office of Education, *Statistics of Public Elementary and Secondary Day Schools*, Fall 1969, and issues for 1964 and 1967. The percentages for the 1960s are probably underestimated because the numerator is students on half-day sessions in states that reported that information, while the denominator is all students in all states.

Table 3-3. Expenditures for Public Elementary and Secondary Schools,
Selected Years, 1929–80

| Year | Total (millions of dollars) | Percent of GNP | | Constant 1972 dollars per student[a] |
		Overall	Per 10 million students	
1929	2,251[b]	2.2	0.86	406
1933	1,948[b]	3.5	1.32	387
1939	2,289[b]	2.5	0.98	430
1940	2,344	2.3	0.92	440
1942	2,323	1.5	0.60	417
1944	2,453	1.2	0.50	423
1946	2,907	1.4	0.59	439
1948	4,311	1.7	0.69	495
1950	5,838	2.0	0.81	596
1952	7,344	2.1	0.79	626
1954	9,092	2.5	0.86	677
1956	10,955	2.6	0.83	701
1958	13,569	3.0	0.90	753
1960[c]	15,613	3.1	0.85	766
1962	18,373	3.3	0.85	799
1964	21,325	3.3	0.83	823
1966	26,248	3.5	0.82	899
1968	32,977	3.8	0.84	965
1970	40,683	4.1	0.90	990
1972	48,300	4.1	0.88	1,048
1974	57,200	4.0	0.88	1,073
1976	71,100	4.1	0.92	1,158
1978	81,200	3.8	0.86	1,208
1980	95,400[d]	3.6	0.87	1,236

Sources: Total expenditures and expenditures per student, 1929–70, are from Bureau of the Census, *Historical Statistics . . . to 1970*, pt. 1, ser. H 492, H 493, pp. 373–74; total expenditures for the 1970s are from Bureau of the Census, *Statistical Abstract of the United States, 1980*, p. 140, and expenditures per student were calculated using these data and numbers of students from table 3-1; total expenditure for 1980 is from Grant and Eiden, *Digest of Education Statistics, 1980*, p. 21. GNP and the GNP deflator for state and local purchases are from the *Economic Report of the President, February 1982*, pp. 233, 237.

a. Deflated by the GNP deflator for state and local purchases.
b. Averages of the adjacent even years.
c. Alaska and Hawaii included for the first time.
d. Estimated.

Two numbers provide a useful summary of the resources devoted to each student—the percentage of gross national product spent per 10 million public school students, and the number of dollars spent per student, corrected for inflation (table 3-3). The concept of the gross national product was defined in measurable terms only during the 1930s, leaving a short historical record to compare with the baby boom era. Of this short record, the 1.32 percent of GNP spent per 10 million students in 1933 is clearly out of line, perhaps reflecting the stickiness of teachers' money wages in a year when the price index hit rock bottom. The remaining prewar years suggest that 0.90 percent of GNP was more typical of the amount spent annually for each 10 million students in public schools. The percentage dropped sharply during the war but began to climb again once the war was over. By 1954, when the first members of the baby boom generation were in the second and third grades, it had regained the level of 1929. It fluctuated around that level through the rest of the 1950s and the 1960s.

A constant percentage of a gross national product that was growing in real terms meant, of course, that a growing quantity of resources was being committed to the education of each student. In short, the huge enrollments did not lead to a reduction in resources per student, nor even in a reduction in the rate of growth in resources per student. This is shown again by the steady rise in the number of inflation-adjusted dollars spent per student. Perhaps rather surprisingly, then, the baby boom generation did not suffer in any obvious way because of its size. Instead it did better than preceding generations, and, in proportional terms, considerably better than the generation that attended school during the 1940s.[32]

The money to finance the public school system had traditionally come from state and local governments, and it continued to come from these sources while the baby boom generation was in school. Their relative shares changed very little after the mid-1940s. The major shift had already occurred during the 1930s, when economic conditions undercut the property tax as a source of revenue and the states came to the aid of local school districts with revenues from newly passed income and sales taxes.[33] During the postwar period the states' share of public school expenditures was consistently near 40 percent, the local share was close to 60 percent, and the federal government supplied only a few percentage points.[34]

32. This conclusion overstates the case a bit, since part of the growth in real resources reflected the higher salaries necessary to attract so many new teachers. But part of the higher salaries paid for the more extensive training required of teachers in the 1950s, and thus for a true increase in resources rather than for a shift in purchasing power.

33. Advisory Commission on Intergovernmental Relations, *Significant Features of Fiscal Federalism, 1979–80 Edition* (GPO, 1980), pp. 95–96.

34. Bureau of the Census, *Historical Statistics . . . to 1970*, pt. 1, ser. H 487–91, p. 373.

The form of state aid had changed considerably in the years preceding the baby boom.[35] State aid was originally distributed as a flat grant per child—of school age, or enrolled in school—with each school district receiving the same amount per child. In the early years of the century, the states began to redesign their aid formulas, or supplement them, to help poor districts more than affluent ones. After 1920 the redesign commonly took the form of a "foundation" program, in which the state declared that a certain minimum expenditure per child was necessary for a decent education. These programs specified the revenue-raising efforts to be made by the district—for example, the minimum percentage tax on each dollar of assessed property value—and the state supplied the difference when local taxes did not produce enough money to achieve the foundation expenditure. The programs often specified as well the conditions under which the districts could spend more per child, with or without state matching funds.[36]

There were urgent calls for federal aid throughout the 1950s, as there had been in earlier decades.[37] The states could not finance the deluge themselves, it was argued, and, in any event, it was in the national interest to equalize expenditures between the states. Three issues blocked the passage of general federal aid to education: the issue of aid to parochial schools, with its implications for the constitutional separation of church and state; the issue of aid to segregated school systems;

35. See Arvid J. Burke, *Financing Public Schools in the United States*, rev. ed. (Harper and Brothers, 1957); and Clayton D. Hutchins and Albert R. Munse, *Public School Finance Programs of the United States*, DHEW, Office of Education, Misc. no. 22 (GPO, 1955).

36. For examples of state foundation programs, see the discussions in Utah Foundation, *Facts, Figures, and Charts on Utah Schools;* Illinois School Problems Commission, *Illinois School Problems;* Ohio School Survey Committee, *Report;* and Texas Research League, *Texas Public Schools under the Minimum Foundation Program: An Evaluation, 1949-1954*, Report 1, Summary of a Survey for the State Board of Education (Austin: Texas Research League, 1954).

37. Walter I. Garms, James W. Guthrie, and Lawrence C. Pierce, *School Finance: The Economics and Politics of Public Education* (Prentice-Hall, 1978), pp. 156–60; Frank J. Munger and Richard F. Fenno, Jr., *National Politics and Federal Aid to Education* (Syracuse University Press, 1962), chaps. 1–3; and Tax Institute, *Financing Education in the Public Schools*, symposium conducted by the Tax Institute, November 3–4, 1955, Princeton, New Jersey (Princeton: Tax Institute, 1956). The major forms of federal aid in place when the baby boom generation started school were grants for vocational education, which began with the Smith-Hughes Vocational Education Act of 1917, and "impact aid," first authorized by the Lanham Act of 1941, for school districts affected by federal employment. Federal aid had also been provided to the schools during the depression through various relief programs.

and the fear that federal funds would bring federal control of education. The specialized programs that were approved—the National Defense Education Act of 1958, the Elementary and Secondary Education Act of 1965, and other, even later, pieces of legislation—have never supplied more than a small proportion of total expenses. State and local governments did finance the deluge themselves after all.

After the Deluge

The number of births was steady at more than 4 million a year from the mid-1950s to 1964. It dropped significantly below that mark for the first time in 1965, and fluctuated just above 3.5 million through 1970. The birth rate—births per 1,000 women of childbearing age—had started to decline even earlier, in the late 1950s.

Observers of the school system in the late 1960s noticed the new developments but did not immediately conclude that the trends of the previous twenty years were about to be reversed.[38] They had good reasons not to. The drop in the birth rate might, of course, be only temporary. But far more persuasive was the fact that the number of women of childbearing age was growing, and was about to start growing very rapidly as the war babies and then the baby boom generation grew up. Even if the birth rate stayed at the new lower level, or dropped a bit further, another baby boom generation would soon begin as the first one married and had children. Although some demographers did speculate that births might remain low, the most likely future seemed to be one of continued growth after a temporary lull. Most people would probably have agreed with the writer who advised school administrators: "Don't stop building!"[39]

And in the meantime enrollments were still increasing. Elementary enrollment would not peak until 1970, and high school enrollment not until the late 1970s. The prospect of a few years of slower growth followed by a few more of stable enrollments was viewed by educators as a welcome breathing space, an opportunity to get ahead of enrollments

38. George J. Collins, "So Get At That Backlog *Now*," *School Management*, vol. 11 (November 1967), pp. 55, 58–59, 124; N. L. Engelhardt, Jr., and Barbara Harrison, "There's a Bigger Boom Ahead . . . ," *School Management*, vol. 11 (November 1967), pp. 54, 57, 124; "Population Trends Signal School Needs," *NEA Research Bulletin*, vol. 46 (March 1968), pp. 24–28; and "Population Trends and School Enrollments," *NEA Research Bulletin*, vol. 47 (March 1969), pp. 25–29.

39. Collins, "So Get At That Backlog *Now*," p. 124.

for a change, ease crowded conditions, and pursue other objectives more vigorously: the expansion of kindergartens and nursery schools, of special programs for potential dropouts and handicapped children, and of special facilities like language laboratories, art rooms, and elementary school libraries.[40]

Then, in the early 1970s, as the second baby boom was supposed to be getting under way, births dropped to a new low, just above 3 million a year, and stayed there. The temporary breathing space began to reveal itself as a long-term decline in enrollments.[41] By this time the enrollment rates of 5- and 6-year-olds, and of teenagers of high school age, exceeded 90 percent and could not do much to offset the declining numbers (table 3-2). Enrollment in the elementary grades began to decline so sharply that total enrollment also declined in spite of the continuing growth in the high schools (table 3-1).

Schools hired teachers at a brisk pace until the end of the 1960s, and with enrollments growing more slowly, class sizes declined at last.[42] But the boom market for teachers ended abruptly when the growth in enrollment ended. It was no longer necessary to hire additional teachers to staff new classrooms full of students. As enrollment declined, it was not even necessary to replace all the teachers who retired or left the profession. The number of teachers employed in the public schools peaked in the mid-1970s at 2.2 million and then turned down, but enrollment fell faster and class sizes continued to drop. The number of teaching jobs available each year was only a fraction of what it had been earlier.[43]

40. Collins, "So Get At that Backlog *Now*"; Engelhardt and Harrison, "There's a Bigger Boom Ahead"; "Population Trends and School Enrollments"; "Outlook in School Enrolment and Teacher Supply," *The Education Digest*, vol. 34 (October 1968), pp. 1–3; and Frederick W. Hill, "School Facilities and Declining Enrollments," *American School and University*, vol. 46 (November 1973), p. 16.

41. George W. Neill, "Statistics Point to a New State of Education," *Compact*, vol. 8 (January–February 1974), pp. 19–21; Cyril G. Sargent, "Fewer Pupils, Surplus Space: The Problem of School Shrinkage," *Phi Delta Kappan*, vol. 56 (January 1975), pp. 352–57; and "Declining Enrollments—the Numbers," *National Association of Secondary School Principals Bulletin*, vol. 60 (May 1976), pp. 92–97.

42. Data on teachers and pupil–teacher ratios in the public schools are from Bureau of the Census, *Historical Statistics of the United States . . . to 1970*, pt. 1, ser. H 420–30, H 523–30, pp. 368, 375; Bureau of the Census, *Statistical Abstract of the United States, 1979* (GPO, 1979), p. 153; and NCES, unpublished data.

43. In Indiana, for example, the number of new hires declined from 3,579 to 1,607 elementary teachers and from 1,494 to 927 secondary teachers between 1970–71 and 1975–76. Indiana State Commission for Higher Education, *Employability of Elementary and Secondary School Teachers in Indiana*, Indiana College-level Manpower Study Report 7 (Indianapolis: The Commission, 1976).

The demand for teachers collapsed only a year or two after the first members of the baby boom generation graduated from college. Encouraged by the boom market they and their siblings had created during the preceding twenty years, they had majored in education in record numbers, and painful adjustments were necessary as this enormous supply met up with the suddenly weak demand. Teachers' salaries peaked relative to wages elsewhere in the economy about 1970 and then declined somewhat.[44] Many disappointed graduates, trained to teach, had to look for other jobs. As incoming college freshmen observed what was happening, the proportion planning to teach plummeted, and the academic qualifications of those who majored in education slipped relative to the qualifications of college students generally.[45]

The need for new classrooms also fell away, and the proportion of total expenditures devoted to construction dropped to lower levels than at any time in this century except during World War II.[46] Voters encouraged the trend by approving only about half the new issues offered them in school bond elections during the late 1960s and the 1970s, compared with more than 70 percent during the height of the baby boom.[47] Where the declines in enrollment were severe, existing buildings were sold, rented, or converted to other uses.[48] Discussions of how to use excess space, or close a school with the minimum of public displeasure, cropped up frequently in school journals.[49]

The total share of GNP going to public elementary and secondary

44. Grant and Eiden, *Digest of Education Statistics, 1980;* and average weekly earnings from *Economic Report of the President, January 1981*, p. 275. For explanation, see note 16.

45. Carroll, "Federal Influence on the Production and Employment of Teachers," p. 112; and W. Timothy Weaver, "The Tragedy of the Commons: The Effects of Supply and Demand on the Education Talent Pool," paper presented at the annual meeting of the American Association of Colleges of Teacher Education, Detroit, February 19, 1981.

46. Bureau of the Census, *Historical Statistics . . . to 1970*, pt. 1, ser. H 492–507, pp. 373–74; Grant and Eiden, *Digest of Education Statistics, 1980*, p. 22; and W. Vance Grant and C. George Lind, *Digest of Education Statistics, 1979* (GPO, 1979), p. 25.

47. Grant and Lind, *Digest of Education Statistics, 1979*, p. 72.

48. Between 1970 and 1976, the year of the intercensal Survey of Income and Education, the population 5 through 14 years of age increased substantially in only three states—Florida, Arizona, and Nevada; it held approximately even in four and declined in all the rest. Bureau of the Census, *Historical Statistics . . . to 1970*, pt. 1, ser. A 195–209, pp. 24–37; and Bureau of the Census, *Current Population Reports*, series P-20, no. 334, "Demographic, Social, and Economic Profile of States: Spring 1976" (GPO, 1979), table 1, p. 10.

49. Harold B. Gores, "Declining Enrollment and Options for Unused Space," *National Association of Secondary School Principals Bulletin*, vol. 60 (May 1976), pp. 92–97; Sargent, "Fewer Pupils, Surplus Space"; and "What To Do If Shrinking Enrollment Forces You to Shut a School," *Nation's Schools*, vol. 91 (February 1973), pp. 12–13.

education leveled off in the 1970s (table 3-3). In part this happened automatically because state aid was linked to enrollment, and in part it happened because voters resisted proposals for further expenditures. Faced with the prospect of declining budgets, some educators urged that the resources be kept in education—even increased—and used to improve quality.[50] The House Select Committee on Population summarized this view: "Society has an opportunity today to improve the entire educational system by allowing the decline in the number of students to result in more resources per student."[51] Oddly enough, the proponents of this view did not seem to realize that resources per student had grown throughout the postwar period and were continuing to grow even as they spoke (table 3-3). Class sizes fell below twenty-five students per teacher, and virtually all teachers had at least a B.A.; indeed, by the mid-1970s, more than a third held master's degrees.[52]

At the end of the 1970s the schools faced a few more years of decline in elementary enrollment and a longer period of decline in the high schools as the small cohorts born during the 1970s worked their way through the system. After that, educators hoped—on the basis of Census Bureau projections—that enrollment would rise somewhat. The problem of the future was how best to manage the schools during a period of fluctuating enrollment.

Higher Education

The history of higher education in the twentieth century has been one of often-explosive growth in enrollments, interrupted from time to time

50. Neill, "Statistics Point to New State of Education"; Duane J. Mattheis, "What Shrinking Enrollments May Mean to America's Schools and Students," *School Management*, vol. 18 (June–July 1974), p. 8; and William F. Keough, Jr., "How to Make the Best of Your School District's Enrollment Slide,"*American School Board Journal*, vol. 162 (June 1975), pp. 40–43.

51. *Domestic Consequences of United States Population Change*, Report prepared by the House Select Committee on Population, 95 Cong. 2 sess. (GPO, 1978), p. 47.

52. *Education Yearbook 1972–73*, p. 536. More resources do not inevitably lead to greater achievement, as the well-publicized decline in college board scores attests. An advisory panel convened by the College Board and Educational Testing Service concluded that most of the decline between 1963 and 1970 was due to the changing composition of the groups taking the test. Only about one-quarter of the decline between 1970 and 1977 was for this reason. The panel was unable to pinpoint the remaining causes, but suggested that several were important—for example, the increasing amount of school time spent on electives, a general decline in seriousness of educational purpose, and television. College Entrance Examination Board, *On Further Examination: Report of the Advisory Panel on the Scholastic Aptitude Test Score Decline* (New York: CEEB, 1977), especially pp. 44–48.

by short, sharp declines brought on by war or depression. Because attendance is voluntary, the number of students in colleges and universities is far more volatile over short periods than the number in elementary and secondary schools. And the longer-term trends have consistently been dominated by the rising proportion of college-age youth who choose to enroll rather than by the size of that age group.[53]

The number of students enrolled in degree programs rose steadily until World War I, dropped by 20 percent between 1916–17 and 1917–18, and continued upward after the war ended (table 3-4).[54] The early years of the Great Depression brought another decline and recovery. Enrollments were depressed again during World War II but shot up after the war as large numbers of returning veterans, far more than anyone had expected, took advantage of the GI bill to continue their education.[55] As late as 1950 veterans accounted for 1 million out of the total of 2.7 million resident students.[56]

The early 1950s were again a period of recession in higher education. Enrollment was down after the veterans graduated, and the more ordinary trends of peacetime did not restore it to the peak reached in 1950 for several years. Real faculty salaries declined,[57] and, for a few years at least, some institutions discussed the possibility of refusing to grant tenure to any more faculty, to keep the proportion of tenured faculty from rising too high.[58]

53. Stephen J. Carroll and Peter A. Morrison, "Demographic and Economic Influences on the Growth and Decline of Higher Education," Rand Paper P-5569 (Santa Monica: Rand, 1967), p. 3. When the enrollment rate is examined in more detail, it turns out that the main factor in its growth has been the rise in the proportion of young people graduating from high school. The proportion of high school graduates going on to college has fluctuated, but shown no longer-term trend, over most of this century. See A. J. Jaffe and Walter Adams, "Trends in College Enrollment," College Board Review, vol. 55 (Winter 1964–65), pp. 27–32; and Robert Campbell and Barry N. Siegel, "The Demand for Higher Education in the United States, 1919–1964," American Economic Review, vol. 57 (June 1967), pp. 482–94.

54. The available data are biennial and do not show the drop between 1916–17 and 1917–18, reported in David D. Henry, Challenges Past, Challenges Present: An Analysis of American Higher Education Since 1930 (Jossey-Bass, 1975), p. 7.

55. Ibid., chap. 4.

56. See Allan M. Cartter, Ph.D.'s and the Academic Labor Market, report prepared for the Carnegie Commission on Higher Education (McGraw-Hill, 1976), p. 11.

57. Howard R. Bowen, "Academic Compensation: Are Faculty and Staff in American Higher Education Adequately Paid?" (New York: Teachers Insurance and Annuity Association–College Retirement Equities Fund, 1978). Bowen shows the entire period 1945–46 to 1951–52 as a period of decline in real faculty salaries in spite of the boom in enrollment because of the veterans. Ibid., table 2.

58. Cartter, Ph.D.'s and the Academic Labor Market, p. 11.

Table 3-4. Higher Education: Enrollment, Faculty, and Degrees Conferred, Selected Years, 1900–80

Thousands

Year	Degree-credit enrollment[a]		Resident instructional staff[d]	Degrees conferred[d]		
	Total[b]	Resident[c]		Bachelor's	Master's	Doctor's
1900	n.a.	238	n.a.	27	2	e
1910	n.a.	355	n.a.	37	2	e
1920	n.a.	598	n.a.	49	4	e
1930	n.a.	1,101	82	122	15	2
1940	n.a.	1,494	111	187	27	3
1942	n.a.	1,404	115	185	25	3
1944	n.a.	1,155	106	126	13	2
1946	2,078	1,677	126	136	19	2
1948	2,403	2,616	174	271	42	4
1950	2,281	2,659	190	432	58	7
1952	2,134	2,302	184	330	64	8
1954	2,446	2,515	207	292	57	9
1956	2,918	2,619	228	310	59	9
1958	3,226	2,900	258	364	66	9
1960[f]	3,583	3,216	282	389	78	10
1962	4,175	3,726	292	414	88	12
1964	4,950	4,296	331	494	106	14
1966	5,928	n.a.	412	551	141	18
1968	6,928	6,659	484	667	177	23
1970	7,920	7,545	551	827	208	30
1972	8,265	n.a.	590	938	253	33
1974	9,023	n.a.	634	1,009	278	34
1976	9,589	n.a.	781	998	313	34
1978	9,790	n.a.	812	998	311	32
1980	n.a.	n.a.	822	929	298	33

Sources: All data for the years 1900–70 are from Bureau of the Census, *Historical Statistics . . . to 1970*, pt. 1, ser. H 699, H 700, H 706, H 752, H 757, H 761, pp. 382–83, 385–86; numbers of degrees conferred, 1972–78, are from Bureau of the Census, *Statistical Abstract of the United States, 1980*, p. 174; enrollments and resident instructional staff, 1972–78, are from Grant and Eiden, *Digest of Education Statistics, 1980*, pp. 89, 106; and 1980 data are from NCES, unpublished.

n.a. Not available.

a. Total enrollment, not full-time equivalent enrollment.

b. Fall enrollment.

c. Enrollment is for the full academic year, 1900–54; for the first term of the academic year, 1956–64; and for the fall of the year thereafter.

d. For the academic year ending in the year shown.

e. Less than 1,000.

f. Data include Alaska and Hawaii in 1960 and later years.

The persistence of the baby boom during these years was beginning to make it clear, however, that higher education could look forward to sharply rising enrollments in the future. Unlike the public school system, the colleges and universities had ample time to see what was coming and plan for it. As early as 1954 the American Council on Education alerted them to the prospects in a pamphlet marked "URGENT" and entitled "A Call for Action to Meet the Impending Increase in College and

University Enrollment."[59] The estimate most frequently mentioned was that enrollment would double between the mid-1950s and 1970.[60] Conferences, workshops, and journal articles were frequently devoted to considering possible responses. Many states commissioned studies of the situation in the mid-1950s so that they could plan for the required financing and institutional growth.[61]

One possible response was to tighten admission requirements as the baby boom generation reached college age so that the enrollment growth would be no more than the institutions could handle comfortably. This possibility was never considered seriously.[62] The prevailing philosophy was that higher education should be made universally available and that enrollment rates should be allowed, even encouraged, to rise further. Plans were drawn up on that basis. Some private colleges did, of course, decide to raise requirements rather than expand enrollments, and others did not intend to expand as much as necessary to maintain their share of enrollments.[63] From the beginning it was clear that public institutions, with their less selective standards for admission, would absorb most of the increase—the more so because projections indicated that the college-age population would grow most in those areas where public institutions were most important.[64]

59. Cited in T. C. Holy, T. R. McConnell, and H. H. Semans, "California Studies Its Needs and Resources in Higher Education," *Educational Record,* vol. 36 (October 1955), p. 291.

60. Richard H. Sullivan, "Cautions and Speculations on Enrollments," *Educational Record,* vol. 35 (October 1954), pp. 250–56; and "Some College Presidents Discuss the Rising Tide," *Educational Record,* vol. 36 (July 1955), pp. 205–10. The President's Committee on Education Beyond the High School predicted in 1956 that enrollment would double by 1970, and might even triple. Henry, *Challenges Past, Challenges Present,* p. 100.

61. A. J. Brumbaugh, "In Anticipation of Increased Enrollments in Florida," *Educational Record,* vol. 36 (April 1955), pp. 129–31; Holy, McConnell, and Semans, "California Studies Its Needs"; John Dale Russell, "Meeting Ohio's Needs in Higher Education: A Report of a Preliminary Survey," *Educational Record,* vol. 37 (October 1956), pp. 303–09; and Allen O. Pfnister, "Missouri Undertakes State-wide Study," *Educational Record,* vol. 38 (October 1957), pp. 340–42.

62. See Henry, *Challenges Past, Challenges Present,* chap. 7; James L. Miller, Jr., "Who Needs Higher Education?" in W. Todd Furniss, ed., *Higher Education for Everybody? Issues and Implications* (Washington, D.C.: American Council on Education, 1971), pp. 94–105.

63. Russell, "Meeting Ohio's Needs"; and Martin Quanbeck, "Implications of Increasing Enrollments for Academic Standards and Methods," *Educational Record,* vol. 38 (April 1957), pp. 127–32.

64. Sullivan, "Cautions and Speculations on Enrollments."

California, which was one of the states where the student population was expected to grow enormously, started early to establish a system to accommodate it. A study conducted in the mid-1950s considered the situation through 1965.[65] It recommended the expansion of the state's system of junior colleges and the enlargement of its existing college and university campuses, but no new ones before 1965; the existing campuses were already located in the areas of greatest projected population growth. The junior colleges would accept virtually all applicants, the state colleges would apply stricter standards, and the universities would apply the strictest of all. To be admitted to the University of California a student had to be in the upper 12.5 percent of the high school graduating class.[66] Graduate training was offered only through the state colleges and the university system, and doctoral programs were run by the university system. The study concluded that "California will be able to support a program of public higher education for the projected enrollments comparable in both scope and quality to that now offered, without unreasonable demands on the state's economy or excessive increase in the burden of taxation."[67]

Thus the administrators and legislators concerned with higher education planned to do far more than simply stay even with the increasing numbers. They also planned to expand access to higher education and even hoped to improve the range and quality of the programs offered. They succeeded in both respects.

Enrollments grew much faster during the 1960s than could be explained by the numbers of children born during the 1940s and 1950s. In 1960, 38 percent of all 18- and 19-year-olds were enrolled in school (a few were in high school) and 19 percent of those 20 and 21 (table 3-2). By 1969 these groups had reached their peak enrollment rates—50 and 34 percent, respectively.[68] Enrollment in degree programs jumped from 3.6 million in 1960 to 7.9 million in 1970 (table 3-4). After 1964, the year the children born in 1946 turned 18, 500,000 students were added each year. Those who could not follow their fathers to Harvard or Yale had

65. Holy, McConnell, and Semans, "California Studies Its Needs."
66. The information in this and the following sentence is taken from Charles J. Hitch, "California's Master Plan: Some Kind of Education for Nearly Everybody," in Furniss, ed., *Higher Education for Everybody?* pp. 23–25.
67. Holy, McConnell, and Semans, "California Studies Its Needs," p. 303.
68. Bureau of the Census, *Current Population Reports,* series P-20, no. 335, "School Enrollment—Social and Economic Characteristics of Students: October 1978," Advance Report (GPO, 1979), p. 4.

to blame the trend toward universal higher education, and the affluence that made it possible, more than their membership in a large generation.

As expected, public institutions absorbed most of the growth. In 1950 they accounted for half the enrollment in institutions of higher education; by 1970 their share was almost three-quarters of the total.[69] Community colleges grew even faster than the public sector as a whole: their share of total enrollment rose from 7 percent in 1950 to 25 percent in 1970.[70]

At the same time, instructional costs per student rose. Expenditures for education per full-time equivalent student in all institutions of higher education, expressed in 1967 dollars, were $1,000 in 1949–50, about $1,500 in 1959–60, and almost $2,000 in 1969–70.[71] This was in sharp contrast to the preceding two decades, when expenditures per student had been essentially constant in real terms. The trend during the 1950s and 1960s reflected the public's desire to see higher education improve. As one observer put it, spending grew "precisely because society was willing to pour rapidly increasing resources into higher education. . . . The public and their leaders . . . wanted the colleges and universities to pay better salaries, to add new buildings and equipment, and to develop larger libraries."[72]

It was the best of times for college faculty. Between 1966 and 1970, the period of fastest growth, the equivalent of more than 20,000 full-time teachers (instructors and above) were added every year.[73] Academic salaries and fringe benefits, which had not risen as fast as those in other occupations during the first half of the century, rose faster after the early

69. David W. Breneman and Chester E. Finn, Jr., "An Uncertain Future," in Breneman and Finn, eds., *Public Policy and Private Higher Education* (Brookings Institution, 1978), p. 22.

70. David W. Breneman and Susan C. Nelson, *Financing Community Colleges: An Economic Perspective* (Brookings Institution, 1981), p. 8.

71. Howard R. Bowen, *The Costs of Higher Education: How Much Do Colleges and Universities Spend per Student and How Much Should They Spend?* report issued by the Carnegie Council on Policy Studies in Higher Education (Jossey-Bass, 1980), p. 38. Expenditures per student might have been even higher in 1970 had not public institutions, which have traditionally spent less per student, grown faster than private institutions over the period.

72. Ibid., p. 37.

73. Carnegie Council on Policy Studies in Higher Education, *Three Thousand Futures: The Next Twenty Years for Higher Education,* Final Report (Jossey-Bass, 1980), p. 81. The actual number of people hired was much larger, as table 3-4 shows, because many were only part-time. The numbers shown in table 3-4 also include teachers below the rank of instructor, the majority of whom are part-time.

1950s and continued to rise faster during the 1960s.[74] In their efforts to attract and hold teachers, institutions bestowed tenure more freely.[75] There was some concern at the time that the strong demand for faculty was forcing institutions to settle for less, lowering the quality, or at least the credentials, of their faculty. Statistics were frequently cited showing that newly hired teachers were less likely than existing faculty to have the Ph.D. But the concern was subsequently discovered to be based on a misinterpretation of incomplete data. Many of the new hires completed their degrees within a few years after starting work, and in such numbers that the proportion of all faculty with the Ph.D. rose from 41 percent in 1953–54 to 51 percent in 1962–63, even before new Ph.D.'s began to flood onto the market in the late 1960s.[76]

The federal government helped finance higher education to a much greater extent than it had elementary and secondary education. In large part this was accidental. Government funding for research and graduate study, stimulated first by the scientific successes of World War II and later by the crisis atmosphere after the launch of Sputnik by the Russians in 1957, reached its peak as a percentage of institutions' income in the late 1960s.[77] But part of the increased aid was intentional, the result of federal programs to help with the construction needed to accommodate rising enrollments, and to provide scholarships and loans to students. The share of educational and general income supplied to institutions of higher education by the federal government rose to almost one-quarter of the total before declining in the 1970s.[78]

State and local governments—primarily state governments—shouldered the largest part of the expense. By 1969–70 they were supplying over 40 percent of the educational and general income for higher education, and their share continued to grow in the 1970s.[79] Tuition and fees accounted for just over one-quarter of the total, somewhat less than

74. Bowen, "Academic Compensation," pp. 8–9.

75. Roy Radner and Charlotte V. Kuh, "Market Conditions and Tenure in U.S. Higher Education: 1955–1973," Technical Report 2 (Carnegie Council on Policy Studies in Higher Education, 1977).

76. Allan M. Cartter, "A New Look at the Supply of College Teachers," Educational Record, vol. 46 (Summer 1965), p. 269.

77. See Henry, Challenges Past, Challenges Present, chap. 8; and Miller, "Who Needs Higher Education?"

78. Carnegie Council on Policy Studies in Higher Education, Three Thousand Futures, p. 140.

79. Ibid.

before World War II,[80] and 7 to 8 percent came from private gifts and grants.[81] The share from endowment income dropped off sharply for many reasons, including the faster growth of public institutions, which have traditionally had only small endowments (or none), and a preference for using gifts and grants immediately to meet operating expenses rather than adding them to the endowment fund.[82]

The boom in higher education came to an end before its time. Although the baby boom generation continued to enter college—the cohort born in 1964 turned 18 in 1982—enrollment rates began to decline after 1969 instead of continuing upward. Between 1969 and 1978 the rate for 18- and 19-year-olds slipped from 50 to 45 percent, and the rate for 20- and 21-year-olds from 34 to 30 percent. Total enrollment continued to grow, but more slowly (table 3-4). The decline in enrollment rates was concentrated among young men, especially those 18 and 19.[83] Faced with a worsening job market for male college graduates (see chapter 4), and no longer in need of draft deferments, they stopped entering college in such numbers. The job market for female college graduates was better, and enrollment rates for young women rose somewhat over the 1970s, but not by enough to prevent the overall rate from declining.

At the same time, an increasingly troubled economy, public reaction to campus disturbances, and growing competition from other claimants for the federal dollar meant that money was no longer so readily available. Many schools found that their costs had been growing faster than their income for some time and were forced first to cut back their plans and then their existing programs.[84] Reflecting the new austerity, educational

80. This is the proportion supplied by gross tuition, which includes veterans' benefits, social security dependents' benefits, and other forms of student aid paid directly to the student and then used by the student to pay tuition. Gross tuition thus overestimates the amount paid by the student and his or her family from their own resources. Susan C. Nelson, "Financial Trends and Issues," in Breneman and Finn, eds., *Public Policy and Private Higher Education*, p. 73. Tuition and fees supplied just under half the income of private institutions during the 1960s, but only between 15 and 20 percent of the income of public institutions. Carnegie Council on Policy Studies in Higher Education, *Three Thousand Futures*, pp. 142–43.

81. Gifts and grants are much more important for private than for public institutions.

82. Henry, *Challenges Past, Challenges Present*, chap. 7.

83. Bureau of the Census, *Current Population Reports*, series P-20: no. 362, "School Enrollment—Social and Economic Characteristics of Students: October 1980" (GPO, 1981), p. 5; and no. 278, "School Enrollment—Social and Economic Characteristics of Students: October 1974" (GPO, 1975), p. 4.

84. Earl F. Cheit, *The New Depression in Higher Education: A Study of Financial Conditions at 41 Colleges and Universities* (McGraw-Hill, 1971).

expenditures per student did not quite stay even with inflation during the 1970s; they were slightly lower in real terms at the end of the decade than at the beginning.[85] Although net additions to faculty were almost as large in the early 1970s as they had been in the late 1960s, the supply of new Ph.D.'s was so much larger and economic conditions so much less favorable that academic salaries no longer kept up with inflation or with salaries in other occupations.[86] By the end of the 1970s, with the prospect that enrollment would actually decline in the 1980s, net additions to faculty dropped almost to zero.

The Carnegie Council on Policy Studies in Higher Education concluded that the 1970s had nonetheless been good years for higher education, years of growth and improvement.[87] The decades ahead promised more turbulence, but no one could be sure how much, or what form it would take. If the historical upward trend in enrollment rates reasserted itself, total enrollment would rise 25 percent between 1980 and 2000. If enrollment rates simply maintained the levels of the late 1970s, enrollment would decline by 25 percent. The council put its bet on a decline of 5 to 15 percent and predicted that not until 2010 would total enrollment regain the level of 1978.[88]

Conclusions

At first glance the school system looks like a particularly clear example of an age-related industry, at least at the elementary and secondary levels. After all, attendance is required by law. Yet the system's development as the baby boom generation progressed through it was anything but a straightforward response to rising numbers of students. There were signs of strain, especially in areas where the youthful population grew especially rapidly, but for the most part these were temporary deviations from a rapidly rising standard of education rather than a sign that standards were deteriorating because of the influx of

85. Bowen, *Costs of Higher Education,* p. 38.

86. Bowen, "Academic Compensation"; and W. Lee Hansen, "An Era of Continuing Decline: Annual Report on the Economic Status of the Profession, 1978–79," *Academe,* vol. 65 (September 1979), pp. 319–67.

87. Carnegie Council on Policy Studies in Higher Education, *Three Thousand Futures,* pp. 9–31.

88. Ibid., pp. 32–48.

students. Throughout the 1950s and 1960s enrollment rates rose as education was made more widely available. The educational qualifications of teachers improved, new school buildings were more comfortable and better equipped than old ones, and course offerings were expanded. To pay for the improvements, the amount spent per student rose steadily in real terms.

The baby boom generation was thus not educationally deprived because of its numbers. More of its members were educated, and more was spent per student on its education than on that of any previous generation. Because of its greater educational opportunities the baby boom generation has achieved a higher level of formal schooling than any previous generation (table 3-5). In 1980 about 85 percent of its members aged 25 through 29 had graduated from high school, compared with only 50 percent of that age group in 1950, and 60 percent in 1960. Also in 1980 almost 45 percent of the same age group had had some college, compared with less than 20 percent in 1950.

Their ultimate academic achievements may be even greater. As the enrollment rates for those in their twenties and early thirties show (table 3-2), many members of the baby boom generation are continuing their education into adulthood. Recent trends in enrollment rates also suggest that an interesting difference may develop between the older and younger members of the generation. Enrollment rates for young women have continued to increase in the 1970s, so that the younger women of the baby boom are likely to achieve a higher level of formal education than the older women, continuing the longer-term trend. But enrollment rates for young men have fallen so much that the younger men are unlikely to exceed the educational attainment of the older ones, and may fall somewhat short of that standard unless they return to school in droves later in life.

It is possible, of course, that the baby boom generation would have done even better had it not been so large, that it suffered in relative if not in absolute terms. But it is hard to believe that any such effect was important—expenditures per student grew steadily throughout the period, the educational preparation of teachers improved, and as the baby boom generation reached the proper ages the proportions of young people enrolled in high school and college rose much faster than before. The affluence of the time and the public's concern for education overwhelmed any generational disadvantage, just as the depression and

Table 3-5. Distribution of Young Adults by Years of School Completed, 1950, 1960, 1970, and 1980

Percent

Year, sex, and age	Elementary	High school		College			High school graduates
		1–3	*4*	*1–3*	*4*	*5 or more*	
1950[a]							
Men 25–29	26.9	21.4	29.0	10.8	9.4[b]	n.a.	49.2
Women 25–29	22.8	21.5	38.7	9.4	5.8[b]	n.a.	53.9
Men 30–34	31.5	21.0	27.7	8.7	8.7[b]	n.a.	45.1
Women 30–34	28.7	21.6	33.6	8.3	5.9[b]	n.a.	47.8
1960							
Men 25–29	19.7	20.7	32.2	13.0	8.4	6.1	59.7
Women 25–29	15.5	23.0	42.6	11.2	6.2	1.6	61.6
Men 30–34	23.9	22.9	28.0	10.7	8.1	6.5	53.3
Women 30–34	18.8	23.3	40.2	10.5	5.5	1.8	58.0
1970							
Men 25–29	9.6	16.2	38.2	16.7	9.7	9.6	74.2
Women 25–29	8.3	18.2	45.3	15.0	9.4	3.8	73.5
Men 30–34	13.3	17.8	37.1	13.4	8.6	9.7	68.8
Women 30–34	11.2	20.2	45.3	12.9	7.3	3.2	68.7
1980							
Men 25–29	4.5	9.9	37.9	23.6	15.1	8.9	85.5
Women 25–29	4.2	10.2	43.8	20.8	14.5	6.4	85.5
Men 30–34	5.2	8.0	32.9	22.6	17.1	14.3	86.9
Women 30–34	5.3	10.6	43.7	19.7	12.6	8.1	84.1

Sources: Bureau of the Census, *United States Census of Population: 1950*, Special Report P-E no. 5B, "Education" (GPO, 1953), table 5, pp. 42–45; Bureau of the Census, *United States Census of Population: 1960, Subject Reports*, Final Report PC(2)-5B, "Educational Attainment" (GPO, 1963), table 1, pp. 1–4; Bureau of the Census, *Census of Population, 1970, Subject Reports*, Final Report PC(2)-5B, "Educational Attainment" (GPO, 1973), table 1, pp. 3–7; and Bureau of the Census, unpublished data for 1980.

n.a. Not available.

a. The percentages do not sum to 100, because those who did not answer this question on the census, never more than 2.5 percent of the age-sex group, were not distributed across the categories on the basis of their other characteristics, as they were in later years.

b. Includes those with five or more years of college.

World War II overwhelmed any advantage of belonging to a small generation for those born in the late 1920s and the 1930s.

The history of the past several decades illustrates the special difficulties that elementary and secondary schools face in planning ahead, especially for the lower grades, because of the short lead time between the publication of birth statistics and the entry of these children into kindergarten and first grade. To make reasonably long-term plans, school administrators must guess about future births. They guessed wrong at both ends of the baby boom—for good, solid reasons based on careful study of past birth rates and projected numbers of young adults. In the postwar period it seemed clear that the long-term decline in birth rates would reassert itself and the baby boom would not last. In the late 1960s it seemed clear that, even if birth rates remained low, total births would increase along with the growing numbers of women of childbearing age. In both cases, predictions based in large part on age structure were confounded by changes in behavior.

The colleges and universities had, of course, ample time to plan ahead, and they appear to have made good use of it. Their experience demonstrates even more clearly that growth in education was not simply a response to age structure. Population was only one factor in the vast expansion of higher education, and not the most important one. Even more than in elementary and secondary education, age structure was dominated by affluence and educational philosophy.

As smaller cohorts of births followed the end of the baby boom in the early 1960s, elementary and then secondary enrollments began to decline. Even with the uncertainty introduced by enrollment rates in higher education, total enrollment in colleges and universities will most likely also begin to decline in the early 1980s, and it may not regain the current level until after the year 2000. Faced with declining numbers of students after so many boom years, educators argue that resources should not be moved out of education—after all, they will be needed again when enrollments turn up—and that they should even be increased. Now, they urge, when the problem of numbers is no longer paramount, is the time to stress quality.

The growth in educational budgets during the 1950s and 1960s, and even the 1970s, was more than a response to the rise in numbers, and future decisions about those resources will be based on more than the decline in enrollments. But one fact stands out. Each sector of the economy through which the baby boom passes will undoubtedly be able to present good arguments why its share of the GNP should be maintained after that generation has gone by. Some of the arguments may be persuasive. But some sectors will have to accept lower shares if the sectors into which the baby boom is moving are to have enough. If the proportion of GNP per 10 million students were kept at the average level of the past several decades (0.85 percent), which would allow students to share proportionately with others in the growth or decline of the economy, the total share of GNP committed to public elementary and secondary education would decline from a high of 4.1 percent in 1970 to 3.4 percent in 1985, freeing resources for other uses.[89]

The coming reallocation of resources will be particularly important for state and local governments. In 1970, when elementary and secondary enrollments peaked and enrollment in higher education was still rising, education accounted for 36 percent of the expenditures of state and local governments.[90] In 1978 it was still 32 percent of the total, by far the largest item of expenditure. As elementary and secondary enrollments reach their low point in the 1980s, and enrollments in higher education begin to decline, the major claim on state and local budgets will ease further. Both levels of government should find themselves in less need of federal funds and better able to pick up expenses in areas other than education.

89. This calculation is based on the Census Bureau's series 2 population projections and the 1978 enrollment rates for children 3 through 17. The complete set of estimates for two different percentages of GNP per 10 million students are as follows:

Percent of GNP per 10 million students	Total share of GNP (percent)				
	1980	1985	1990	1995	2000
0.85	3.5	3.4	3.6	3.9	4.0
0.90	3.8	3.6	3.8	4.1	4.2

These can be compared with the historic trend in GNP share shown in table 3-3.

90. Bureau of the Census, *Statistical Abstract of the United States, 1980* (GPO, 1980), p. 296.

chapter four The Labor Market

After 1962 the labor force began to grow rapidly as succeeding waves of the baby boom generation reached the official working age of 16. The impact of the large cohorts of young people was reinforced by simultaneous changes in labor force participation rates. An unusually high percentage of the generation sought work during its teen years, and young women also entered the labor force in greater and greater numbers.[1] All during the 1960s the fastest growing groups in the labor force were teenagers and young women, and then, as the 1960s gave way to the 1970s and the first members of the baby boom generation entered their twenties, young adults generally.

The economy was able to absorb most of the new workers. Employment grew almost as fast as the labor force over these years (in fact, faster during the 1960s), and the proportion of the population in civilian jobs was at a postwar high during the 1970s. But the unemployment rate was also high by postwar standards, in spite of rates of inflation that had, in the past, signaled tight labor markets. Unemployment among teenagers reached unprecedented levels. Earnings corrected for inflation stagnated after two decades of steady growth, and young college graduates had difficulty finding jobs.[2] The baby boom generation's first years in the labor market fell considerably short of the expectations its members had formed growing up in the 1950s and 1960s.

As these conditions persisted, analysts argued with increasing frequency that the conjunction of events was not accidental, that the

1. The participation rates of older women, which had risen sharply during the 1950s, rose only modestly during the 1960s and 1970s. Participation rates from Bureau of Labor Statistics, *Handbook of Labor Statistics 1975—Reference Edition*, Bulletin 1865 (Government Printing Office, 1975); and *Employment and Earnings*, vol. 27 (January 1980), and previous January issues.

2. *Economic Report of the President, January 1979*, pp. 214–16, 224–25; and Richard B. Freeman, *The Overeducated American* (Academic Press, 1976).

economy was showing the strains of trying to absorb so many additional workers, many of them inexperienced, in such a short time. They reasoned that the baby boom generation was not only contributing to the problems of the economy but that it was, in part, the cause of its own problems in the labor market.

This chapter examines the baby boom's experience in the labor market, compared with that of other generations and compared with what that experience might have been had the generation been smaller, and considers the evidence that the size of the generation has been a major factor in its experience. Two subjects are investigated in particular—unemployment and the earnings of young workers.

As background for the chapter, table 4-1 shows the changes that have taken place in the size and age structure of the labor force since 1950. The labor force grew by more than 30 million workers between 1965 and 1980, compared with 12 million between 1950 and 1965; the total stood at 105 million in 1980. As mentioned, the growth was concentrated in the young age groups—the more so because the small cohorts born during the 1930s were reaching middle age at the same time.

The share of the young in the labor force was at its lowest point in the mid-1950s. In 1955 teenagers accounted for 6.3 percent of the labor force and young adults for 8.7 percent—a total of 15.0 percent between them. From then on, their shares rose—first because of the cohorts born during World War II, and later because of the baby boom generation itself— and were at their peak in 1978: teenagers had grown to 9.5 percent of the labor force and those 20 through 24 to 14.9 percent—a total of 24.4 percent.[3] The projections for 1985 and 1990 show that the share of teenagers and young adults in the labor force is expected to decline in the future as the baby boom generation ages and is replaced by the smaller cohorts born since the mid-1960s.

The Effect of Age Structure on the Unemployment Rate

In the early 1960s the Council of Economic Advisers established 4 percent as the overall unemployment rate that could be achieved by means of fiscal and monetary policies without causing substantial infla-

3. Almost all the change was due to the change in the age structure of the population; if labor force participation rates had been the same in 1978 as in 1955, the percentage would have been reduced only slightly, to 23.3 percent.

Table 4-1. Distribution of the Civilian Labor Force, by Age and Sex, Selected Years, 1950–80, and Projections, 1985 and 1990

Percent unless otherwise indicated

Age-sex group	1950	1955	1960	1965	1970	1975	1980	1985a	1990a
Total number (thousands)	62,208	65,023	69,628	74,455	82,715	92,613	104,719	114,985	122,375
16–17									
Total	2.7	2.6	3.0	3.3	3.8	4.0	3.6	3.2	2.8
Women	1.0	1.0	1.2	1.3	1.6	1.8	1.7	1.5	1.4
Men	1.7	1.7	1.9	2.1	2.2	2.2	2.0	1.6	1.4
18–19									
Total	4.1	3.7	3.9	4.6	5.0	5.5	5.2	4.3	4.1
Women	1.8	1.7	1.8	2.1	2.3	2.6	2.5	2.1	2.1
Men	2.3	2.0	2.2	2.5	2.7	2.9	2.7	2.2	2.0
20–24									
Total	11.8	8.7	9.6	11.1	12.8	14.5	14.7	13.8	11.6
Women	4.3	3.8	3.7	4.5	5.9	6.6	6.8	6.7	5.8
Men	7.5	5.0	5.9	6.6	6.9	8.0	7.9	7.1	5.8
25–34									
Total	23.5	23.2	20.7	19.1	20.6	24.1	26.9	28.6	28.6
Women	6.6	6.5	5.9	5.8	6.9	9.1	11.3	13.0	13.5
Men	16.9	16.6	14.7	13.3	13.7	15.0	15.6	15.6	15.1
35–44									
Total	22.4	23.7	23.4	22.6	19.9	18.1	19.3	22.5	25.5
Women	6.7	7.4	7.6	7.7	7.2	7.0	8.2	10.1	11.9
Men	15.7	16.3	15.8	14.9	12.7	11.1	11.1	12.4	13.6
45–54									
Total	18.4	20.0	21.3	21.2	20.5	18.5	16.2	14.7	15.8
Women	5.4	6.4	7.6	7.7	7.9	7.2	6.7	6.2	6.8
Men	13.1	13.6	13.8	13.5	12.6	11.3	9.5	8.5	9.0
55–64									
Total	12.3	13.1	13.5	13.9	13.6	12.1	11.2	10.3	9.1
Women	3.0	3.7	4.3	4.8	5.0	4.6	4.4	4.1	3.7
Men	9.3	9.4	9.2	9.1	8.6	7.5	6.8	6.2	5.4
65 and over									
Total	4.9	5.1	4.6	4.2	3.9	3.2	2.9	2.6	2.5
Women	0.9	1.2	1.3	1.3	1.3	1.1	1.1	1.0	1.0
Men	3.9	3.9	3.3	2.9	2.6	2.1	1.8	1.6	1.5

Sources: Data for 1950–75 are from Bureau of Labor Statistics, *Handbook of Labor Statistics 1978,* Bulletin 2000 (Government Printing Office, 1979), pp. 21, 28–29; for 1980, from BLS, unpublished data; and projections are from Howard N. Fullerton, Jr., "The 1995 Labor Force: A First Look," *Monthly Labor Review,* vol. 103 (December 1980), pp. 11–21. Figures are rounded.
a. BLS intermediate projections.

tion.[4] This target was based on studies of the economy's performance during the 1950s and, of necessity, accepted the underlying economic conditions of that time, including the rate of technological change, the structure of markets, and many other factors. Most important for this chapter, the target implicitly incorporated the labor force composition

4. *Economic Report of the President, January 1962,* pp. 40–49.

Table 4-2. Unemployment Rates of the Civilian Labor Force, by Age and Sex, Selected Years, 1950–80

Percent

Age-sex group	1950	1955	1960	1965	1970	1975	1980
All	5.3	4.4	5.5	4.5	4.9	8.5	7.1
16–17							
Women	14.2	12.0	15.4	17.2	17.4	21.2	19.5
Men	13.3	12.5	15.5	16.1	16.9	21.6	20.4
18–19							
Women	9.8	9.1	13.0	14.8	14.4	18.7	15.6
Men	12.3	10.8	15.0	12.4	13.4	19.0	16.7
20–24							
Women	6.9	6.1	8.3	7.3	7.9	12.7	10.3
Men	8.1	7.7	8.9	6.3	8.4	14.3	12.5
25–34							
Women	5.7	5.3	6.3	5.5	5.7	9.1	7.2
Men	4.4	3.3	4.8	3.0	3.4	7.0	6.7
35–44							
Women	4.4	4.0	4.8	4.6	4.4	6.9	5.3
Men	3.6	3.1	3.8	2.6	2.4	4.9	4.1
45–54							
Women	4.5	3.6	4.2	3.2	3.5	5.9	4.5
Men	4.0	3.2	4.1	2.5	2.4	4.8	3.6
55–64							
Women	4.5	3.8	3.4	2.8	2.7	5.1	3.3
Men	4.9	4.3	4.6	3.3	2.8	4.3	3.4
65 and over							
Women	3.4	2.3	2.8	2.8	3.1	5.1	3.1
Men	4.8	4.0	4.2	3.5	3.3	5.4	3.1

Sources: Bureau of Labor Statistics, *Handbook of Labor Statistics, 1978*, pp. 176–80; and BLS, unpublished data.

of the 1950s, when teenagers and young adults made up an unusually small share of the labor force.

Teenagers have had much higher unemployment rates than adults throughout the postwar period (table 4-2). In 1955, for example, unemployment was 12 percent for 16- and 17-year-olds and about 10 percent for 18- and 19-year-olds. By contrast, the rate for men between 25 and 55 was just over 3 percent. Moreover, young adults have had higher rates than older adults, and women have usually had higher rates than men of the same age. While the level for each group rises and falls with the business cycle, the pattern of differences between groups has persisted over the years. Thus the unemployment rate that could be achieved through the management of aggregate demand could be expected to change with the composition of the labor force. And, in particular, the target level would have to be set higher when the share of young people in the labor force rose substantially.

The council recognized that the unemployment target could not be fixed at a given number for all time. It reflects contemporary economic conditions and must be changed to reflect changes in those conditions. The council considered, but rejected, arguments that several character-istics of the economy of the early 1960s—such as a more rapid rate of technological change and the entry of the baby boom generation into the labor force—were already putting the 4 percent target beyond reach. The 1965 report granted the significance of the baby boom, stating that the "great increase in the number of young, inexperienced workers constitutes the most important change in the labor force during this decade."[5] But the council believed that other factors counterbalanced the influx of young workers, and that government programs aimed at reducing particular pockets of unemployment would help still more, making it possible to achieve overall rates even lower than 4 percent.

During the 1970s, it proved impossible to maintain unemployment at 4 percent, or even at somewhat higher levels. One reason was that the composition of the labor force continued to shift toward groups with high unemployment rates. The target rate needed to be adjusted to give a fairer picture of what the economy could do and of how well or poorly it was doing. Further, it was increasingly apparent that it would be useful to quantify the effect of the changes in the labor force, to test the claims about its importance for the unemployment rate.

The effect can be estimated in either of two ways. The first is to adjust the unemployment target for changes in labor force composition and compare the adjusted and unadjusted targets. The second is to adjust the unemployment rate itself and compare the adjusted and unadjusted rates.

Adjustment of the target begins with the observation that an overall rate of 4 percent corresponds to widely different rates for different groups. If 4 percent is the lowest rate that can be achieved by aggregate demand management, then the component group rates must be at or near their minima as well, given the underlying structure of the economy. These component rates can thus be applied to the labor force composition of a given year to produce an overall target appropriate to that year. The logic behind this adjustment is that the target for each year is then based on the assumption that people with similar characteristics have the same

5. *Economic Report of the President, January 1965*, p. 124.

Figure 4-1. The Unemployment Rate Compared with the Adjusted Target, 1947–80

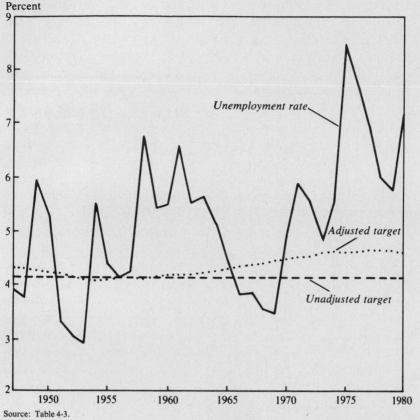

Percent

Source: Table 4-3.

degree of difficulty finding jobs as they had in the base year. All that changes is the number of people in a given group.

The adjusted target, based on unemployment rates by age for 1956, when overall unemployment was 4.14 percent, began to rise in the 1960s as larger numbers of teenagers and women entered the labor force (figure 4-1 and table 4-3, column B).[6] By 1970 it was one-third of a percentage point higher than the 1956 rate, and by 1980 it had been steady at about

6. Adjusted targets using 1956 component rates are presented in the *Economic Report of the President, January 1972,* and *January 1979.* Some results based on 1957 rates are reported in the *Economic Report* of 1966. The formula for the adjusted target is $\Sigma u_{i56}w_{it} \div \Sigma w_{it}$, where u_{i56} is the unemployment rate of group i in 1956 and w_{it} is the number of group i in the labor force in year t. The sixteen age-sex groups shown in tables 4-1 and 4-2 were used in the calculations. The formula is from Paul O. Flaim, "The Effect of Demographic Changes on the Nation's Unemployment Rate," *Monthly Labor Review,* vol. 102 (March 1979), pp. 13–23.

Table 4-3. Estimates of the Effect of Changes in Labor Force Composition on Unemployment, 1947–80

Year	Unemployment rate (A)	Unemployment target adjusted for changes in labor force (B)	Estimate 1: adjusted target (B) − 4.14 percent (C)	Unemployment rate standardized for changes in labor force (D)	Estimate 2: actual (A) − standardized unemployment rate (D) (E)	Difference between the estimates (E − C) (F)
1947	3.90	4.30	0.16	3.67	0.23	0.07
1948	3.75	4.30	0.17	3.58	0.17	0.00
1949	5.94	4.27	0.13	5.71	0.23	0.09
1950	5.28	4.25	0.11	5.15	0.12	0.01
1951	3.32	4.21	0.07	3.31	0.01	−0.06
1952	3.02	4.16	0.03	3.00	0.02	−0.01
1953	2.92	4.12	−0.02	2.93	−0.01	0.01
1954	5.55	4.10	−0.03	5.59	−0.04	0.00
1955	4.39	4.11	−0.03	4.42	−0.03	0.00
1956	4.14	4.14	0.00	4.14	0.00	0.00
1957	4.26	4.14	0.00	4.26	0.00	0.00
1958	6.80	4.13	0.00	6.80	−0.01	0.00
1959	5.46	4.16	0.02	5.44	0.02	0.00

Year						
1960	5.53	4.20	0.06	5.46	0.06	0.00
1961	6.66	4.20	0.07	6.58	0.08	0.02
1962	5.54	4.20	0.07	5.48	0.07	0.00
1963	5.67	4.24	0.10	5.54	0.13	0.03
1964	5.18	4.28	0.14	4.98	0.20	0.06
1965	4.53	4.32	0.19	4.30	0.23	0.05
1966	3.80	4.38	0.25	3.52	0.28	0.03
1967	3.84	4.39	0.26	3.52	0.32	0.07
1968	3.58	4.40	0.27	3.24	0.34	0.07
1969	3.51	4.44	0.30	3.13	0.38	0.08
1970	4.94	4.48	0.34	4.44	0.50	0.16
1971	5.94	4.51	0.37	5.32	0.63	0.26
1972	5.58	4.57	0.43	4.87	0.70	0.27
1973	4.85	4.61	0.48	4.13	0.72	0.24
1974	5.58	4.64	0.50	4.75	0.84	0.34
1975	8.47	4.64	0.50	7.44	1.03	0.53
1976	7.69	4.65	0.51	6.69	1.00	0.49
1977	7.03	4.66	0.52	6.05	0.99	0.46
1978	6.03	4.67	0.54	5.09	0.94	0.40
1979	5.80	4.66	0.52	4.92	0.88	0.36
1980	7.10	4.63	0.49	6.18	0.92	0.43

Sources: Author's calculations based on unemployment rates and numbers in the civilian labor force, by age and sex, from Bureau of Labor Statistics, *Handbook of Labor Statistics 1978*, and BLS, unpublished data.

one-half a point higher for years (column C in table 4-3).[7] But even with
the target adjusted to take account of changes in the age structure of the
labor force, the conclusion that unemployment was relatively high during
the 1970s is unaffected. Actual unemployment was well above the
adjusted target in every year except 1970 and 1973.

The second method for estimating the effect of demographic changes
starts by calculating what the unemployment rate would have been in a
given year if the composition of the labor force had been the same as in
some base year. This calculation uses the actual unemployment rate for
each age-sex group in the given year (which may be quite different from
the rate in the base year) and applies the base-year age-sex profile. The
difference between the resulting standardized, or fixed weight, rate and
the actual rate provides a second estimate of the effect of changes in
labor force composition. And if unemployment in the base year was
close to the 4 percent target, the standardized rate can be compared with
the base year rate to assess the performance of the economy.

Comparison of the standardized rate with the rate in 1956 of 4.14
percent shows again that the performance of the economy was not
particularly good during the 1970s (figure 4-2 and table 4-3, column D).[8]
And the difference between the actual unemployment rate and the
standardized rate (column E in table 4-3) reinforces the earlier conclusion
that changes in labor force composition first became an important factor
in the late 1960s. Before 1966 the two series did not disagree by more
than one-quarter of a percentage point. Thereafter the gap between them
grew rapidly until, by the mid-1970s, unemployment was a full percentage
point higher than it would have been had the composition of the labor
force not changed.

The two estimates of the effect of changes in the composition of the
labor force differ considerably for the 1970s. For the mid-1970s the
difference is about half a percentage point (table 4-3, column F), and the

7. Comparisons of the new and old targets must take 4.14 percent as the old target; no
year during the 1950s produced an overall rate of exactly 4 percent, and an adjusted target
based on components corresponding to some other rate must be compared to that rate.

When the base year for the calculations is taken from the 1950s, virtually all the
difference between the new and old targets can be attributed to the change in the age
structure of the population for most years. Changes in participation rates are important
for the middle and late 1970s, but not before, and even then the major part of the estimated
effect is due to the age structure of the population. See Flaim, "Effect of Demographic
Changes."

8. The formula in this case is $\Sigma\, u_{it}w_{i56} \div \Sigma\, w_{i56}$. As before, it is taken from Flaim,
"Effect of Demographic Changes," p. 14.

**Figure 4-2. The Unemployment Rate Compared with the Standardized
Unemployment Rate, 1947–80[a]**

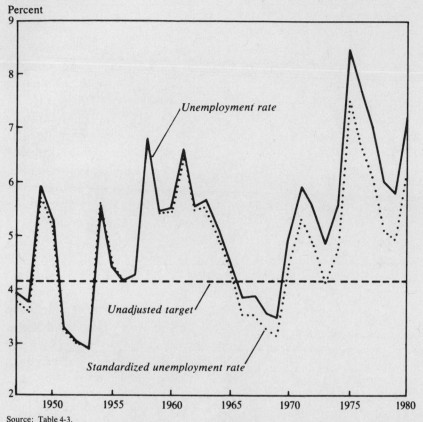

Percent

Source: Table 4-3.
a. From 1956 through 1958 the unemployment rate and the standardized unemployment rate were identical.

estimate produced by the second method is approximately double the
estimate produced by the first. The disagreement arises because the two
methods differ in their treatment of the interaction between changes in
labor force shares and changes in group unemployment rates.[9] There is
no right way to divide this interaction between the two kinds of change,
and the two estimates take up the extreme positions: the first excludes

9. The difference between the two estimates is

$$\frac{\Sigma\, \Delta u_i w_{it}}{\Sigma\, w_{it}} - \frac{\Sigma\, \Delta u_i w_{i56}}{\Sigma\, w_{i56}}.$$

Restating the $w_i/\Sigma w_i$ terms as proportions, p_i, this becomes $\Sigma\, \Delta u_i(p_{it} - p_{i56}) = \Sigma\, \Delta u_i \Delta p_i$.

Figure 4-3. Unemployment Rates Corrected for the Business Cycle, 1947–80

Unemployment rate (percent)

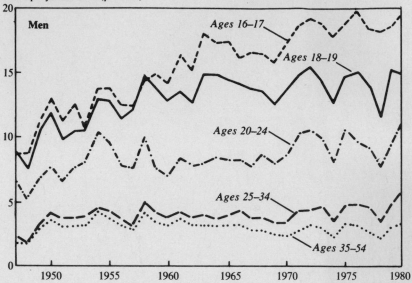

Unemployment rate (percent)

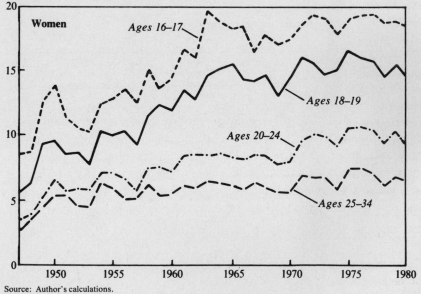

Source: Author's calculations.

the interaction, the second includes all of it. They thus show the minimum and maximum values, respectively, for the effect on unemployment of changes in the age structure of the labor force.

Unemployment Rates of Young Workers

Judging from the past, the baby boom generation could have expected to experience high unemployment during its first years in the labor force. In fact, its unemployment rates turned out to be even higher than those of preceding generations. Rates of 10 percent or more were common in the 1970s even for those aged 20 through 24, and teenage unemployment was stuck in the 15 to 20 percent range. Figure 4-3 shows that correcting for the business cycle does not change the story.[10]

Explanations for the Trends

During the 1960s and 1970s, the *Economic Report of the President* repeatedly examined possible reasons for differences in group unemployment rates, emphasizing in particular the high rates of the young. It was impossible to decide whether anything could, or should, be done until the reasons for the differences were better understood. More generally, if an overall unemployment target is to be considered something more than an unsatisfactory but necessary short-term compromise, the component rates must be acceptable. Their acceptability depends on their levels and, especially when a group suffers unusually high unemployment rates, on the reasons for those levels. The aim of these examinations by the Council of Economic Advisers was sometimes to determine whether these differences were acceptable, and at other times to make the case that they were.

As a starting point, the council assumed that a certain amount of "frictional" unemployment is unavoidable, even desirable, in a free economy. People just entering the labor force may take time to choose a job, even when jobs are readily available. Others will leave the jobs they have to look for new ones they like better. Still others will be laid off because of temporary or permanent declines in the fortunes of the

10. Each unemployment series was regressed on the ratio of real GNP to its trend value. The series was then adjusted by subtracting the variation that could be attributed to the difference between the GNP ratio in a given year and 100 (GNP = trend).

firms they work for. This kind of unemployment allows the economy to adjust to new markets and new technologies and is inevitable if workers are to have the freedom to choose their occupation, location, and so on. Frictional unemployment is usually considered acceptable for these reasons, the more so when it involves primarily short-term unemployment and when much of it can be linked to the preferences of individual workers.

Frictional unemployment is distinguished from "structural" unemployment, which in its pure form arises because certain features of product and labor markets prevent the free movement of workers. These features range from the pension rights that may discourage older workers from leaving an employer during a temporary layoff to union rules against hiring certain workers, from racial discrimination to the minimum wage. Although some kinds of unemployment can be clearly labeled frictional or structural, the distinction is often not clear. The *Economic Report* of 1962 observes that "structural unemployment may be regarded as an extreme form of frictional unemployment. It occurs when inability or failure to make the necessary adjustments concentrates unemployment of long duration on displaced workers in particular areas and occupations, while elsewhere jobs are seeking workers of quite different qualifications."[11] As a rule, structural unemployment differs from frictional unemployment in that it often lasts a long time and is due to causes beyond the worker's control. For these reasons it tends to be considered unacceptable.

The general explanation offered for the high unemployment rates of young people (and women) is that their rates of frictional unemployment are high because they enter, leave, and reenter the labor force often.[12] Most people enter the labor force for the first time during their teens or early twenties. Many young people are in school for a large part of the year and enter the labor market only to find summer work or part-time jobs. In addition, young people change jobs more often than older people as they look for work that suits them, and they may be unemployed for short spells in the process. The 1975 *Economic Report* calculated

---

11. *Economic Report of the President, January 1962*, p. 45.

12. See the *Economic Report of the President, January 1979*, p. 119; and reports for *February 1975*, pp. 86–91; *February 1974*, pp. 58–62; *January 1972*, pp. 113–16; *February 1971*, pp. 40–41; *February 1970*, pp. 152–56; and *January 1967*, pp. 100–08, for statements of this explanation. A person is considered to be in the labor force if he or she is employed or actively looking for work. If the person quits a job (or is fired) *and* does not actively look for another, he or she is counted as having left the labor force.

unemployment rates that excluded entrants and reentrants, leaving only those who lost or quit their jobs.[13] The adjusted unemployment for teenagers was much lower than the rate for all teenagers—5.7 percent for job losers and leavers as against 16.0 percent for all teenage workers in 1974—but still higher than the adjusted rates for adult workers. The adjusted unemployment rates were 3.0 percent for adult men and 3.2 percent for adult women in the same year (the unadjusted rates were 3.8 and 5.5 percent, respectively). Thus a large part of the difference between the unemployment rates of teenagers and adults appears to be due to frictional causes. This is comforting, although neither the data nor the underlying explanation is detailed enough to justify the size of the difference.

But something more is needed to explain, even in general terms, why these already high rates increased still further during the 1960s and 1970s. One common explanation is that frictional levels of unemployment increased for young workers because of the growth in the number who were enrolled in school at the same time that they were looking for work. Students enter and leave the labor force frequently and when in the labor force are less flexible than nonstudents about season, hours, and location of work. Thus it could be argued that the level of unemployment due to entrants and reentrants had increased. Statistics showed that, by the late 1960s, about half of unemployed teenagers were students, and the proportion for those 20 through 24, while lower, was rising. It was also true that for those 16 through 21, or even 16 through 24, the unemployment rate was higher for students than nonstudents.[14] The *Economic Report*s of 1970, 1971, 1972, 1975, and 1977 accordingly argued that the rise in school enrollment explained the rise in unemployment rates.

The explanation is plausible but wrong. The unemployment statistics for broad age groups of young people do show that student rates are higher, but this is due to the very different age distributions of students and nonstudents. Unemployment rates decline with age (table 4-2), and nonstudents are much more heavily concentrated at the older ages than students. Unemployment rates for finer age groupings show that, for

13. *Economic Report of the President, February 1975*, p. 103.

14. The statistics are based on surveys taken in October each year and count only people who are simultaneously enrolled in school and looking for work. They do not reflect students looking for work during the summer vacation. *Economic Report of the President, February 1971*, p. 41; BLS, *Handbook of Labor Statistics 1975—Reference Edition*, pp. 87–89; and BLS, *Handbook of Labor Statistics 1978*, Bulletin 2000 (GPO, 1979), pp. 106–08.

nearly every group in every year, students have had lower unemployment rates than nonstudents.[15] The growth in school enrollments should have contributed to lower, not higher, unemployment.

The major alternative explanation is that the large numbers of young workers were responsible not only for a purely compositional effect on overall unemployment, already documented, but for the rise in their own unemployment rates. According to this hypothesis, as supplies of young workers grew rapidly, and remained high relative to more experienced workers, the labor market had difficulty absorbing them all and their unemployment rates rose accordingly. If this explanation is correct, an even larger part of the current overall unemployment rate can be attributed to age structure—some portion of the increased unemployment that affects all young people should be added to the estimates given in table 4-3.[16]

A crude test of the hypothesis is to examine the timing of the rise in unemployment rates. Two possible patterns seem logical. If employers distinguish among workers by age in some detail, then each group's unemployment rate would have been affected only when the number in that age group began to grow. If, on the other hand, employers view a wide range of ages as more or less interchangeable, then the unemployment rates of all young people would have been affected as soon as any of the groups started to grow. In either case, because of the pattern of growth in the labor force, unemployment rates should have been stable or declining to the mid-1950s and rising after that, with the largest increases coming in the mid-1960s.

The unemployment rates shown in figure 4-3 do not conform to either of these patterns. The rates for teenagers rose over the entire postwar period, and more rapidly during the earlier part of the period than later.

15. Ibid. The only important exceptions are 1969, when student unemployment rates were higher for four of six detailed groups (women 18–19, men 18–19, women 20–24, and men 20–24), and 1965, when three of six student rates were higher.

16. If unemployment in the base year is expressed as the sum of the weighted rates for detailed age-sex groups, $\Sigma\, u_{ib}p_{ib}$, then the difference between the base year and some subsequent year is $\Sigma\, (\Delta u_i p_{ib} + \Delta p_i u_{ib} + \Delta u_i\, \Delta p_i)$. Both estimates presented in table 4-3 included $\Delta p_i u_{ib}$ and the second method of estimation added $\Delta u_i\, \Delta p_i$ to that. If some portion, k, of Δu_i can be clearly linked to age structure, then a third estimate would consist of $\Delta p_i u_{ib} + k\, \Delta u_i\, \Delta p_i + k\, \Delta u_i p_{ib}$.

Although the two effects arise from the same cause—age structure—they should not evoke the same reaction. The compositional effect means that there are more people in groups with normally high unemployment rates; those people may have no more difficulty finding jobs than smaller generations. But higher rates, if caused by age structure, mean that through no fault or wish of their own, people in these groups have more trouble finding jobs.

The rising trend for young adults is more modest and also shows no sign of a specific response to the arrival of the baby boom generation. The true pattern may be obscured, however, by the changes made in the labor force survey in 1967.[17] These changes reduced measured unemployment rates for teenagers, by approximately 1 percentage point in 1966 (when the new and old surveys were run side by side), just when the effects of the baby boom should have been most pronounced.

Regression Tests

Two studies have used regression techniques and times series data to test whether the unemployment rates of the young are affected by their labor force share. In a study based on data for detailed age-sex groups for the years 1948–75, Michael Wachter found that the unemployment rates of teenagers and young adults were indeed higher when people 16 through 24 accounted for a larger proportion of the working-age population.[18] Joseph Anderson got similar results when he regressed the unemployment rates of three age groups—people 14 through 24, 25 through 54, and 55 and older—on the corresponding shares of the labor force; in each case, the group's unemployment rate was higher when its labor force share was higher.[19]

On closer examination the evidence offered by these studies is not as strong as it appears at first. For each age-sex group, two regressions are shown in table 4-4. The first is similar to Wachter's specification;[20] the

17. Robert L. Stein, "New Definitions for Employment and Unemployment," *Employment and Earnings*, vol. 13 (February 1967), pp. 3–27.

18. Michael L. Wachter, "The Changing Cyclical Responsiveness of Wage Inflation," *Brookings Papers on Economic Activity, 1:1976*, pp. 115–59.

19. Joseph M. Anderson, "An Economic-Demographic Model of the United States Labor Market" (Ph.D. dissertation, Harvard University, 1977). These results were not repeated when Anderson regressed the unemployment rates of sixteen age-sex groups on several broadly defined labor force shares. Only occasionally in these regressions was a group's unemployment rate shown to be higher when the labor force aggregate to which it belonged was a larger share of the total labor force.

20. The business cycle is represented by the ratio of real GNP to its trend value, instead of the unemployment rate of men 25–54, which Wachter uses in "Changing Cyclical Responsiveness." (The trend value is the value predicted by a regression of the natural logarithm of real GNP on time.) Wachter's measure is inappropriate in equations to explain the unemployment rates of men 25–34, 35–44, and 45–54 because the dependent variable in each case is related to the independent variable by definition; this is signaled by the extraordinarily high *t*-scores he reports in these equations. It may be inappropriate in the equations for other groups as well. If age structure affects unemployment rates, an unemployment measure of the business cycle will include some of the effect of age structure. Also, the measured unemployment rate for men 25–54 was affected by the survey changes in 1967; as a result of these changes it was reduced.

Table 4-4. Unemployment as a Function of the Business Cycle and the Population Share of the Young, 1947–80[a]

Age-sex group	Constant	Business cycle: ratio of real GNP to trend	Percent of the working-age population 16–24	Time trend	Summary statistics	
					Corrected R^2	Durbin-Watson
16–17						
Women	33.223	−0.389	1.055	. . .	0.53	0.40
	(2.3)	(2.8)	(5.6)			
	49.540	−0.371	−0.113	0.326	0.80	0.90
	(5.1)	(4.1)	(0.5)	(6.5)		
Men	45.889	−0.504	0.980	. . .	0.58	0.39
	(3.6)	(4.1)	(5.7)			
	62.289	−0.486	−0.194	0.327	0.89	1.31
	(8.7)	(7.3)	(1.2)	(8.8)		
18–19						
Women	29.588	−0.366	0.964	. . .	0.54	0.30
	(2.3)	(2.9)	(5.7)			
	44.829	−0.349	−0.127	0.304	0.82	0.77
	(5.4)	(4.5)	(0.7)	(7.1)		
Men	81.082	−0.756	0.366	. . .	0.65	0.73
	(7.8)	(7.5)	(2.7)			
	92.303	−0.743	−0.437	0.224	0.83	1.52
	(12.2)	(10.5)	(2.6)	(5.7)		
20–24						
Women	35.265	−0.383	0.536	. . .	0.60	0.35
	(4.5)	(5.0)	(5.1)			
	45.448	−0.372	−0.193	0.203	0.89	1.20
	(10.8)	(9.4)	(2.0)	(9.3)		
Men	72.784	−0.691	0.228	. . .	0.74	1.04
	(9.8)	(9.6)	(2.3)			
	79.246	−0.683	−0.234	0.129	0.82	1.53
	(12.4)	(11.5)	(1.6)	(3.9)		

a. Linear regressions. All variables are expressed as percents. Numbers in parentheses are *t*-statistics.

second adds a time trend to that specification. The purpose of the time trend is to force the age structure measure to prove that it is not simply standing in for a smooth sequence of changes over time that might have been caused by any of a number of other factors. Many phenomena rise or fall smoothly over time (GNP or labor force participation rates, for example), and the use of a time trend is a standard statistical device for determining whether the factor of interest is a better explanation than the general flow of events. It is perhaps too strict a test, since a smooth trend in unemployment rates might well be the consequence of age structure. But the alternative, to assign the trend automatically to age structure, is not strict enough. The basic problem is lack of enough variation in age structure even over a period of thirty years and will be solved only when data are available for a much longer period.

When the time trend is left out, the regressions show that the unemployment rates of young people have been higher when their share of the population is high. The effect is strongest and largest for 16- and 17-year-olds and women 18 and 19: an increase of 1 percentage point in the population share raises the unemployment rates of these groups by about 1 percentage point. The effect is smaller and weaker for the other groups, especially men 20 through 24. To their credit, these results are achieved in spite of the fact that the 1967 changes in the survey made it more difficult for the effects of age structure to show up because they lowered the measured unemployment rates of teenagers at the time when changes in age structure should have been pushing them higher.[21]

But when the time trend is included, the coefficient for age structure is no longer positive in any of the equations. In two cases—men 18 and 19, and women 20 through 24—the coefficient is not only negative but statistically significant, implying that their unemployment rates are *lower* when young people are a large share of the population. Generally speaking, then, age structure cannot be distinguished from a smooth trend, and thus it is impossible to prove that it is uniquely associated with higher unemployment rates for young workers.

Indeed, there is reason to question the ability of these data even to separate correct hypotheses from incorrect ones, let alone to measure the relative strengths of competing correct hypotheses. Regressions to test the hypothesis that unemployment rates have risen because of the increase in the number of young workers who are also students provide strong support for the hypothesis when the time trend is omitted (table 4-5), and some support for it even when the time trend is included. Yet the evidence discussed earlier shows that this hypothesis is wrong.

The fairest conclusion appears to be that, although it is plausible that the unemployment rates of young people are higher when there are more of them, the shortcomings of the time series data make it impossible to derive solid evidence from that source. It is doubly impossible to estimate the size of any effect. The search for evidence can be extended in several

21. Wachter, in ibid., argues that the rising number of young people has also affected the unemployment rates of adults, raising those of women and lowering those of men. He interprets his results as showing that women are substitutes for young workers, and men are complements. It is equally plausible, however, that the pattern he observes is the result of the 1967 changes in the labor force survey. These raised the rates for women and lowered them for men. Regressions replacing the labor force share of the young with a binary variable set at one for 1967 and later years, and zero earlier, confirms the pattern of changes and does as good a job of explaining these unemployment rates as the age structure variable. The correlation between the two variables is 0.90.

Table 4-5. Two Explanations of Unemployment: Age Structure and School Enrollment[a]

Age-sex group and period	Constant	Business cycle: ratio of real GNP to trend	Percent of the work-ing-age population 16–24	Percent of labor force group en-rolled in school (October)	Summary statistics Corrected R²	Durbin-Watson
16–17 (1953–80)						
Women	50.835	−0.531	0.925	. . .	0.76	0.87
	(5.3)	(5.7)	(7.8)			
	50.778	−0.486	. . .	0.198	0.76	1.69
	(5.3)	(5.2)		(7.9)		
Men	67.895	−0.694	0.873	. . .	0.88	1.31
	(9.9)	(10.3)	(10.3)			
	66.157	−0.651	. . .	0.217	0.87	1.13
	(9.1)	(9.2)		(9.6)		
18–19 (1947–80)						
Women	29.588	−0.366	0.964	. . .	0.54	0.30
	(2.3)	(2.9)	(5.7)			
	40.471	−0.342	. . .	0.313	0.80	0.61
	(5.0)	(4.2)		(10.8)		
Men	81.082	−0.756	0.366	. . .	0.65	0.73
	(7.8)	(7.5)	(2.7)			
	96.964	−0.890	. . .	0.193	0.82	1.50
	(13.1)	(11.8)		(6.4)		
20–24 (1948–80)						
Women	40.101	−0.430	0.537	. . .	0.72	0.53
	(6.2)	(6.9)	(6.4)			
	44.109	−0.389	. . .	0.291	0.86	1.28
	(9.8)	(8.7)		(10.4)		
Men	75.000	−0.712	0.229	. . .	0.76	1.08
	(10.2)	(10.0)	(2.4)			
	79.915	−0.733	. . .	0.142	0.79	1.17
	(11.9)	(10.8)		(3.1)		

a. Linear regressions. All variables are expressed as percents. Numbers in parentheses are *t*-statistics.

directions—to other countries, to cross-section data for the United States, and to other consequences of the baby boom.[22] Only the last is pursued in this book. If the evidence for other consequences is strong, the case for the effect of generation size on unemployment rates is made stronger by association. In the meantime, however, it requires a small leap of faith to believe that the age structure of the labor force has had an important effect on the unemployment rates of young people.

22. Using 1960 data for seventy-five cities, Kalachek found that teenage unemployment rates were higher where teenagers were a larger proportion of the population. Edward Kalachek, "Determinants of Teenage Unemployment," *Journal of Human Resources*, vol. 4 (Winter 1969), pp. 3–21.

Earnings

The young adults of the baby boom generation have earned, and are earning, more than earlier generations did at the same ages. Table 4-6 shows that the real incomes of young men and women in the late 1960s and the 1970s were higher than the real incomes of their predecessors in the 1950s and early 1960s. But real incomes failed to grow during the 1970s (this was true for older groups as well). The expectations of steady growth built up during the two preceding decades were disappointed, and later cohorts of the baby boom started out at real incomes no higher than those of earlier cohorts.

Earnings Profiles

The baby boom generation is doing well, but it might be doing still better if it were not so large. The reasoning behind the hypothesis that age structure affects the unemployment rates of the young suggests that it may also affect earnings, since the ease of hiring from an abundant supply of workers allows employers to lower wages or, in inflationary times, to increase them more slowly. Thus it is reasonable to ask not only what this generation is earning, but what it might have earned if the change in age structure had not occurred.

The best test would match the profile of earnings for the baby boom cohorts over their working lives against the earnings of cohorts similar in every respect except that of belonging to such a large generation. The closest practicable approximation to this would be an analysis of the earnings over time of different cohorts, which adjusted for as many of the differences between the cohorts as possible—in the performance of the economy during their working lives, and in their levels of education, skills, and other characteristics. By permitting income comparisons for different cohorts at the same age, such an analysis would make it possible to estimate differences due to membership in an unusually large cohort.

The development of earnings profiles over time is hampered by the brevity of the published time series for either earnings or income (besides earnings, income includes receipts from interest and rental income, veterans' benefits, pensions, alimony, welfare, and other sources). The more narrowly defined the series—hence the better it controls for important differences among individuals—the shorter it is. Average

Table 4-6. Median Incomes of Full-Time Year-Round Workers, Selected Age Groups, 1955–80

Constant 1967 dollars

Year	Women			Men		
	20–24	25–34	45–54	20–24	25–34	45–54
1955	3,451	3,559	3,490	4,113	5,383	5,611
1956	3,306	3,807	3,563	4,308	5,577	5,772
1957	3,437	3,807	3,641	4,227	5,722	5,972
1958	3,370	3,652	3,670	3,998	5,827	5,978
1959	3,522	3,890	3,717	4,262	6,094	6,187
1960	3,557	4,001	3,716	4,415	6,144	6,401
1961	3,508	4,016	3,702	4,515	6,311	6,570
1962	3,511	3,993	3,981	4,597	6,372	6,767
1963	3,602	4,079	4,045	4,612	6,628	6,847
1964	3,831	4,191	4,064	4,671	6,759	7,085
1965	3,929	4,295	4,179	4,980	6,915	7,236
1966	3,909	4,272	4,312	5,186	7,132	7,612
1967	3,970	4,491	4,445	5,312	7,275	7,851
1968	4,044	4,736	4,471	5,431	7,525	8,014
1969	4,233	4,874	4,829	5,618	7,903	8,476
1970	4,237	5,093	4,805	5,722	7,847	8,539
1971	4,270	5,091	4,773	5,502	7,820	8,812
1972	4,278	5,352	4,943	5,602	8,243	9,449
1973	4,155	5,324	5,014	5,614	8,509	9,584
1974	3,960	5,148	4,982	5,219	8,150	9,236
1975	4,093	5,212	4,950	5,286	7,926	9,186
1976	4,086	5,243	5,012	5,249	7,765	9,319
1977	4,131	5,258	5,037	5,399	7,785	9,382
1978	4,154	5,193	5,120	5,328	7,870	9,562
1979	3,944	5,129	5,031	5,279	7,727	9,413
1980	3,812	4,939	4,909	4,906	7,182	9,045

Sources: Data for 1955–77 are from Bureau of the Census, *Current Population Reports*, series P-60, no. 118, "Money Income in 1977 of Families and Persons in the United States" (GPO, 1979), pp. 179–83, and earlier editions; and for 1978–80, from Bureau of the Census, unpublished data.

annual income for all workers has been published since the 1940s, for all full-time year-round workers since 1955, and for full-time workers by education since 1967. The detailed data for individuals that are necessary for a really careful analysis of earnings are also available for only short spans of time.

Because of these difficulties, much analysis has concentrated on the cross-section profile of earnings by age—the earnings of people of different ages in the same year. The basic shapes of these profiles have remained much the same for decades. Figure 4-4 shows the profiles for

Figure 4-4. Age Profiles of Earnings of Full-Time Year-Round Workers, by Sex, 1960 and 1970

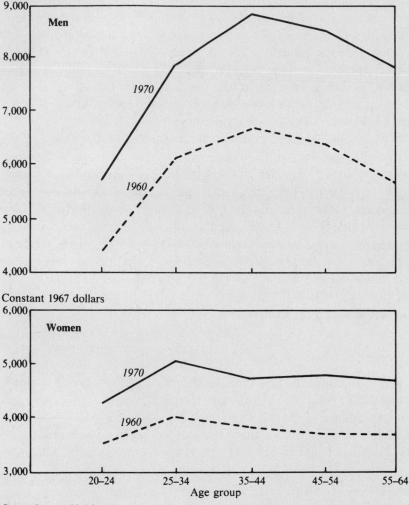

Constant 1967 dollars

Source: Same as table 4-6.

men and women in 1960 and 1970. In both years men's incomes rise sharply from the first age group (20–24) to the second (25–34), and rise again, but less sharply, to the next age group; for men 45 and older they decline. Women's incomes follow a different but equally stable pattern.They rise from the first to the second age group and show little change over the remaining groups.

These cross-section profiles will be higher or lower in different years depending on such factors as the price level, the stage of the business cycle, and the average level of productivity. But the relationship between different age groups will change only when these factors affect groups differently (for example, if the earnings of young people fluctuate with the business cycle more than those of older people) or when the collective characteristics of an age group—its education, experience, and size—change as new generations reach it. Trends in these characteristics could be expected to produce a related trend in the earnings of the affected group relative to those of other age groups.

Thus income profiles for different years can be examined for changes that might have resulted from the changing age structure of the labor force. If younger and older workers are perfect substitutes, no change would be observed, because a larger number of young workers would mean lower earnings for all workers. Since they are not, the brunt of the increased supply should have fallen on the baby boom generation itself, causing its earnings to decline relative to those of older workers. Because other factors could also produce changes in the income profile, the question is not only whether changes occurred but whether the timing, direction, and size of the changes suggest that the baby boom, and not some other factor, was responsible.

Trends in the Earnings of Young Workers

For men, the statistics indicate that the baby boom generation's earnings may be affected by its size. The incomes of the two youngest groups—20 through 24 and 25 through 34—fell relative to the incomes of men 45 through 54 from about 1969–70 on (figure 4-5 and table 4-7).[23] It is hard to pinpoint exactly when the decline started, but it was clearly

23. The income data are based on a sample, as are the unemployment rates discussed in the preceding section, and some of the fluctuation in the ratios from year to year is caused by sampling variability. This variability is less for 1967 and later years, when the sample was doubled in size from about 25,000 households to about 50,000.

The data for full-time workers used here omit the variations in hours and weeks worked that affect income data when part-time workers are included. The proportion working full time fluctuated around 40 percent over the period for men 20–24, and between 70 and 80 percent for those in the three age groups between 25 and 54 (25–34, 35–44, and 45–54). For women, the percentages reflect rising labor force participation rates and were, in every case, higher in the late 1970s than in 1955. In the three groups aged 25–54, 20 percent or less of each group was working full time in 1955. By 1978 more than 30 percent of each group was working full time. The proportion started higher and rose less for women 20–24—it was 23 percent in 1955 and 28 percent in 1978.

Figure 4-5. Ratios of Incomes of Younger Men to Those of Men Aged 45 through 54, 1955–80[a]

Income ratio

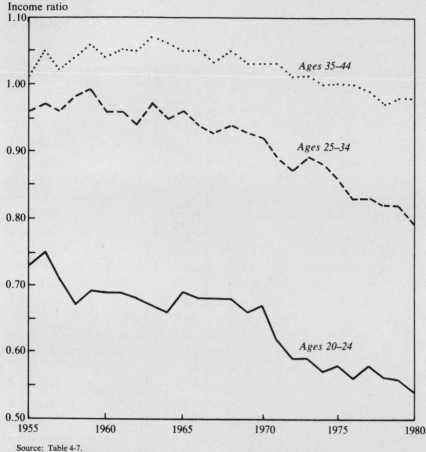

Source: Table 4-7.
a. Only full-time year-round workers are included.

under way by 1971 in both cases. The median income of men 20 through 24 was just over two-thirds that of men aged 45 through 54 between 1958 and 1970. By the late 1970s the ratio had dropped to approximately 0.56, a decline of more than 15 percent. The median income of men 25 through

Using only full-time workers also helps to minimize the difference between income and earnings; in 1975, 1976, and 1977, when data were published showing sources of income by age, the amount of total income derived from earnings was never less than 95 percent for full-time workers under 55. Bureau of the Census, *Current Population Reports*, series P-60: no. 118, "Money Income in 1977 of Families and Persons in the United States" (GPO, 1979), pp. 192–202; no. 114, "Money Income in 1976 of Families and Persons in the United States" (GPO, 1978), pp. 192–210; and no. 105, "Money Income in 1975 of Families and Persons in the United States" (GPO, 1977), pp. 194–212.

Table 4-7. Percent Growth in the Numbers of Younger Workers and Their Median Incomes Relative to Those of Workers Aged 45 through 54, 1955–80ᵃ

Year	Percent growth in civilian labor force						Relative income					
	Ages 20–24		Ages 25–34		Ages 35–44		Ages 20–24		Ages 25–34		Ages 35–44	
	Women	Men	Women	Men	Women	Men	Women	Men	Women	Men	Women	Men
1955	0.9	5.5	0.9	0.3	2.0	0.8	0.99	0.73	1.02	0.96	1.02	1.01
1956	0.4	8.2	0.6	−1.1	4.7	0.6	0.93	0.75	1.07	0.97	1.00	1.05
1957	−0.5	4.1	−0.5	−1.1	1.7	0.6	0.94	0.71	1.05	0.96	0.99	1.02
1958	2.4	4.0	−1.5	−0.9	1.4	1.0	0.92	0.67	1.00	0.98	1.03	1.04
1959	−1.1	4.5	−2.5	−1.2	0.8	0.5	0.95	0.69	1.05	0.99	1.00	1.06
1960	4.3	4.6	1.0	−0.9	1.5	0.6	0.96	0.69	1.08	0.96	1.03	1.04
1961	4.5	3.2	0.3	−0.7	1.6	0.4	0.95	0.69	1.09	0.96	1.07	1.05
1962	3.9	0.6	−1.0	−2.5	1.6	0.9	0.88	0.68	1.00	0.94	0.97	1.05
1963	5.6	5.5	1.7	−0.5	2.3	0.7	0.89	0.67	1.01	0.97	1.00	1.07
1964	8.5	5.3	0.1	0.0	0.3	−0.3	0.94	0.66	1.03	0.95	1.02	1.06

Year												
1965	4.8	2.9	3.6	0.3	1.9	−0.3	0.94	0.69	1.03	0.96	1.03	1.05
1966	6.7	−1.5	4.1	0.5	0.6	−1.2	0.91	0.68	0.99	0.94	0.99	1.05
1967	10.5	4.6	7.5	2.6	1.5	−1.1	0.89	0.68	1.01	0.93	0.98	1.03
1968	6.8	0.5	5.2	4.0	0.4	−1.2	0.90	0.68	1.06	0.94	1.00	1.05
1969	8.6	4.2	5.8	3.1	0.6	−1.6	0.88	0.66	1.01	0.93	0.99	1.03
1970	6.0	8.1	5.6	3.4	1.1	−0.9	0.88	0.67	1.06	0.92	0.99	1.03
1971	4.0	8.5	4.1	3.0	−0.2	−1.4	0.90	0.62	1.07	0.89	1.00	1.03
1972	4.8	8.1	9.9	4.8	1.1	0.0	0.87	0.59	1.08	0.87	1.01	1.01
1973	5.2	5.8	10.2	5.3	2.1	−0.5	0.83	0.59	1.06	0.89	1.02	1.01
1974	4.3	2.4	8.7	4.2	3.3	0.4	0.80	0.57	1.03	0.88	1.01	1.00
1975	4.1	2.0	8.2	3.4	2.2	−0.2	0.83	0.58	1.05	0.86	1.01	1.00
1976	3.5	3.6	8.3	3.8	4.7	0.8	0.82	0.56	1.05	0.83	1.02	1.00
1977	4.4	2.8	7.5	3.5	5.2	2.4	0.82	0.58	1.04	0.83	1.02	0.99
1978	4.6	2.4	7.1	2.7	6.8	3.5	0.81	0.56	1.01	0.82	1.02	0.97
1979	2.5	2.2	5.9	3.3	6.4	3.2	0.78	0.56	1.02	0.82	1.02	0.98
1980	0.9	0.6	6.0	3.4	5.8	2.6	0.78	0.54	1.01	0.79	1.01	0.98

Sources: Labor force data for 1955–77 are from Bureau of Labor Statistics, *Handbook of Labor Statistics 1978*, pp. 28–29; income ratios are calculated from same sources as table 4-6; and data for 1978–80 are from BLS and Bureau of the Census, unpublished.

a. Only full-time year-round workers are included.

34, relative to that of men 45 through 54, appears to have fallen slightly during the 1960s and then more rapidly during the 1970s. Between 1970 and 1980 the ratio fell from 0.92 to 0.79. A hint of decline appears as well in the income ratios for men 35 through 44.

The timing of the declines in relative incomes corresponds closely to the onset of steady, rapid growth in the respective labor force groups. The number of men aged 20 through 24 in the labor force grew especially quickly from 1969 to 1972, and steadily but more slowly afterwards (table 4-7). The number of men 25 through 34, which had actually declined during the early 1960s, started to grow at rates exceeding 3 percent annually toward the end of the 1960s. At the same time, the number of women 25 through 34 in the labor force was growing even faster, particularly during the 1970s, when their numbers increased 8 to 10 percent a year for several years.

But it is important to keep in mind that the comparison group—45-through 54-year-old men—began to decline at almost the same time, as the small cohorts born during the late 1920s and 1930s aged into it. If large numbers lead to lower earnings, then smaller numbers should lead to higher earnings, and this group is generally believed to have done exceptionally well during its years in the labor force. Thus the income ratios of the 1970s could be as much a consequence of the good fortune of the comparison group as they are of the poorer experience of the baby boom generation. And the coincidence in timing of the two changes would reinforce the timing of the downturn in the ratios.[24]

The income statistics for women give a somewhat different picture (figures 4-6 and 4-7 and table 4-7). Median income for women 20 through 24 fell relative to that of older women from the late 1960s on, when the number of young women began to grow very rapidly. But the incomes of women 25 through 34 do not appear to have been affected by the changing age structure of the labor force. Their relative incomes did not fall, in spite of growth rates for the group of better than 5 percent annually during the late 1960s and extremely rapid growth, already mentioned, during the 1970s.

A possible explanation is that expanding opportunities for women, and their growing commitment to careers, combined to offset any effects of age structure. Just as their rapidly growing numbers were beginning to depress earnings, better jobs and more continuous experience in the labor market should have been giving women an earnings profile more

24. The decline in the labor force participation rates of older men might also have contributed to the downturn if older men with low earnings are more likely than those with high earnings to drop out of the labor force.

Figure 4-6. Ratios of Incomes of Younger Women to Those of Women Aged 45 through 54, 1955–80[a]

Income ratio

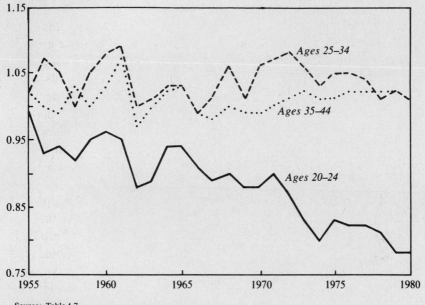

Source: Table 4-7.
a. Only full-time year-round workers are included.

Figure 4-7. Ratios of Incomes of Women Aged 20 through 24 to Those of Women Aged 25 through 34, 1955–80[a]

Income ratio

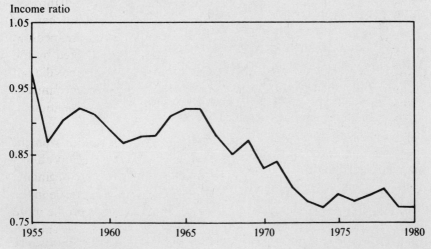

Source: Table 4-7.
a. Only full-time year-round workers are included.

like that of men, with large increases from one age group to the next until middle age. If so, the incomes of women 25 through 34 should have risen relative to those of women aged 20 through 24—alternatively, the younger women's incomes should have declined in relative terms—and figure 4-7 shows that this did in fact happen. Another sign of the change would be an increase in the earnings of women relative to men, particularly after the first few years in the labor market, as more recent cohorts of women accumulated more experience than earlier cohorts. There is some support for this hypothesis as well. For the youngest group, 20 through 24, women's incomes declined slightly relative to men's. But the incomes of women 25 through 34 rose relative to those of men of the same age, to a ratio of about 0.67 in the 1970s—having earlier declined from that level in the 1950s to about 0.62 in the 1960s.

Except for women 25 through 34, then, the relative incomes of young workers did decline as more of them entered the labor force. The effect appears to have been smaller for older cohorts, although it is too soon to conclude that this will always be the case—the oldest members of the baby boom generation were only 34 in 1980. As of 1980, however, the relative incomes of men 20 through 24 had fallen by a larger percentage than those of men 25 through 34. The same statement is true of women, but in a trivial sense, since the incomes of women 25 through 34 did not appear to be affected by the baby boom.

The drop in relative incomes was not evenly spread over all members of an age group but was concentrated on those who entered the most crowded areas of the labor market. In particular, with so many members of the baby boom generation going on to college after high school, the number of young workers with college degrees grew much faster than the total—more than 12 percent annually for a time during the early 1970s (table 4-8). Median incomes by education and age have been published for full-time workers only since 1967, but they suggest that college graduates suffered relatively greater declines in income because of their relatively greater numbers. For both men *and* women, the incomes of college graduates aged 25 through 34 fell relative to the incomes of high school graduates of the same age. The incomes of young graduates fell relative to those of older graduates as well, although the timing in this case did not follow as closely on the influx of new graduates.[25]

25. For high school graduates, the incomes of younger men fell twice during the period relative to those of older men but recovered after each fall. The incomes of young men with one to three years of college declined slightly relative to those of older men with the

Table 4-8. Percent Growth in the Number of Workers Aged 25 through 34 with a
College Degree, and Their Median Incomes Relative to Those of High School
Graduates and Older College Graduates, 1967–80

Year	Percent growth in young workers with college degrees		Income relative to that of high school graduates		Income relative to that of college graduates 45–54	
	Women	Men	Women	Men	Women	Men
1967	4.9	4.2	1.42	1.30	0.87	0.71
1968	12.0	6.1	1.44	1.33	0.89	0.76
1969	14.2	4.2	1.44	1.35	0.89	0.76
1970	7.6	7.8	1.45	1.35	0.88	0.72
1971	13.1	3.5	1.44	1.32	0.87	0.69
1972	18.7	13.7	1.42	1.31	0.85	0.69
1973	17.2	6.5	1.44	1.22	0.90	0.69
1974	21.3	15.6	1.36	1.19	0.84	0.67
1975	11.5	12.3	1.36	1.21	0.82	0.65
1976	13.4	8.8	1.32	1.21	0.78	0.63
1977	13.7	7.7	1.29	1.19	0.80	0.62
1978	3.5	1.9	1.28	1.15	0.80	0.64
1979	6.5	4.3	1.33	1.19	0.83	0.65
1980	9.2	2.4	1.34	1.21	0.86	0.64

Sources: Labor force and income data are as of March of each year. Labor force data for 1967–78 are from Bureau of
Labor Statistics, *Educational Attainment of Workers—Some Trends from 1973 to 1978*, Special Labor Force Reports,
and previous issues; income data are from same sources as table 4-6; and data for 1979 and 1980 are from BLS and
Bureau of the Census, unpublished.

Survey of Regression Studies

Several regression studies have tried to determine more precisely the
effect of age structure on earnings, after allowing for at least some of the
other factors that might be involved in the historical trends. Three are
described here.

FREEMAN. Richard Freeman analyzes income ratios like the ones
just discussed, except that he uses mean rather than median incomes,
for men 20 through 24 and 25 through 34 over the period 1955–74.[26]
Besides a measure of age structure, Freeman uses a measure of the
business cycle (the ratio of real GNP to its trend value) and a time trend
to explain the changes in these ratios. The business cycle is included to
capture any shifts in the cross-section income profile that may have

same education. There was no trend in the income ratios for women in either of these
educational groups.

26. Richard B. Freeman, "The Effect of Demographic Factors on Age-Earnings
Profiles," *Journal of Human Resources*, vol. 14 (Summer 1979), pp. 289–318. The oldest
members of the baby boom generation proper turned 28 in 1974.

occurred because different age groups are affected differently by the business cycle. The reasoning behind the time trend is the same as it was for the unemployment regressions—to determine whether the association between age structure and relative incomes can be distinguished from a smooth trend.

The regressions in table 4-9 apply Freeman's specification to the income ratios reported in table 4-7 for the years 1955–80, for men *and* women. Age structure is measured by the number of younger people in the civilian labor force, whether full time or part time, per 100 workers aged 45 through 54 of the same sex. The results for men are similar to Freeman's. In every case, even when the time trend is included in the equations, the coefficients for age structure are statistically significant and show that young men's incomes are relatively lower when there are relatively more of them in the labor force. The regressions for women, like the tabular analysis presented earlier, do not offer much support for the importance of age structure. The ratio of younger to older workers is significant only in the equation for 20- through 24-year-olds, and then only when the time trend is omitted.[27]

The best equation for men 20 through 24 is probably the one without the time trend; the trend adds nothing to the explanatory power of the specification and introduces considerable collinearity, so that the age structure coefficient is, while larger, not measured with much precision. The time trend greatly improves the fit of the equation for men 25 through 34 and does not affect the significance of the age structure coefficient, although its size is cut in half. This age group is perhaps the best test of age structure available in the data. The ratio of younger to older workers is clearly distinct from a trend, falling to a low point in the mid-1960s and rising thereafter.

The sizes of the estimated effects in these equations are reasonable and suggest that most of the decline in the income ratios of young men during the 1970s can be attributed to age structure. Since the regressions are estimated in log-linear form, the coefficients are elasticities and show the percentage drop in the income ratio associated with each 1 percent increase in the worker ratio. For men 20 through 24 the worker ratio rose 52 percent between 1970 and 1980. Based on the equation without the time trend, this should have caused a decline in the income ratio of 18

27. Regressions that used people 35–44, rather than 45–54, in the denominators of the income and worker ratios produced essentially the same results for both men and women. So did regressions that defined the worker ratio to include both sexes rather than the one for which the income ratio was defined.

Table 4-9. Incomes of Young Workers Relative to Those of Workers Aged 45 through 54, as a Function of the Business Cycle, Age Structure, and Time, 1955–80[a]

Age-sex group	Constant	Business cycle: ratio of real GNP to trend	Ratio of young workers to workers 45–54[b]	Time	Summary statistics Corrected R^2	Durbin-Watson
20–24						
Women	−0.778	0.358	−0.235	. . .	0.82	1.43
	(0.9)	(1.9)	(10.5)			
	−1.044	0.298	−0.090	−0.005	0.85	1.65
	(1.3)	(1.7)	(1.4)	(2.3)		
Men	−1.002	0.421	−0.346	. . .	0.95	1.84
	(1.5)	(3.0)	(21.2)			
	0.128	0.289	−0.495	0.005	0.95	2.06
	(0.1)	(1.7)	(4.7)	(1.4)		
25–34						
Women	0.766	−0.148	−0.010	. . .	−0.06	1.52
	(0.8)	(0.7)	(0.5)			
	0.829	−0.157	−0.016	**	−0.10	1.53
	(0.8)	(0.8)	(0.5)	(0.2)		
Men	2.917	−0.266	−0.375	. . .	0.73	0.37
	(2.5)	(1.1)	(8.1)			
	0.842	−0.004	−0.178	−0.005	0.96	1.83
	(1.7)	(*)	(7.3)	(11.7)		

* Less than 0.05.
** Less than 0.0005.

a. The dependent variable is the median income for full-time year-round workers in the age-sex group, divided by the median income of full-time year-round workers 45–54 of the same sex, for the years 1955–80. All variables except time are in natural logarithms. Numbers in parentheses are t-statistics.

b. Number of people in the age-sex group in the labor force, divided by the number of people 45–54 and of the same sex in the labor force.

percent; the measured decline was only slightly larger—19 percent. The worker ratio for men 25 through 34 rose 51 percent between 1970 and 1980. The equation for this group, with time included, implies an associated drop in the income ratio of 9 percent; the actual drop was 14 percent.

Two other analysts—Plantes and Welch—tackle the same issue but use different approaches and data. Like Freeman, both limit their investigation to men. Unlike Freeman, both use sources that provide data for individuals, although they aggregate the data before computing regressions.

PLANTES. Mary Kay Plantes uses the Continuous Work History Sample, a sample consisting of one out of every 1,000 holders of a social security card.[28] Data are available for longer, but she limits her analysis

28. Mary Kay Plantes, "Work Experience, Economic Activity and Lifetime Earnings: An Intercohort Analysis" (Ph.D. dissertation, Massachusetts Institute of Technology, 1978).

to the years 1957–73 to avoid the complications created by changes in the coverage of the program before 1957. And because the primary focus of the analysis is work experience and its effects on earnings, she further limits the analysis to men who turned 16 in 1957 or some later year; the record of their experience in the labor force is complete from the beginning. This means, however, that the oldest men in the sample were only 32 in 1973, the last year included. Plantes then groups the individuals in the sample according to age, experience, and race, and computes the average earnings in each year for each group. These group averages, deflated by the consumer price index to yield earnings in constant dollars, are analyzed in the regressions.

In the regressions of greatest interest, annual earnings are explained by the age, experience, and race of each group, a time trend, the gap between measured and potential GNP, and cohort size.[29] The results show that large cohorts of men have lower earnings and that the effect is greater for the youngest men. For every 1 percent increase in cohort size, measured as the percentage of men 16 through 65 accounted for by the age group, the annual earnings of teenagers are lower by about 0.25 percentage point. The depression is slightly smaller—about 0.21 percentage point—for men 20 through 24, and smaller again—0.17 percentage point—for men 25 through 34. (Recall that no one in the sample reached the age of 25 until 1965.)[30]

WELCH. Finis Welch uses the Current Population Surveys for the years 1967–75 for his study.[31] These surveys are the source of the published averages shown in tables 4-6, 4-7, and 4-8 and used by Freeman in his work. Because Welch is particularly interested in whether the effects of cohort size differ by level of education, he analyzes four groups separately—white men between the ages of 14 and 65 with eight to eleven years of school, with a high school degree, with one to three years of college, and with a college degree. Since direct information about work experience is not available from the survey, a probable level of experience is assigned to each man on the basis of other information about him. The men in each of the four schooling groups are then subdivided

29. No information about education is available from the sample, so this factor could not be included.

30. Later regressions introduce a number of variables that are so highly correlated with cohort size, a set of cohort binaries in particular, that the results are muddied. The differences between age groups remain, but large cohort size is associated with higher earnings in these regressions, with the advantage greater at older ages.

31. Finis Welch, "Effects of Cohort Size on Earnings: The Baby Boom Babies' Financial Bust," *Journal of Political Economy*, vol. 87, pt. 2 (October 1979), pp. S65–S97.

according to experience, and (geometric) mean earnings are computed for each subgroup in each year. These averages, corrected for inflation, serve as the basis for the regression analysis.

Cohorts are defined as groups of men with the same number of years of experience rather than with the same year of birth, and there are forty-four of these cohorts, one for each year of experience. Nine years of earnings are available for each cohort. Like Plantes's data, then, Welch's consist of a set of overlapping time series. Looked at slightly differently, both studies combine time series (the years of earnings for each cohort) with cross-section data (many different cohorts); Welch's data provide more cohorts than Plantes's but fewer years. In effect, both studies splice the experience of the baby boom onto the experience of preceding generations, on the hypothesis that this fairly represents the path the earnings of the baby boom will follow over time. In both samples, all the young men were born during the baby boom, or shortly before, so that comparisons between different cohorts of young men are essentially comparisons of the baby boom generation with itself.

To explain annual earnings, Welch uses experience, a time trend, the unemployment rate for men, and several other variables in addition to cohort size. Cohort size is entered in the form of two variables—one measures a constant effect and the other tests for the possibility that the effect is greater for workers who have just entered the labor force.

The results support both ideas. On the basis of the regressions, Welch estimates that a 1 percent increase in the size of the (experience) cohort depresses the annual real earnings of new entrants by 0.24 percentage point for workers with eight to eleven years of schooling, by 0.37 for high school graduates, by 0.51 for men with some college, and by 0.91 for college graduates. Applying 1975 labor force shares by education produces a weighted average effect of 0.52 percentage point for all new entrants. But over the first six to nine years in the labor force (depending on the educational group), the effect of cohort size diminishes considerably, and converges to about the same level for all four groups. Each 1 percent addition to cohort size causes a persistent reduction in annual real earnings of about one-fifth of a percentage point for college graduates and those with some college, less than one-tenth of a point for high school graduates, and about one-quarter of a point for men with eight to eleven years of schooling.[32]

32. Welch, ibid., also finds that cohort size affects weeks and hours of work for new workers (which is consistent with the results for unemployment in the last section), but that these effects disappear as the cohort gains experience.

DISCUSSION. The results of the three studies agree closely in spite of their differences in approach and data. All three conclude that large cohorts of young men have had lower earnings than smaller cohorts and that the relationship is statistically significant even when a time trend is present in the equation. They agree that the effect has so far been greater for men in their early twenties, which suggests that it wears off as the cohort ages and that the experience of a large cohort is not as bad in the longer run as it is initially. Plantes and Welch produce nearly identical estimates of this longer run, or persistent, effect on annual earnings.[33] Plantes estimates that a 1 percent increase in cohort size causes a reduction of 0.17 percent in the annual real earnings of men 25 through 34. When Welch's estimates of the persistent effect for each schooling group are weighted by the groups' shares in the labor force aged 25 through 34 in 1975 and summed, the resulting average indicates that a 1 percent increase in cohort size causes a reduction in earnings of 0.16 percent.

Even in the face of such impressive agreement, there are reasons to remain skeptical about the strength of the evidence, and even more, about the precision of the estimated effects. All three studies are mining the same rather limited period of time; lack of data for earlier years gives them no choice in the matter. The time series used in Freeman and table 4-9 are the only data that include young people born much before the baby boom itself, and this gain comes at the cost of an inability to control for many of the other factors that might have influenced the ratios. In all cases the time period includes essentially only one observation on cohort size—the shift from the small cohorts born during the 1930s to the baby boom cohorts. If there were important special circumstances during this period in addition to the baby boom itself, and these were correlated with it, none of the studies would be able to identify the effect of age structure precisely, or perhaps at all.

One of the special circumstances might be trends in the demand for workers, which are not accounted for in any of the studies. Dresch has pointed out that the pattern of industry growth in the 1950s and 1960s

33. The comparison is valid because Plantes, *Work Experience,* and Welch, ibid., use reasonably similar specifications of the earnings function—annual real earnings are specified as a function of the percentage of the male work force or population belonging to the particular birth or experience cohort. Freeman's estimate ("Effect of Demographic Factors") for men 25–34, and the one in table 4-9, are not comparable with the other two studies because the income variable is a ratio, and the age structure variable is also a ratio rather than a percent.

produced strong demands for college graduates.[34] The number of professionals and managers grew 3 percent annually between 1950 and 1970 (table 4-10). During the years 1970–75—when enormous numbers of new college graduates were entering the labor force—the growth in professional and managerial jobs was considerably slower. More recently, it has moved back up to the 3 percent rate. But the slowdown was so timed as to reinforce any effects of age structure, and age structure may well have received the credit for what was in fact the consequence of many factors. Further, if changes in demand affect new workers the most, these changes might have been partly responsible for the finding that the effects of age structure are greatest for young workers.

More detailed examination of the occupations of young adults indicates that differences in demand probably account for much of the difference in the earnings experience of men and women during the 1970s. After rising steadily during the 1950s and 1960s, the proportion of men aged 25 through 34 employed in the professions remained constant throughout the 1970s, at about 20 percent. Thus professional employment for young men grew as fast as the age group over the decade, but not as fast as in previous decades, and not fast enough to match the rapidly growing number of college graduates. Similarly, the proportion of men 25 through 34 employed as managers was steady at about 13 percent of the age group in the 1970s.[35]

By contrast, the proportion of women aged 25 through 34 employed in these occupations continued to rise during the 1970s. In 1970 about 20 percent of the women in this age group were employed in the professions, and the percentage moved a few points higher during the decade. The proportion employed in managerial posts, which was the same in 1970

34. Stephen P. Dresch, "Demography, Technology, and Higher Education: Toward a Formal Model of Educational Adaptation," *Journal of Political Economy*, vol. 83 (June 1975), pp. 535–69.

35. The statements in this and the following paragraph are based on data from the 1950, 1960, and 1970 Censuses: Bureau of the Census, *Census of Population, 1970*, vol. 1: *Characteristics of the Population*, pt. 1: *United States Summary*, sec. 2 (GPO, 1973), table 226; *U.S. Census of Population: 1960, United States Summary*, Final Report PC(1)-1D, *Detailed Characteristics* (GPO, 1963), table 204; and *U.S. Census of Population, 1950, U.S. Summary*, Report PC-1, *Detailed Characteristics* (GPO, 1953), table 127; and on unpublished tabulations from the Current Population Surveys for 1968 through 1979, supplied by the Bureau of Labor Statistics. The numbers reported by the Census and the Current Population Survey for 1970, the year for which data are available from both sources, sometimes differ. The largest difference is in the proportion of men 25–34 reporting employment as managers—10 percent in the Census, 13 percent in the Survey.

Table 4-10. Average Annual Rate of Growth in Total Employment and in Employment of Professional and Managerial Workers, Selected Periods, 1951–80
Percent

Period	Total	Professional and managerial	Professional	Managerial
1951–60	1.11[a]	3.14	5.06	1.43
1960–70	1.80	2.94	4.08	1.61
1970–75	1.52	2.18	2.73	1.41
1970–80	2.15	3.17	3.43	2.79

Sources: Data for professional and managerial employment are from Bureau of the Census, *Current Population Reports,* series P-50, no. 40 "Annual Report on the Labor Force, 1951," p. 26; *Employment and Training Report of the President, 1976* (GPO, 1976), p. 234; and BLS, unpublished data. Total employment data are from the *Economic Report of the President, January 1981,* p. 266.

a. 1950–60.

as in 1950, rose rapidly during the 1970s, from about 3 percent at the beginning of the decade to more than 6 percent at the end. The growing employment of women in these better-paid occupations helps to explain why women's relative incomes held steady while men's fell.

This evidence underlines yet again an important weakness in the case for the effect of age structure on the earnings of the baby boom generation—the absence of a good study of its effects on women workers. It is important to know whether a force as general as age structure has affected women workers and to disentangle its effects from those of other changes occurring at the same time. A convincing explanation of the role of age structure must account for the different experiences of men and women. It may turn out that much of the shift in men's incomes is due not to age structure but to some other factor, such as an improvement in women's position in the job market relative to that of men.

Conclusions

Because teenagers and young people have higher rates of unemployment than adults, even at the best of times, the entry of the baby boom generation into the labor force caused the overall rate of unemployment to rise substantially. By the mid-1970s it was at least half a percentage point higher than it would have been otherwise, and perhaps as much as a full percentage point higher. While that was not enough to explain the levels of unemployment reached during the 1970s, it was clear that 4 percent, set by the Council of Economic Advisers as the lowest overall rate that could be achieved without significant inflation, was no longer a reasonable target.

Further, as the number of young people in the labor force grew, their unemployment rates rose to levels even higher than those recorded in the 1950s. A plausible case can be made that the higher group rates were also a consequence of the changes in the age structure of the labor force, because the labor market could not absorb so many new and inexperienced workers in such a short time. The statistical evidence is consistent with this idea, but weak; the effects of age structure cannot be distinguished from a smooth trend, which might have been caused by many factors other than, or in addition to, age structure.

The evidence is somewhat stronger that the influx of young workers may have caused a decline in their relative earnings. Three studies, approaching the question from different perspectives and with different sets of data, agree that large cohorts of men have had lower earnings than small cohorts, other things equal. The reduction appears to be greatest at the beginning of the career and to diminish thereafter. The two studies that are roughly comparable on conceptual grounds estimate that each 1 percent increase in the size of a cohort, with size measured by the cohort's percentage share of the male work force or population, reduces the annual earnings of an average member of that cohort by 0.16 to 0.17 percentage point after the first few years in the labor force.

Because the arguments underlying the hypotheses are related, the results for earnings reflect on the results for unemployment and suggest that age structure has probably had an effect there as well, even though it cannot be clearly demonstrated. But the tests of both hypotheses are necessarily based on such a short span of time that neither can be accepted as well established. Age structure changes slowly, and in spite of the many years covered by some of the studies, there has been essentially only one observation on the phenomenon of interest: the shift from the small cohorts born during the late 1920s and the 1930s to the large cohorts of the baby boom. Other changes have taken place over the same period that may have had similar effects. The growth in professional and managerial employment slowed during the early 1970s, just as large numbers of college graduates were looking for their first jobs. And although the numbers of young women in the labor force grew much faster than the numbers of young men, the little evidence available does not show much effect of age structure on their relative earnings.

It is important to keep in mind that the issues raised here concern *relative* changes in incomes. Are the members of the baby boom generation earning less than they would have had their generation been smaller? Are they earning less relative to older workers than young workers of the 1950s or 1960s earned relative to the older workers of those years? Regardless of what the definitive answers to these questions turn out to be, it remains true that, throughout its years in the labor force, the baby boom generation has earned real incomes as high as, or higher than, those of any preceding generation (table 4-6). But this fact has been overshadowed by disappointment because earnings, of older workers as well as younger ones, did not continue to grow during the 1970s as they had during the 1950s and 1960s.

No employment policies specific to the problems of the baby boom generation as such have been undertaken in the United States.[36] There has been discussion of measures to ease young people's entry into the labor force, particularly the idea of setting a lower minimum wage for teenagers, but nothing has been done. Broader measures to compensate the baby boom generation would probably be unwise, even if they were feasible—the affected group is too large relative to the population, and the evidence on which to base compensation is too weak. The programs actually undertaken have instead focused on disadvantaged subgroups. The various programs to give training and summer jobs to disadvantaged young people are the major example.

In any event, as the baby boom generation advances into middle age, the need for programs to deal with its youthful unemployment problems is passing. The generations immediately following, whatever their problems, will not suffer from being too numerous. A longer-lasting consequence of the baby boom may be its implications for the interpretation of economic statistics, particularly a major signpost like the unemployment rate. The baby boom is one of several factors that have stimulated a new examination of unemployment statistics—what they measure and should measure, how they should be calculated and how presented.

In separate papers, Cain, and Watts and Skidmore, argue that unemployment is better viewed as a measure of economic performance than of economic hardship, one that measures how well the economy is able

36. Some European countries have recently introduced programs aimed specifically at the employment problems of young people, but there too the main response has been to expand existing programs aimed at more general employment problems. Organization for Economic Cooperation and Development, *Youth Unemployment*, vol. 1, Report on the High Level Conference, 15–16 December 1977 (Paris: OECD, 1978).

to make use of the labor offered for paid market work.[37] Cain suggests that this performance would be better indicated if the reported unemployment rate were standardized by using the age composition of the labor force in some base year, along the lines of the standardization for age and sex discussed earlier in this chapter. Unemployment would then be a fixed-weight index, like the consumer price index.

But the two indexes differ in some important respects. From the point of view of the consumer, or economic policy, an increase in the price of one item in the CPI is not usually considered important as long as it is balanced by a decline in the price of another. This is not as true of the unemployment rates of different subgroups in the labor force; while a decline in the rate for one group may cancel the rise in that of another group arithmetically, it does not balance it in the sense of rendering it acceptable or unimportant. The group rates have importance in their own right. Further, the weights in the consumer price index are not held constant over long periods of time. The purpose of the CPI is to measure the rate of inflation faced by an average household, and the expenditure weights have been replaced approximately every ten years to achieve that purpose. The purpose of the unemployment rate is analogous—to reflect the experience of the "average" worker. A standardized rate would reflect that experience less and less well with the passage of time.

The National Commission on Employment and Unemployment Statistics considered a recommendation that an age-adjusted unemployment rate be presented each month, along with the unadjusted rate, and rejected it for reasons similar to those just outlined. The commission argued that a standardized rate would conceal more than it revealed precisely because high-unemployment groups would have less weight in it than they do in the current labor force, and that it would not give an accurate picture of the economy's performance in keeping the existing labor force employed.[38]

The basic reason for standardizing the unemployment rate is that the unadjusted rate cannot be fairly compared with a target rate that was

37. Glen G. Cain, "Labor Force Concepts and Definitions in View of Their Purposes," Special Report 20 (University of Wisconsin, Institute for Research on Poverty, 1978); and Harold W. Watts and Felicity Skidmore, "The Implications of Changing Family Patterns and Behavior for Labor Force and Hardship Measurement," Special Report 21 (University of Wisconsin, Institute for Research on Poverty, 1978). Both papers were prepared for the National Commission on Employment and Unemployment Statistics.

38. National Commission on Employment and Unemployment Statistics, *Counting the Labor Force* (GPO, 1979), pp. 281–82.

established when conditions were different. It follows, therefore, that, rather than adjusting the unemployment rate to an outdated labor force composition in order to be able to compare it with an outdated target, one might better adjust the target so that it can be fairly compared with current unemployment experience. This was the first adjustment procedure presented earlier in this chapter.

Adjusting the target has its own problems. To begin, it is necessary to choose unemployment rates for the subgroups in the labor force. As discussed earlier, these rates should in some sense be acceptable. The component rates for an overall rate of about 4 percent were granted a qualified acceptability in the early 1960s because 4 percent was believed to be the lowest rate that could be achieved without serious inflation. Ideally, the groups into which the labor force is divided should be reasonably homogeneous and should differ from one another in ways that bear a strong and consistent relationship to their market behavior. Divisions by age (and sex) may not be the best choice, because they are only proxies for divisions by such characteristics as experience, skill, commitment to paid market work, mobility, and preference for full-time or part-time work. The less closely the divisions are linked to these characteristics, the more variation there will be over time in the unemployment rates of subgroups. The need to devise new explanations for the unemployment rates of young people illustrates the difficulty. Watts and Skidmore have recommended that labor force groups be redefined and based directly on such factors as experience, and that unemployment rates be reported separately for at least some of these groups.

Perhaps the major argument in favor of adjusting the target is that adjustment would serve as a reminder that the target is not, and cannot be, a fixed number, and would help prevent thinking of the sort that led to the enshrinement of the 4 percent target of the early 1960s in the Humphrey-Hawkins Full Employment and Balanced Growth Act of 1978. The case against an age-adjusted target is that it would become accepted as the "right" number, when in reality many factors influence the target, and most of them cannot be quantified. This argues against an automatic adjustment procedure based on one or a few factors and in favor of a more thorough and judgmental review.[39]

39. Some of the discussions included in the *Economic Report of the President,* cited in footnote 12 above, are partial reviews of this sort.

chapter five Patterns of Consumption

As they approached the end of their formal education and entered the labor force, increasingly in full-time jobs, successive cohorts of the baby boom generation also began to establish their own households. The number of households headed by an 18- through 24-year-old rose from 4.6 million in 1970 to 6.4 million in 1980, and those headed by someone between the ages of 25 and 34 grew from fewer than 12 million to nearly 18 million (table 5-1). This chapter explores some of the implications of so large an increase in young households for consumer spending, in total and in different sectors of the economy.

Here again, as with labor force behavior, age is important not in itself but because it is closely related to other characteristics that directly affect the way consumers spend their money. Analysts of consumer behavior often group these characteristics—particularly whether a person is married or not, and the number and ages of any children—to describe distinct stages of the household life cycle. The groupings used by different analysts are variations on a familiar sequence of events.[1] As people age, they leave their parents' homes and live on their own, they marry and have children, their children grow up and move away, and they return to a family of two, or, through death or divorce, to living alone again. The household's spending patterns reflect these family groupings and responsibilities—from the initial move to separate living quarters, to the need for more space when children are born, toys when they are young and college educations when they are older, and the

1. J. B. Lansing and J. N. Morgan, "Consumer Finances over the Life Cycle," in L. H. Clark, ed., *Consumer Behavior,* vol. 2: *The Life Cycle and Consumer Behavior* (New York University Press, 1955); Kevin F. McCarthy, "The Household Life Cycle and Housing Choices," Rand Paper P-5565 (Rand Corporation, 1976); and Patrick E. Murphy and William A. Staples, "A Modernized Family Life Cycle," *Journal of Consumer Research,* vol. 6 (June 1979), pp. 12–22.

Table 5-1. Number of Households, by Age of Head, Selected Years, 1950–80

Thousands

Year	All ages	Age group					
		18–24	*25–34*	*35–44*	*45–64*	*65–74*	*75 and over*
1950	42,210	1,984	8,679	9,610	15,523	4,559	1,855
1960	52,988	2,663	9,763	11,711	19,566	6,420	2,865
1970	63,477	4,553	11,678	11,827	23,178	7,780	4,462
1980	79,064	6,354	17,901	13,903	24,757	9,937	6,212
		Percent change					
1950–70	50	130	35	23	49	71	141
1970–80	25	40	53	18	7	28	39

Sources: Bureau of the Census, *U.S. Census of Population: 1950*, Special Report P-E no. 2D, *Marital Status* (Government Printing Office, 1953), table 1; Bureau of the Census, *U.S. Census of Population: 1960, Subject Reports,* Final Report, PC(2)-4B, *Persons by Family Characteristics* (GPO, 1963), table 2; Bureau of the Census, *Census of Population, 1970, Subject Reports,* PC(2)-4B, *Persons by Family Characteristics* (GPO, 1973), table 2; and data for 1980 from the *Current Population Reports,* series P-20, no. 365, "Marital Status and Living Arrangements: March 1980" (GPO, 1981), table 2.

return to the habits and tastes of a small household, this time of older adults, when the children are gone.[2]

The growth in young households must be set in proper perspective. It is not the only important force operating on the number of households and their distribution by age, nor is it solely a product of the baby boom as such. The number of households headed by people 65 or older has also been rising rapidly. And in every age group the number of households has grown far more rapidly than can be explained by the changes in the corresponding population groups, because of sharply rising rates of household incidence.[3] Before 1950 these rates were stable for many decades, going back to the last century.[4] The trends since 1950 are a new and important phenomenon.

2. This chapter is concerned with the kinds of expenditures that each household makes for itself out of its own (after-tax) income. Education and medical care are examples of expenditures that are also affected by age structure, but they have come to be provided collectively for the most part, through public spending or, in the case of medical care, through both public spending and private insurance. Education is the subject of chapter 3, and medical care is discussed in chapter 6.

3. The rate of household incidence for an age group is the number of households headed by people of that age per 1,000 population of the same age. The Census Bureau defines a household as a group of people who occupy separate living quarters. The number of households is thus equal to the number of occupied housing units. The criteria for separate living quarters have to do with separate kitchen facilities and access to the outside. Bureau of the Census, *Census of Population, 1970, Subject Reports,* Final Report PC(2)-4A, *Family Composition* (Government Printing Office, 1973), p. VIII.

4. Burnham O. Campbell, *Population Change and Building Cycles* (Bureau of Economic and Business Research, University of Illinois, 1966); and Frances E. Kobrin, "The

The increases in household incidence have been greatest in the youngest and oldest age groups (table 5-2), reinforcing the effects of the changing age structure of the population. In 1980 the number of households per 1,000 for people 25 through 34 was much closer to the rates for people between 35 and 64 than it had been in 1950. The rate for those 18 through 24 had also risen but was still well below that of any other age group. The changes in the oldest age groups have been perhaps the most amazing. In 1950 the rates for people 65 and older were about the same as those for people in middle age. By 1980 they were much higher, particularly for the 75 and over group, which, at 719 households per 1,000 population, far outdistanced every other age group.

The rising rates of household incidence show clearly that, while it is useful to think about consumers' behavior in terms of stages of the life cycle, these stages are not fixed in length or content. Nor is their relationship to age invariant. The households of the baby boom generation are different from those of their predecessors not only in numbers but also in ways that are important to their spending decisions. It is worthwhile to explore in more detail some of the trends that have made them different.

The driving force behind the changes in household incidence has been the rise of the "primary individual," a term used by the Census Bureau to refer to a household head who lives alone or with nonrelatives.[5] Most of the growth in the rates has come about because more adults have been choosing to live alone. Table 5-2 shows that the number of families per 1,000 population rose in the younger groups at first, although not as much as the number of primary individuals. Since 1970, however, the number of families has been constant in these groups, or even declined, and all the growth in households per 1,000 has been due to the increasing tendency for adults to live alone. In the older age groups—45 and over— the number of families has been virtually constant throughout. Thus, in these older groups, all the growth in household incidence has been due to the primary individual.

At the same time that families have been declining in importance relative to primary individuals, they have been changing in character. The Census Bureau defines a family as two or more persons who live

---

Fall in Household Size and the Rise of the Primary Individual in the United States," *Demography*, vol. 13 (February 1976), pp. 127–38.

5. Bureau of the Census, *Census of Population, 1970,* Final Report PC(2)-4A, *Family Composition,* pp. VIII–IX. The overwhelming majority of primary individuals live alone (Kobrin, "Fall in Household Size").

Table 5-2. Households per 1,000 Persons, by Type of Household and Age of Person, Selected Years, 1950–80[a]

Year and household type	18–24	25–34	35–44	45–64	65–74	75 and over
1950						
All households	127	371	457	518	555	509
Families	116	355	431	455	415	338
Primary individuals	11	16	26	63	139	171
All household heads plus spouses	353	759	856	857	763	595
1960						
All households	173	432	491	545	605	576
Families	150	404	458	461	416	339
Primary individuals	23	28	33	84	190	237
All household heads plus spouses	425	849	914	904	837	683
1970						
All households	196	474	515	559	639	644
Families	150	424	474	463	395	320
Primary individuals	46	49	41	96	244	323
All household heads plus spouses	411	874	930	932	888	766
1980						
All households	225	508	549	569	658	719
Families	131	390	480	460	399	321
Primary individuals	93	118	69	109	260	398
All household heads plus spouses	389	852	939	938	929	860

Sources: Same as table 5-1.
a. Based on noninstitutional population.

together and are related by blood, marriage, or adoption, and distinguishes three general types—husband-wife families (in which, until the 1980 census, the husband was automatically designated the head), other families headed by men, and families headed by women.[6] Other families headed by men have never been more than a few percent of all families, but families headed by women have grown at the expense of husband-wife families since 1950. In 1980 they were 19 percent of all families headed by a 15- through 24-year-old and 16 percent each of families headed by people 25 through 34 and 35 through 44; the corresponding

6. Bureau of the Census, *Census of Population, 1970,* Final Report PC(2)-4A, *Family Composition,* p. VIII; and Paul C. Glick and Arthur J. Norton, "Marrying, Divorcing, and Living Together in the U.S. Today," *Population Bulletin,* vol. 32 (October 1977, rev. ed. February 1979).

proportions in 1950 were 4, 4, and 7 percent. Reflecting the drop in the birth rate, young families of the 1970s were smaller than those of the 1950s or 1960s, and a higher proportion of young couples had no children. And, of course, the labor force participation of women has grown so rapidly, particularly among the younger age groups, that many more families now have two earners. In the late 1970s more than half of all married women under 45 and living with their husbands were in the labor force, compared with approximately 30 percent in the late 1950s.[7]

As of 1980, then, the baby boom generation—whose oldest members were 34 in that year—was forming more separate households than earlier generations. With marriage coming later, if at all, and divorce rates high, the big difference was not in the number of families but in the number of people living on their own.[8] In 1950 primary individuals accounted for only 4 percent of all households headed by a person aged 25 through 34. In 1980 primary individuals made up more than 20 percent of the households in this age group. Further, the composition and character of family households had changed in important ways. The families headed by members of the baby boom generation were smaller than the young families of the generations just preceding, they were less likely to be headed by a married couple, and when they were, both members of the couple were likely to be in the labor force.

While it is impossible to say which of these trends will continue, and which will not, one can get a better sense of the limits on further increases in rates of household incidence by examining the number of households

7. Statistics on families are from Bureau of the Census, *U.S. Census of Population: 1950*, Special Report P-E no. 2A, *General Characteristics of Families* (GPO, 1955); Bureau of the Census, *U.S. Census of Population: 1960, Subject Reports*, Final Report PC(2)-4A, *Families* (GPO, 1964); Bureau of the Census, *Census of Population, 1970*, Final Report PC(2)-4A, *Family Composition;* and Bureau of the Census, *Current Population Reports*, series P-20, no. 366, "Household and Family Characteristics: March 1980" (GPO, 1981). Statistics on the labor force participation of married women are from Bureau of Labor Statistics, *Handbook of Labor Statistics, 1975—Reference Edition*, Bulletin 1865 (GPO, 1975), table 5, p. 40; and BLS, *Handbook of Labor Statistics, 1978*, Bulletin 2000 (GPO, 1979), table 5, p. 39.

8. A reader has suggested that later marriage and more frequent divorce among young people may be a reaction to their relatively disappointing economic position, as Richard Easterlin argues in *Birth and Fortune: The Impact of Numbers on Personal Welfare* (Basic Books, 1980). Whatever the truth of the argument, there is no necessary connection between those trends and the rising number of households per 1,000 population among young adults. Historically, most single adults lived with their relatives or in group quarters such as boarding houses or shared apartments. A generation feeling constrained by its economic circumstances should logically have reverted to the historic pattern rather than continuing the trend toward more single-person households.

plus spouses per 1,000 population. This ratio allows for the fact that both members of a couple have moved out of their parents' homes and consider themselves to be independently established, even though they count as only one household. As table 5-2 shows, in 1980 households plus spouses were near the maximum of 1,000 for people between the ages of 35 and 74. The ratio was high but still left some room for growth in the 25 through 34, and 75 and older, groups. Thus future increases in numbers of households will have to come primarily from continued growth in single-adult households. This in turn requires further delays in marriage, more people who decide not to marry at all, and still higher divorce rates among those already married. Household formations are the result of many individual decisions shaped by incomes, the availability of housing, personal preference, and other factors. Whether these trends will continue is anyone's guess, but if they do, the implications for the characteristics of households are obvious.

Aggregate Consumption and Saving

In 1960 Ansley Coale observed that, ever since the appearance of Keynes's *General Theory of Employment, Interest and Money* in 1936, with its emphasis on the determinants of consumer spending, business investment, and government outlays, economists have been intrigued by the possibility that demographic factors strongly influence the level of economic activity.[9] The potential role of age structure has been frequently discussed because of the differences in spending patterns of households at different stages of the life cycle. For example, in 1949 Dorothy Brady reviewed survey evidence showing the consumption behavior of different age groups, and stressed the idea that changes in the age structure of the population could change the relationships among aggregate income, consumption, and savings.[10] Coale's own observation introduced a paper in which he attempted to quantify the importance of several demographic factors, including age structure. In 1968 Richard Easterlin set out the hypothesis that the formation of unusual numbers

9. Ansley J. Coale, "Population Change and Demand, Prices, and the Level of Employment," in *Demographic and Economic Change in Developed Countries* (Princeton University Press for the National Bureau of Economic Research, 1960), pp. 352–71.

10. Dorothy S. Brady, "Influence of Age on Saving and Spending Patterns," *Monthly Labor Review*, vol. 78 (November 1955), pp. 1240–44.

of new households generated long-term spending commitments that might explain the long swings in economic activity earlier identified by Simon Kuznets—commitments entailed by the purchase of housing and associated durable goods and by the establishment of new businesses.[11] And from time to time during the 1950s and 1960s demographic forces were mentioned in the pages of the *Economic Report of the President* as potentially important for the size and composition of aggregate consumption.[12]

The baby boom generation is associated with shifts in the distribution of households by age that could obviously affect patterns of consumption in important ways. Households headed by someone under 35 accounted for 31 percent of all households in 1980, compared with 23 percent in 1960 (table 5-1). As the baby boom generation ages, the bulge in the distribution of households will age with it. Later sections of the chapter consider the effects these shifts have had, and will have, on housing and durable goods. This section reviews recent studies that have dealt with a more difficult question: whether the changes in age structure have altered total consumption and saving, and the relation of consumption and saving to income.

Analytical Problems

One problem facing studies of this question is that the effects of age structure on aggregate consumption are not generally direct, but occur indirectly through numbers of households and their composition. Household composition is in turn only one influence on household choices about spending. Both speculation about the effects of age structure and rigorous studies of the subject assume that these intervening links are relatively stable. But they are not. As a result, it becomes much more difficult to predict the effects of a given age structure—they can be amplified or muted by changes in the intervening variables.

The previous section showed that rates of household incidence, and the composition of households, have been anything but stable in the

11. Richard A. Easterlin, *Population, Labor Force, and Long Swings in Economic Growth* (Columbia University Press for the National Bureau of Economic Research, 1968). Easterlin noted that in the past the new households were the result of waves of immigration. More recently they have reflected the age structure of the population together with changes in patterns of household formation.

12. *Economic Report of the President, January 1953*, pp. 94–96; *January 1958*, p. 51; *January 1962*, p. 141; and *January 1965*, pp. 92–95.

period since World War II. And surveys of consumer expenditure suggest that patterns of expenditure by age of household head have often not been stable over time. Certain patterns may be more or less pronounced in different surveys, or fail to appear altogether in others. Here again, as in other areas, any study of the effects of age structure must examine the stability of the behavior that is supposed to link age structure to its expected effects.

Measuring the effects of age structure on aggregate consumption has been further complicated by the way in which the theory of consumer behavior has developed. For purposes of macroeconomic policy the relevant aggregates are current consumption expenditures in relation to current income. Modern consumption theory posits, however, that consumers base their spending decisions—especially for long-lived items such as housing and durable goods—on their expectations about usual or lifetime income, not solely on the income of the current year. Further, consumption is measured as the stream of services received rather than as current expenditures. For nondurable goods and services the two are considered equivalent, but for housing and durable goods they are not. With any luck, an appliance bought for cash in a given year will provide services for many years. Consumption is thus defined as the services received from the appliance each year, conceptually equivalent to its depreciation, rather than as the full expenditure in the first year and nothing in subsequent years. Analogously, saving by households is defined to include net investment in housing and sometimes in durables, as well as the more familiar, financial forms of saving—net additions to checking and saving accounts, to holdings of stocks and bonds, and so on.

Because of the difficulties of specification and estimation created by this view of consumption, and by the data defined in accordance with it, studies of the effects of age structure on consumption have often excluded part or all of current expenditures on housing and durables. As a result, the estimates produced in the studies appear counterintuitive and not particularly relevant to the question at hand.

Survey of Studies

Consider first studies of aggregate consumption. Surveys show that young households spend beyond their incomes more often than older households, and take on larger amounts of debt, even though their current incomes are lower.[13] Thus it seems reasonable to believe that their average propensity to consume (defined as total consumption expenditures divided by after-tax income) and their marginal propensity to consume (the proportion of an *addition* to income spent on consumption) are higher than those of other age groups.

The measure of consumption used in these studies is crucial for the outcome. In a study of the relation of current consumption to current income, Dale Heien omitted housing and durables because of the difficulties associated with them, and concluded that the marginal propensity to consume rises, rather than falls, as the median age of the population rises.[14] But expenditures on nondurables and services are not the quantity of interest for macroeconomic policy, and the estimated marginal propensity to consume them alone would be of limited value in gauging, for example, the likely effects of a cut in the income tax. Charles Lieberman and Paul Wachtel produced a similar result—that the marginal propensity to consume is higher for older age groups—in a time series analysis based on consumption statistics that estimate the flow of services from housing (and, in one case, durables), rather than the current expenditures on them, and that include those service estimates in after-tax income.[15] By contrast, Richard Parks and Anton Barten were unable to find any connection between age structure and the marginal propensity to consume in a cross-national study of expenditures on food, clothing, rent, and durables.[16]

The complement of the average propensity to consume is the average propensity to save, and other studies have approached the issue of age structure and its effects from this perspective. The results here depend

13. See, for example, Lansing and Morgan, "Consumer Finances over the Life Cycle"; and the statistics on net liability in BLS, *Consumer Expenditure Survey Series: Interview Survey, 1972–73,* Bulletin 1985 (GPO, 1978), table 12.

14. Dale M. Heien, "Demographic Effects and the Multiperiod Consumption Function," *Journal of Political Economy,* vol. 80 (January–February 1972), pp. 125–38.

15. Charles Lieberman and Paul Wachtel, "Age Structure and Personal Saving Behavior," in George M. von Furstenberg, ed., *Social Security versus Private Savings* (Ballinger, 1979), pp. 315–57. The time series analysis is repeated for each of two sets of income and consumption data—from the national income and product accounts and from the data bank for the Federal Reserve–MIT–Pennsylvania econometric model.

16. Richard W. Parks and Anton P. Barten, "A Cross-Country Comparison of the Effects of Prices, Income and Population Composition on Consumption Patterns," *Economic Journal,* vol. 83 (September 1973), pp. 834–52. Actually, the marginal propensity to consume durables does show a relationship to age structure, but the authors conclude that when the results for all the categories of expenditure are combined, there is no evidence that age structure alters the overall marginal propensity to consume.

on how saving is defined. It is usually defined, following the national income accounts, to include net investment by consumers in housing (gross investment less depreciation). Two studies based on saving rates that include net investment in housing find that age structure has not had, and will not have, much effect on saving. Lieberman and Wachtel conclude that the effect of age structure alone is almost completely offset by the decline in an age group's average income as its numbers rise; when both changes are allowed for, saving is unaffected.[17] A study by Roger Brinner summarizes an analysis of the period 1950–90 as follows: "Demographic shifts have not and will not produce major changes in aggregate personal savings. Despite relatively large differences in savings rates across age groups, the most substantial result of population composition changes has been a minor, one-third percentage point reduction in the aggregate savings rate during the past five years [1970–1975]. The major fluctuations observed in the personal savings rate have been due to cyclical phenomena—tax cuts, buying confidence, and consumer debt burdens."[18]

Since both studies use household survey data, it is worthwhile to consider the stability of the saving patterns shown by these data. The Brinner study averages the saving rates by age from six surveys—four from the years 1946–50 and two from the early 1960s.[19] In general, the rates for households headed by someone under 25 or over 65 are lower than those for other age groups. But the two sets of surveys differ substantially in what they show for households headed by people in the four age groups between 25 and 65. The surveys from 1946–50 support the often-described pattern of saving rates rising with age until just before retirement. But those from the early 1960s suggest that the saving rates for these four age groups are virtually the same. The suggestion is repeated by data from the 1972–73 Consumer Expenditure Survey, which show the saving rate to be about 9 percent for each of the three age groups 25 through 34, 35 through 44, and 45 through 54. The rate is slightly higher for the 55-through-64 group, about 6 percent for those 65

17. Lieberman and Wachtel, "Age Structure and Personal Saving Behavior." Their time series analysis, however, implies that the average propensity to save rises when there are more young households.

18. Roger E. Brinner, "The Outlook for Savings," Special Study (Data Resources, Inc., Lexington, Mass., n.d.), p. I.84.

19. The source of the data is Dorothy S. Projector, *Survey of Changes in Family Finances* (Board of Governors of the Federal Reserve System, 1968), p. 14.

and older, and a negative 7 percent for those under 25.[20] These numbers help explain why Lieberman and Wachtel, who used saving rates from the early 1960s, found that saving was virtually unaffected by age structure, and suggest that had the Brinner study eliminated the early postwar surveys, it might have found even less effect than it did.

It is also important to remember that both studies define saving to include net investment in housing—a broader definition than many people have in mind when they express concern about trends in saving. Often the concern has to do with the saving that the household sector makes available to the rest of the economy for investment purposes. This is net financial saving—financial saving less the change in debt assumed by the household sector.

From the perspective of saving broadly defined, then, the question might be not whether the level of saving has been affected by age structure, but whether the composition of saving, and specifically the level of net financial saving, has been affected. The saving rate could remain constant while its composition shifted toward homeownership and away from financial assets. For example, data from the 1963 Survey of Changes in Family Finances show that households headed by someone younger than 35 did relatively more of their saving in the form of net investment in a home (and in noncorporate business and automobiles) than households headed by older people.[21] But examination of the components of annual saving by individuals since 1946—increase in financial assets, net investment in tangible assets, and net increase in debt—do not reveal the shifts suggested by the hypothesis.[22] The data are subject to error, of course, and errors could disguise a modest shift; but, if anything, the ratios of the components have moved in the opposite

20. The saving rates were calculated, in accordance with the definition followed by Dorothy Projector for the 1960–61 Consumer Expenditure Survey, as the household's net change in assets and liabilities divided by its after-tax income. The data come from BLS, *Consumer Expenditure Survey Series: Interview Survey, 1972–73*, Bulletin 1985, table 12.

21. Projector, *Survey of Changes in Family Finances*, p. 214.

22. Two ratios were calculated for the period 1946–79 on the basis of annual data supplied by the Federal Reserve Board: the ratio of the increase in financial assets to net investment in tangible assets (which includes owner-occupied homes and consumer durables), and the ratio of the increase in financial assets to the net increase in debt. The hypothesized effects of age structure would have caused both ratios to be lower during the 1970s than earlier. Instead, the first ratio was consistently higher. The second ratio varied a great deal, but the years in which it was a bit below the values usual in the 1950s and the 1960s were balanced by the years in which it was above those values. Ratios involving financial assets and subcomponents of tangible assets and debt also failed to show any evidence for the hypothesis.

direction from that expected to result from an increase in young households.[23]

This chapter does not try to settle the issue of the effect on aggregate consumption and saving of age structure in general, or of the baby boom generation in particular. Instead, it turns to two more specific areas of consumption—housing and durables. If the large number of young households has had significant effects on consumption, they should show up most clearly in these two areas. The *Economic Report of the President* for January 1965, looking back at the small cohorts that had reached adulthood in the 1950s, and forward to the coming of age of the baby boom generation, observed: "The forthcoming changes in the age-structure of the population will have their primary influence on over-all demand by affecting spending for durables and housing."[24] The following sections try to determine how great that primary influence has been.

Housing

In the early 1960s many observers predicted that an unprecedented demand for housing would develop later in the decade as the oldest members of the baby boom generation reached adulthood. The subject was first mentioned in the *Economic Report of the President* in 1962, when the Council of Economic Advisers urged the importance of improving housing quality in the first half of the decade, before the need for quantity became overriding.[25] The 1968 *Economic Report* predicted that 20 million units would be required during the 1970s "to meet the needs of the post–World War II baby boom."[26]

In a book published in 1966, Burnham Campbell analyzed the historical relationship between the housing market and the size and age structure of the population. He found that the relationship had been stable for many years before World War II, with changes in the housing stock

23. In their cross-section analysis based on survey data, Lieberman and Wachtel, "Age Structure and Personal Saving Behavior," find that age structure alone would have caused net financial saving to decline substantially in the 1970s. But when they adjust further for the growth in the number of primary individuals, and the saving behavior associated with them, they find that net financial saving did not decline after all. Their analysis shows the importance of considering the changes in household type that have accompanied changes in age structure, rather than assuming that they remain constant.

24. *Economic Report of the President, January 1965*, p. 93.

25. *Economic Report of the President, January 1962*, p. 141.

26. *Economic Report of the President, February 1968*, p. 151.

following population changes rather closely, but that rising rates of household incidence since World War II had meant that housing markets continued to do well after the postwar backlog had been eliminated, even though population trends were working against them. He was therefore understandably cautious in predicting the effects of the baby boom, observing that "if population changes alone can still lead to boom conditions," they would be most likely to do so between 1970 and 1975. More generally he predicted that "the 1970's and perhaps the early 1980's should see a major residential construction boom—a boom that will first involve construction of dwelling units almost entirely for people under 35 and that will have to adjust successfully from rental to sales orientation in the mid-seventies."[27]

Growth of the Housing Stock, 1950–80

As promised, housing construction hit record levels in the 1970s (table 5-3). Housing starts exceeded 2 million a year in 1971, 1972, and 1973, and again in 1977 and 1978. The totals are even larger when mobile homes are included—almost 3 million new units in the peak year of 1972.

The rapid growth in the housing stock has often been discussed as though it were due entirely to the baby boom generation, for obvious reasons.[28] The true situation is more complicated. Three demographic factors have been involved: the growth in the youngest age groups (people under 35) because of the baby boom; the growth in the oldest age groups (people 55 or older); and the rising rates of household incidence in all age groups. These three factors can be separated to gain a clearer picture of the baby boom generation's contribution to the housing market in the past and its potential future contribution.

The definitions used by the Census Bureau guarantee that each household is associated with one and only one occupied housing unit. Thus additions to the occupied housing stock associated with a particular

27. Campbell, *Population Change and Building Cycles*, pp. 151, 160.

28. Two examples are the quotation from the *Economic Report of the President, February 1968*, given in the first paragraph of this section, and a recent OMB report which asserts that "between 1970 [and] 1978, approximately 1.6 million units per year were required to meet demographic demands generated by the baby boom." Office of Management and Budget, "Impact of Changing Demographic Patterns on Future Housing Needs, 1980–2000," Interim Report (OMB, 1979), p. 1. Both statements attribute the entire amount of construction, or increase in the occupied housing stock, to the requirements of the baby boom generation.

Table 5-3. Housing Starts and Mobile Home Shipments, 1947–80

Thousands

Year	Housing starts			Mobile home ship-ments	Housing starts plus mobile home shipments
	Total[a]	Single unit[b]	Multi-unit		
1947	1,292	n.a.	n.a.	60	1,352
1948	1,385	n.a.	n.a.	86	1,471
1949	1,489	n.a.	n.a.	46	1,535
1950	1,973	n.a.	n.a.	63	2,036
1951	1,514	n.a.	n.a.	67	1,581
1952	1,527	n.a.	n.a.	83	1,610
1953	1,461	n.a.	n.a.	77	1,538
1954	1,574	n.a.	n.a.	76	1,650
1955	1,668	n.a.	n.a.	112	1,780
1956	1,372	n.a.	n.a.	124	1,496
1957	1,248	n.a.	n.a.	119	1,367
1958	1,405	n.a.	n.a.	102	1,507
1959	1,554	1,251	303	121	1,675
1960	1,296	1,009	287	104	1,400
1961	1,365	989	376	90	1,455
1962	1,492	996	496	118	1,610
1963	1,635	1,013	622	151	1,786
1964	1,561	972	589	191	1,752
1965	1,510	965	545	216	1,726
1966	1,196	780	416	217	1,413
1967	1,322	845	477	240	1,562
1968	1,545	900	645	318	1,863
1969	1,500	811	689	413	1,913
1970	1,469	815	654	401	1,870
1971	2,085	1,153	932	497	2,582
1972	2,379	1,311	1,068	576	2,955
1973	2,057	1,133	924	567	2,624
1974	1,352	889	463	329	1,681
1975	1,171	896	275	213	1,384
1976	1,548	1,166	382	246	1,794
1977	2,002	1,451	536	277	2,267
1978	2,036	1,433	587	276	2,299
1979	1,760	1,194	551	277	2,026
1980	1,313	852	440	229	1,542

Sources: Bureau of the Census, *Historical Statistics of the United States: Colonial Times to 1970* (GPO, 1975), pt. 2, ser. N 156-70, pp. 639–40; Bureau of the Census, *Construction Reports*, series C20, no. 82-1 (GPO, 1982), tables 1, 6; and author's estimates. Figures are rounded.

n.a. Not available.

a. Farm plus nonfarm. Housing starts for 1947–58 are author's estimates based on a regression of total on nonfarm starts for 1959–69. Nonfarm starts for 1947–58 were adjusted upward by means of the regression.

b. Private starts only.

age group over a particular period are the number of households in that age group at the end of the period less the number at the beginning— namely, the net change in the number of households. But this calculation, which Burnham Campbell labels *actual additions,* combines changes in the size of the age group with changes in its behavior as reflected in its household incidence.[29] Campbell uses the term *required additions* to refer to those additions that can, strictly speaking, be attributed to the change in the size of the age group. Required additions are the number of additional housing units that would have been required if the population had changed as it actually did while its rate of household incidence remained at the level of the beginning of the period. The difference between actual and required additions is due to changes in household incidence.[30] Actual or required additions for the entire population are derived by summing the additions for each age group.

Table 5-4 shows required additions, actual additions, new housing starts, and housing starts plus mobile homes for each five-year period from 1950 to 1980. (Required additions are calculated by using the rates of household incidence by age for the first of the five years in each period.) Housing starts plus mobile homes exceed actual additions by a large margin in every period and exceed required additions by an even larger margin. Except during the period 1975–80, actual additions to the occupied housing stock never accounted for more than two-thirds of the new units, and required additions never more than 50 percent. The gap arises because some new housing is built to replace older housing, to allow for vacancies and second homes, and to house migrants to growing areas; migration may mean, of course, that housing stands unoccupied in declining areas. Thus some of the new construction (including mobile homes) is required for these other purposes and cannot be linked, at

29. Campbell describes his methodology in chapter 3 of *Population Changes and Building Cycles*.

30. More precisely, the difference between actual and required additions is the sum of (1) population at the beginning of the period times the change in the rate of household incidence, and (2) an "interaction term" that is the product of the change in population and the change in household incidence. This interaction term cannot be attributed to population or household incidence alone, since it is the product of changes in both. It has been included in the difference between actual and required additions here, hence implicitly attributed to changes in household incidence. This makes little difference to the analysis, the more so since with household incidence rates held constant over periods of only five years, the interaction term is never more than 10 percent as large as the effect of changes in household incidence.

Table 5-4. Required and Actual Additions to the Occupied Housing Stock, Housing Starts, and Housing Starts plus Mobile Home Shipments, 1950–80
Thousands

Period	Required additions	Actual additions	Housing starts[a]	Housing starts plus mobile home shipments[a]
1950–55	3,112	5,544	8,049	8,415
1955–60	3,099	5,011	7,247	7,825
1960–65	3,004	4,636	7,349	8,003
1965–70	3,813	5,968	7,073	8,477
1970–75	5,187	7,716	9,342	11,712
1975–80	6,008	7,960	8,481	9,770

Sources: Author's calculations based on data supplied by the Bureau of the Census, and table 5-3.
a. Summed over the periods 1950–54, 1955–59, 1960–64, 1965–69, 1970–74, 1975–79.

least not directly, to either population changes or changes in rates of household incidence.

Further, actual additions consistently exceed required additions. Since required additions represent the additions attributable to age structure alone, the large differences between the two measures demonstrate the importance of changes in household incidence rates. Comparison of the trends in required additions with those in actual additions or new units shows in still another way that age structure has not been the only important influence on additions to the housing stock. The three series move together much of the time, but not always, and the sizes of the changes in each series often differ substantially. For example, although required additions and new units were both at their highest levels during the 1970s, required additions rose in the second half, while starts plus mobile homes fell.

The overall relationship between actual and required additions holds for the various age groups as well (table 5-5). With three exceptions—households headed by people aged 45 through 54 in 1960–65, 55 through 64 in 1970–75, and 65 through 74 in 1975–80—actual additions are larger than required additions for every age group in every period, usually substantially larger, or the reduction in actual additions is less than the reduction in required additions, reflecting once again the steady rise in the incidence of households in every age group.

The progress through the housing market of the small cohorts born during the late 1920s and the 1930s shows up clearly in table 5-5. These cohorts appear as negative required additions beginning in the under 30 group in 1950–55 and moving up to the 45-through-54 group by 1975–80. They illustrate the looseness of the link between required and actual additions—that is, between age structure and housing—particularly well. For example, during the 1955–60 period required additions declined by 466,000 as the small cohorts moved into the 25-through-34 age groups, while actual additions grew by 409,000.

Perhaps most important, the table shows the impact of the growing numbers of older people on the occupied housing stock. Year after year they have added substantially to the number of required additions, and even more substantially to actual additions. They have been major contributors to the trends so often attributed solely to younger age groups.

The effects of the baby boom are apparent in the numbers for 1970–75 and 1975–80. In the first half of the decade, the baby boom generation proper—that is, the cohorts born between 1946 and 1964—was under 30. Had household incidence remained at the levels of 1970, these young households would have required 1,862,000 additional housing units over the next five years, 36 percent of total required additions. When changes in household incidence are included, they accounted for 3,151,000, or 41 percent, of actual additions. Another 20 percent of actual additions were provided by households in the 30-through-34-year-old category (the young adults just ahead of the baby boom generation), and the remainder—almost 40 percent—by older households, especially those headed by someone over 45.

By the second half of the decade, the baby boom generation had aged to include all households under 35. Based on the rates of household incidence for 1975, required additions for these households totaled 2,673,000 units, or 45 percent of all required additions. Actual additions were 3,479,000, or 44 percent of total actual additions. As before, the remaining actual additions came from the cohorts just ahead of the baby boom generation and from cohorts over 55. If the war generation—aged 35 through 40 in this period—could be separated from the 35-through-44 group, its contribution would probably be in the neighborhood of 20 percent again. Households headed by someone 45 through 54 years old actually served to reduce both required and actual additions.

These numbers may appear inconsistent with some of the commonly cited statistics about apartment renters and home buyers. For example, surveys of buyers of new homes show that over half were between 25

Table 5-5. **Additions to the Occupied Housing Stock, by Age of Household Head, 1950–80, and Projections to 2000**
Thousands

Period and type of addition	Under 25	25–29	30–34	35–44	45–54	55–64	65–74	75 and over	Total
1950–55									
Required	−22	−193	327	596	659	585	775	385	3,112
Actual	128	32	603	1,375	1,019	917	945	525	5,544
1955–60									
Required	280	−276	−190	627	933	585	673	466	3,099
Actual	414	231	178	629	1,324	694	876	665	5,011
1960–65									
Required	664	159	−387	108	667	799	481	511	3,004
Actual	854	491	−288	395	645	1,001	793	745	4,636
1965–70									
Required	609	1,008	208	−641	776	892	363	598	3,813
Actual	928	1,344	481	−224	817	1,231	433	958	5,968
1970–75									
Required	421	1,441	1,166	−166	242	646	849	587	5,187
Actual	1,493	1,658	1,537	76	576	470	1,304	602	7,716
1975–80									
Required	90	922	1,661	1,510	−581	812	1,034	561	6,008
Actual	528	1,102	1,849	2,049	−340	880	1,028	865	7,960
1980–85									
Required	−419	777	1,061	3,058	−134	310	675	874	6,202
1985–90									
Required	−602	−194	823	2,771	1,566	−564	807	827	5,435
1990–95									
Required	−66	−1,178	−215	1,905	3,018	−108	269	757	4,383
1995–2000									
Required	452	−563	−1,260	619	2,780	1,563	−505	793	3,881

Sources: Actual additions, same as table 5-4; required additions, author's calculations.

and 34 years of age in the late 1970s, although this age group accounted for a much smaller share—37 percent—of the actual additions to the occupied housing stock.[31] The explanation is that the rising rates of household incidence among older people mean, in large part, not the creation of new households, but the decision not to disband existing ones when a single person or couple retires, or a spouse dies. With older people continuing to occupy the existing stock of housing, young people must buy new houses if they are to set up on their own. Thus they account for a much larger share of new home purchases than of additions to the housing stock.

Future Growth

What about the future of the housing market, and the role of the baby boom generation in that future? Required additions can be predicted with reasonable confidence to the year 2000, because the population that will be 25 or older in that year was already born when the population projections were made; younger cohorts—whose numbers must be based on guesses about birth rates—are not an important factor in housing. But the link between the housing market and the size and age structure of the population has obviously been quite loose since World War II. The validity of required additions as a forecast of future housing demand depends on future trends in household incidence.

It was noted earlier in the chapter that the scope for further increases in household incidence is limited simply because the rates are already so high. The decision to form a separate household depends on personal preferences and circumstances, and involves a number of related decisions—such as the decision to enter the labor force, to marry or divorce, or to have a family. In 1977 Frieden and Solomon examined the trends in some of these related decisions and in economic conditions and concluded that rates of household incidence were indeed likely to level off during the 1980s.[32] If they are right, required and actual additions will be quite close in the next decade or so, as they were for many decades

31. Michael Sumichrast, Gopal Ahluwalia, and Robert S. Sheehan, *Profile of a New Home Buyer: 1979 Survey of New Home Owners* (Washington, D.C.: National Association of Home Builders, 1979), p. 11.

32. Specifically, they considered marital status, family size, the availability of relatives to live with, income and wealth, the cost of separate households, and the match between types of housing and types of households. Bernard J. Frieden and Arthur P. Solomon, *The Nation's Housing: 1975 to 1985* (Harvard-MIT Joint Center for Urban Studies, 1977).

before World War II, and population size and age structure will once again offer a reliable clue to housing trends.

Table 5-5 projects required additions through the year 2000 on the assumption that household incidence will remain at the levels of 1980. The projections suggest that unless there are offsetting changes in the incidence of households, demand for housing will remain strong in the 1980s, and the baby boom generation will contribute more to that demand than in the 1970s. Older groups will begin to decline in importance as the small cohorts of the late 1920s and the 1930s age into them.

At 6,202,000, required additions are slightly higher for the period 1980–85 than they were for 1975–80. The members of the baby boom generation cannot be identified precisely in the later period, when they are between the ages of 21 and 39, but they probably account for about two-thirds of total required additions, considerably more than at any time during the 1970s. Required additions are modestly lower in the next five years (1985–90), but the baby boom is equally important. Then between the ages of 25 and 44, its members account for 3,400,000, or 63 percent, of total required additions. In the 1990s required additions will drop to much lower levels as the small cohorts of the late 1920s and the 1930s continue to age and the small cohorts born after the baby boom reach adulthood.

Renting versus Owning

The growth or decline of different age groups affects not only the number of units but the type of housing demanded—apartments, mobile homes, or single-family houses. In turn, housing type is closely linked to the choice between renting and owning, although the correspondence is not perfect. While most single-family houses are owned, some are rented, and cooperatives and condominiums make it possible to buy rather than rent an apartment.

Different ages are associated with different types of housing because age brings with it changes in family responsibilities and income that make particular choices both desirable and possible. The familiar pattern is that young single people rent apartments, while middle-aged married couples—especially those with children—buy single-family houses. Older people sometimes move to an apartment once their children are grown. A study of housing choices in a county in Wisconsin, for example, found that more than 90 percent of the young single people lived in apartments, but that the situation was reversed for older married couples

with children—by this stage, more than 90 percent of the families owned
their own homes.[33] And families with children who rented often rented
single-family houses rather than apartments. Nationally, more than 90
percent of new home buyers are married couples.[34]

If the housing choices of different age groups had remained constant
over the last thirty years, the age structure of the population would have
produced a trend toward homeownership in the 1950s, then toward
apartments and renting as the baby boom generation grew up in the 1960s
and early 1970s, and then back to homeownership in the later 1970s and
beyond. It was for this reason that Campbell predicted, again with well-
founded caution, not only a residential construction boom during the
1970s and early 1980s but also a shift from rental housing at the beginning
of the boom to sales housing toward the end.

But here as elsewhere, age is an imperfect guide to behavior. In the
1950s young adults married and had children earlier than preceding
generations. Since then, the trends have been in the direction of delayed
marriage and childbearing, more frequent divorce, and an increasing
number of one-person households in all age groups, but especially the
youngest and oldest. Thus households that are less likely to buy their
own homes have become a larger share of the total.

Further, the choice of housing made by a given type of household is
not fixed. It depends on the household's current and prospective income,
the prices of different types of housing, the financing available, and the
attractiveness of housing as an investment. These factors, which make
up the cost of housing, are discussed in more detail later. Suffice it to
say here that, on balance, they have combined to make homeownership
increasingly attractive since World War II. And during much of the
period the federal government has aided and abetted this process,
actively promoting homeownership through a variety of programs to
make mortgage money more easily available.[35]

33. McCarthy, *Household Life Cycle and Housing Choices*.
34. Sumichrast and others, *Profile of a New Home Buyer*, p. 13.
35. Discussions of federal policy and of programs to support the mortgage market can
be found in various issues of the annual *Economic Report of the President*. For example,
page 79 of the 1956 report, page 140 of the 1962 report, and page 43 of the 1969 report.
Gibson provides a discussion of the major federal programs for insuring and purchasing
mortgages and providing interest subsidies. William E. Gibson, "Protecting Homebuilding
from Restrictive Credit Conditions," *Brookings Papers on Economic Activity, 3:1973*, pp.
647–91 (hereafter BPEA). Jaffee and Rosen analyze the importance of money market
certificates in maintaining the flow of funds to thrift institutions, which make most mortgage
loans. Dwight M. Jaffee and Kenneth T. Rosen, "Mortgage Credit Availability and
Residential Construction," *BPEA, 2:1979*, pp. 333–76.

Table 5-6. Homeowners as a Percentage of Husband-Wife Households and of All Households, by Age of Household Head, Selected Years, 1940–80

Year and type of household	Under 25	25–29	30–34	35–44	45–54	55–64	65 and over	All ages
Husband-wife								
1940	11.8	18.8	27.1	39.2	55.4		68.5	43.2
1960	24.4	44.5	61.9	71.5	74.5		77.7	67.1
1970	26.1	48.8	66.0	77.1	81.1		78.8	71.1
1976	31.3	55.3	74.2	81.1	86.0		82.8	75.9
1980	35.0	57.7	75.8	83.7	89.1		84.9	79.0
All								
1960	20.4	51.8		67.0	64.8	69.0	71.4	62.6
1970	20.8	49.9		69.4	73.7	72.3	68.1	63.3
1976	21.1	52.3		71.2	77.0	77.3	71.0	65.1
1980	24.3	54.8		73.4	79.2	81.0	72.3	66.3

Sources: Data for 1940 and 1960 husband-wife households are from Bureau of the Census, *U.S. Census of Population: 1960, Subject Reports, Final Report PC(2)-4A, Families* (GPO, 1964), table 1; 1960 data for all households are derived from Bureau of the Census, *U.S. Census of Housing: 1960, Final Report HC(4), pt. 2-1, Components of Inventory Change: 1957–1959 Components* (GPO, 1962); and Bureau of the Census, *Current Population Reports*, series P-20, no. 296, "Households and Families by Type" (GPO, 1976), tables 3, 6; data for 1970 are from Bureau of the Census, *Census of Population, 1970, Subject Reports, Final Report PC(2)-4A, Family Composition* (GPO, 1973); table 1; and data for 1976 and 1980 are author's calculations based on the Bureau of the Census, Current Population Survey Public Use Datatapes for March of each year.

For a given type of household and a given age group, economic factors should dominate. The data for husband-wife households, the life cycle stage for which homeownership has become the norm, show that the rise in homeownership was extremely rapid for all age groups between 1940 and 1960; the proportion of all married couples who owned their own homes rose from 43 percent in 1940 to 67 percent in 1960. Between 1960 and 1970 homeownership grew more slowly—the largest increase was in the 45-through-64 age group. Then in the 1970s the rate of increase picked up again, particularly among younger couples, where the percentages were lowest to start with. Between 1970 and 1980 the proportion of homeowners rose from 49 to 58 percent for the 25-through-29 age group, and from 66 to 76 percent for those 30 through 34.

The trends in homeownership for all households of a given age show that since 1960 the shift away from husband-wife households has largely offset their higher rates of homeownership in the youngest and oldest age groups. For all households, the proportion of homeowners hovered around 21 percent in the under-25 group during the 1960s and early 1970s, before rising to 24 percent in 1980. For the 25-through-34 and 65-and-over groups the proportion fell slightly between 1960 and 1970 and then rose a bit above its 1960 value by 1980. Ownership rose steadily in the middle age groups, where husband-wife households are the dominant type, but not as sharply as for husband-wife households alone.

The trend in homeownership for all households of all ages taken together is the combined result of economic factors, household composition (alternatively, stage of the life cycle), and age structure. Sternlieb and Burchell report that in 1940, just at the end of the depression, 44 percent of all households owned their homes.[36] The proportion rose rapidly to 55 percent in 1950 and 63 percent in 1960 (table 5-6). It was still 63 percent in 1970. During the 1970s economic factors, perhaps with some help from age structure, slightly outweighed the offsetting effects of changes in household composition, and homeownership rose to 66 percent of all households in 1980.

Since 1979 economic conditions have not been so favorable to homeownership as they were earlier. And if rates of household incidence level off in the 1980s, as Frieden and Solomon predict, the shift away

36. George Sternlieb and Robert W. Burchell, *Multifamily Housing Demand, 1975–2000*, study prepared for the Subcommittee on Priorities and Economy in Government of the Joint Economic Committee, 95 Cong. 2 sess. (GPO, 1978), p. 2. The number for 1950 is also from Sternlieb and Burchell.

Table 5-7. Required Additions to the Housing Stock, by Type of Unit and Age of Household Head, 1975–80, and Projections to 1995–2000

Thousands

Period and type of unit	Under 25	25–34	35–44	45–54	55–64	65 and over	Total
1975–80							
Sales	19	1,351	1,075	−447	628	1,132	3,758
Rental	71	1,232	435	−134	184	463	2,251
1980–85							
Sales	−88	961	2,177	−103	240	1,100	4,287
Rental	−331	877	881	−31	70	449	1,915
1985–90							
Sales	−127	329	1,973	1,206	−436	1,160	4,105
Rental	−475	300	798	360	−128	474	1,329
1990–95							
Sales	−14	−728	1,356	2,324	−83	728	3,583
Rental	−52	−665	549	694	−25	298	799
1995–2000							
Sales	95	−953	441	2,141	1,208	204	3,136
Rental	357	−870	178	639	355	84	743

Sources: Tables 5-5 and 5-6.

from husband-wife households should level off too. Table 5-7 shows how required additions will be split between rental and sales housing in the future if the proportions of homeowners and the distribution of households by type remain at the levels of 1976, so that age structure can act unimpeded.

Rental units diminish steadily in importance as the baby boom generation reaches middle age in the 1980s, while the small cohorts of the 1920s and the 1930s enter old age and those of the late 1960s and the 1970s become adults. In the 1975–80 period rental units were 37 percent of total required additions. By the end of the 1980s they should decline to about 25 percent, and then to about 20 percent in the 1990s. Thus, as Campbell predicted, future changes in age structure should produce a shift away from rental housing toward owned housing, and the proportion of households who own their homes should rise.

But age structure may be offset or reinforced by other factors as it has been for the last thirty years. For example, economic conditions might combine to raise the cost of housing and cause homeownership to decline. This section concludes by examining recent trends in the cost of housing.

Cost of Housing

During the 1970s house prices rose considerably faster than the prices of other goods and services (figure 5-1 and table 5-8).[37] Mortgage interest rates soared to unprecedented levels. To all appearances, homeownership was increasingly out of the reach of most households, especially young ones, and the situation was a frequent source of comment among journalists, scholars, and the public at large.[38] Yet, as has just been shown, married couples—the traditional home buyers—bought houses in greater numbers than ever before, young ones no less than older ones. Surprisingly few people were deterred by the high prices.

The truth of the matter was that the cost of homeownership rose less than other prices during the 1970s, despite appearances. It even rose less than rents, which lagged behind other goods and services from the late 1960s on (table 5-8). The reasons lay in several factors that are familiar to anyone who has ever considered buying a house, but that are not reflected in the usual price indexes.

For example, most people recognize the advantage of fixed mortgage payments in periods of serious inflation like the 1970s. Rising prices and mortgage interest rates affect new buyers, but they do not change the payments of existing owners. For all homeowners, once the purchase is made, the fixed mortgage payments become easier to meet as incomes rise in line with inflation. Indeed, payments that are onerous during the first few years rapidly become less so if inflation continues. Many new

37. The price of the average new house includes changes in quality as well as true changes in price. Between 1969 and 1972 the index of new house prices, shown in the first column of table 5-8, lagged behind other prices in large part because new federal subsidies encouraged the construction of more small, low-quality units during those years. Anthony M. Rufolo, "What's Ahead for Housing Prices?" *Federal Reserve Bank of Philadelphia, Business Review* (July–August 1980), pp. 9–15.

The table does not include the home purchase component of the consumer price index. This component is based on the sales prices of houses insured by the Federal Housing Administration and is believed to be unrepresentative of the broader housing market. For example, the home purchase index rose at about the same rate as the index for other goods and services during the 1970s rather than faster. For a discussion of the problems with the home purchase component, see Alan S. Blinder, "The Consumer Price Index and the Measurement of Recent Inflation," *BPEA, 2:1980*, especially pp. 550, 551.

The rise in rents is modestly understated by the rent index in table 5-8, because as fuel prices rose over the period more landlords separated heating bills from the rest of the rental payment.

38. For example, Frieden and Solomon, *Nation's Housing, 1975 to 1985*.

Table 5-8. Price Indexes of Selected Components of Housing Costs, Selected Years, 1950–80

Index 1967 = 100

Year	Purchasing costs				Cost of upkeep			Goods and services other than housing[c]
	Sales prices of single-family houses			Financing, taxes, and insurance	Maintenance and repair	Fuel and other utilities	Rent	
	New	New, constant quality[a]	Existing[b]					
1950	n.a.	n.a.	n.a.	n.a.	n.a.	n.a.	70	73
1955	n.a.	n.a.	n.a.	n.a.	74	85	84	81
1960	n.a.	n.a.	n.a.	n.a.	85	96	92	89
1965	87	93	n.a.	n.a.	91	98	97	95
1970	108	116	125	142	124	108	110	114
1971	115	123	136	144	134	115	115	119
1972	124	131	146	151	141	120	119	123
1973	144	142	160	161	151	127	124	131
1974	158	156	174	181	172	150	131	146
1975	173	171	189	202	188	168	137	159
1976	195	186	205	213	200	183	145	168
1977	220	208	233	227	215	202	154	179
1978	254	258	269	258	233	216	164	191
1979	292	271	312	309	256	239	176	211
1980	310	301	353	396	286	279	192	236

Sources: Bureau of the Census, *Construction Reports*, series C25, *New One-Family Houses Sold and for Sale*, various issues; National Association of Realtors, *Existing Home Sales*, various issues; and for consumer price index and components, Bureau of Labor Statistics.

n.a. Not available.

a. The price of a house with ten major characteristics specified and held constant over time (for example, floor space); eight characteristics were used before 1974.

b. A price for 1967 was not available from the National Association of Realtors. The 1967 value was estimated by extrapolation to allow this index to have the same base year as the others in the table.

c. Consumer price index less shelter.

Figure 5-1. Price Indexes for Housing and Consumer Goods Other Than Housing, 1963–80[a]

Index (1967 = 100)

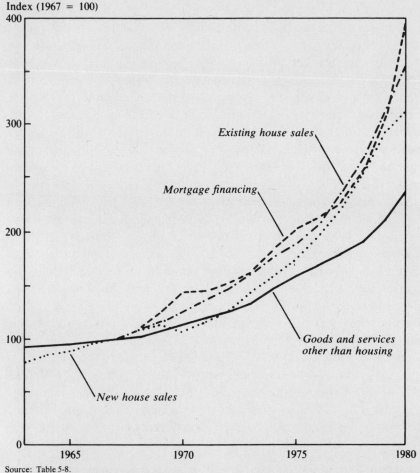

Source: Table 5-8.
a. 1967–80 for existing housing and mortgage financing.

buyers of the 1970s recognized this fact and, betting (correctly, as it turned out) that inflation would continue, took on heavy payments.

And, of course, rising house prices have advantages as well as disadvantages. While they mean that new buyers find it increasingly expensive to buy a house, they also mean that houses are a good investment. Looked at this way, the price indexes in table 5-8 show that investing in houses was an excellent way to maintain the value of a capital sum during the 1970s, and, even better, to make substantial capital gains. Few other investments, if any, did as well.

The favorable tax treatment accorded homeowners also makes buying a house a better choice than the indexes suggest. A renter must pay the full cost of his or her shelter—a rental payment that covers maintenance, taxes, financing costs, depreciation, and a return to the landlord—out of after-tax income. By contrast, owners can deduct mortgage interest payments and property taxes from their taxable income.[39] In addition, by living in the house, they receive housing services in excess of their direct payments, services analogous to the depreciation and return charged by the landlord. Since these services are received as such, rather than in the form of money payments, they are not taxed, and the owner is effectively the beneficiary of some tax-free income. The higher the household's marginal tax rate, the greater the tax advantages of home-ownership.

The combined effect of all the advantages of homeownership has been substantial. Patric Hendershott calculated that throughout the 1960s and most of the 1970s the actual cost of owning a house declined relative to the prices of other goods and services.[40] It declined relative to the cost of renting as well, so that owning rather than renting became an increasingly attractive choice. But Hendershott also found that the decline was abruptly reversed in 1979 and 1980, when skyrocketing interest rates outstripped the various tax and investment advantages, and the cost of owning a house began to rise faster than other prices.

Anthony Downs and S. Michael Giliberto calculated that real mortgage interest rates—that is, rates adjusted for inflation and tax deductions—declined during the 1960s and 1970s.[41] In fact, from the mid-1960s on, real after-tax rates were actually negative. Thus while nominal before-tax financing costs appeared prohibitive, real after-tax financing

39. Walter S. Salant has pointed out that the home buyer's advantage over a renter is the same whether the buyer pays cash or takes out a mortgage, because the deductibility of mortgage interest means that all interest payments, made or received, are treated the same under the federal income tax. To see the essential point, suppose that the interest rate on mortgages, r, is the same as the rate of return on investment. If the buyer pays cash, he or she gives up the opportunity to invest the money and receive a return of $r(1 - t)$, where t is his or her marginal tax rate. If the buyer takes out a mortgage, he or she pays at the rate of $r(1 - t)$ on the loan, since the interest payments are deductible. The after-tax income forgone under the first method of financing is exactly the same as the after-tax income paid out under the second.

40. Patric H. Hendershott, "Real User Costs and the Demand for Single-Family Housing," *BPEA, 2:1980*, especially pp. 405–07.

41. Anthony Downs and S. Michael Giliberto, "How Inflation Erodes the Income of Fixed-Rate Lenders," *Real Estate Review*, vol. 11 (Spring 1981), pp. 43–51 (Brookings Reprint 372). See also Anthony Downs, "Too Much Capital for Housing?" *The Brookings Bulletin*, vol. 17 (Summer 1980), pp. 1–5.

costs—the costs of concern to the buyer—offered a powerful incentive to buy. And people did. After reviewing recent developments in the housing market, Downs concluded that during the 1970s "a majority of American households have discovered the advantages of using financial leverage to make real estate investments during inflationary periods—in this case, investments in their own homes."[42]

At the same time that the actual cost of owning a house was rising more slowly than other prices, incomes were rising almost as fast as the price indexes in table 5-8. This fact was obscured because house prices were usually compared with average family income. Because of the shift away from families headed by married couples, and the recent influx of young families, average family income is not a well-defined benchmark. Two better measures, both largely free of the effects of changes in household composition, are the incomes of young married couples and per capita disposable income. Both measures show that income lagged only a bit behind house prices during most of the 1970s, and stayed well ahead of the actual cost of owning a house. Here again, however, the situation began to change in the late 1970s as house prices began to rise somewhat faster than incomes.[43]

Thus the older members of the baby boom generation appear to have encountered a more favorable housing market than preceding generations, rather than a less favorable one, and to have been quick to respond to the opportunities presented. Recent trends suggest that the situation may be different for the younger members of the generation. But any changes that occur are less likely to arise from the effect of these cohorts on the housing market than from the future course of prices and interest rates, and their interaction with the tax code.

Durable Goods

As they set out on their own, buy houses, and start families, young people invest in many kinds of durable goods for the first time—

42. Anthony Downs, "Public Policy and the Rising Cost of Housing," *Real Estate Review*, vol. 8 (Spring 1978), p. 38 (Brookings Reprint 344). None of the discussion to this point recognizes the importance of mobile homes as a low-cost alternative for some buyers. In 1979, when the average price of a new house was $71,800 and that of an existing house $64,200, the price of a mobile home averaged only $17,600 (without land), and some models were available for considerably less. Many households chose this form of housing, especially during the early 1970s; mobile homes stayed consistently at about 20 percent of total housing starts plus mobile homes during this period (table 5-3).

43. Based on per capita disposable income, and average incomes for families headed by someone aged 25–34, or 35–44, from the Census Bureau.

Table 5-9. Expenditures per Household on Household Furnishings and Automobiles, by Age of Household Head, 1960–61 and 1972–73

Survey period and expenditure	Under 25	25–34	35–44	45–54	55–64	65 and over
1960–61						
Household furnishings and equipment						
Amount (dollars)	283	330	341	293	221	121
Percent of after-tax income	6.7	5.8	5.1	4.4	4.1	3.6
Percent of before-tax income	6.0	5.2	4.5	3.8	3.6	3.3
Automobiles						
Amount (dollars)	788	805	853	837	609	292
Percent of after-tax income	18.6	14.0	12.6	12.5	11.4	8.7
Percent of before-tax income	16.8	12.7	11.3	11.0	9.9	8.1
1972–73						
Household furnishings and equipment						
Amount (dollars)	301	495	524	457	320	167
Percent of after-tax income	5.1	4.8	4.1	3.3	2.9	2.8
Percent of before-tax income	4.4	4.1	3.5	2.8	2.4	2.6
Automobiles						
Amount (dollars)	858	881	976	1,041	732	282
Percent of after-tax income	14.5	8.6	7.7	7.5	6.7	4.8
Percent of before-tax income	12.5	7.3	6.5	6.3	5.6	4.4

Sources: Data for 1960–61 are from BLS, *Consumer Expenditures and Income: Cross-Classification of Family Characteristics*, BLS Report 237-93, suppl. 2 (USDA Report CES 30) (BLS, 1966), table 14; and for 1972–73, from BLS, *Consumer Expenditure Survey Series: Interview Survey 1972–73*, Bulletin 1985 (GPO, 1978), table 12.

particularly automobiles, furniture, and household appliances. Statistical studies have repeatedly confirmed that young households spend relatively more on durable goods than older households.[44] In the broad view of saving discussed earlier, young households do more of their saving in the form of these material goods, while older households do more of theirs in the form of financial assets. Once again, of course, the relationship between age and behavior arises primarily because age is associated with differences in family responsibilities and income.

Table 5-9 shows the average expenditure by households for two broad groups of durable goods—automobiles, and household furnishings and equipment—based on surveys carried out in 1960–61 and 1972–73. Expenditures for automobiles are the sum of net outlays (purchase price less trade-in allowance) for cars and trucks and the interest charges on

44. Harold Lydall, "The Life Cycle in Income, Saving, and Asset Ownership," *Econometrica,* vol. 23 (April 1955), pp. 131–50; Janet A. Fisher, "Consumer Durable Goods Expenditures, with Major Emphasis on the Role of Assets, Credit and Intentions," *Journal of the American Statistical Association,* vol. 58 (September 1963), pp. 648–57; and Gilbert R. Ghez and Gary S. Becker, *The Allocation of Time and Goods over the Life Cycle* (Columbia University Press for the National Bureau of Economic Research, 1975).

loans taken out to finance those purchases. "Household furnishings and equipment," though not precisely the same set of items in the two surveys, includes the general categories of furniture, rugs, linens, appliances of all sorts, and housewares.

In both surveys middle-aged households spent the largest dollar amounts on durable goods, but young households invariably spent a larger percentage of their incomes. For example, in 1972–73 households headed by someone under 25 years of age spent an average of 14.5 percent of their after-tax income on automobiles; the percentage declined steadily with age—to 4.8 percent for households with a head aged 65 or older. Although expenditures are more logically related to after-tax income—the income actually available to spend on goods and services— the table also shows expenditures as a percentage of before-tax income. These percentages are required for projecting the effect of changes in age structure. Fortunately, the pattern across age groups is quite similar regardless of the measure of income used.

At each age the percentages spent on durables were lower in 1972–73 than in 1960–61 because expenditures did not rise as fast as income. But despite the differences between the two surveys in percentages spent— due partly to the differences in income, and, among younger households, in household size—the relative standings of the age groups remained much the same. For automobiles, the percentage spent by each age group relative to the percentage spent by households aged 45 through 54 was virtually the same in 1972–73 as in 1960–61 except for the very youngest households. The ratios were not quite as stable for household furnishings, but this may reflect the differences in the items included.

Since younger households spend relatively more of their income on durable goods, the average percentage of total household income spent on these goods should rise when young households claim a larger share of household income, and fall as their share declines. Table 5-10 shows the shifts in the distribution of total money income among age groups that occurred between 1967 and 1975 and that are projected to occur between 1980 and 1995.[45] These shifts suggest that the average percent-

45. Income was first published for households for the year 1967. Before then, it was published only for families and unrelated persons. The difference between the two ways of counting heads is greatest for the young age groups.

The projected income distribution in table 5-10 is based on the assumption that household incidence rates will rise only slightly above the level of 1977, the base year. (The methods for projecting household incidence rates are described in Bureau of the Census, *Current Population Reports,* series P-25, no. 805, "Projections of the Number of

Table 5-10. Percent Shares of Total Money Income, by Age of Household Head, Selected Years, 1967–75, and Projections for 1980–95

Year	Under 25	25–34	35–44	45–54	55–64	65 and over	Total (millions of dollars)
1967	4.6	18.3	23.9	25.1	17.4	10.8	495,174
1970	5.2	19.0	22.2	25.0	18.0	10.6	643,804
1975	5.3	21.6	20.8	23.3	17.2	11.9	1,004,034
1980	5.3	23.1	21.9	20.9	17.0	11.8	1,310,580
1985	4.8	23.6	24.6	19.0	16.1	11.9	1,496,760
1990	4.0	22.9	26.8	20.0	14.4	12.0	1,690,140
1995	3.6	20.3	27.7	23.0	13.4	12.0	1,882,780

Sources: Bureau of the Census, *Current Population Reports,* series P-60, no. 104, "Household Money Income in 1975 and Selected Social and Economic Characteristics of Households" (GPO, 1977), table 7, and previous issues, nos. 62, 79, for years shown; and Bureau of the Census, *Current Population Reports,* series P-60, no. 122, "Illustrative Projections of Money Income Size Distributions, for Households: 1980 to 1995" (GPO, 1980), pp. 26, 54, 82, 110.

ages spent on durables should have risen during the 1970s, and should continue to rise during the 1980s before declining in the 1990s as the baby boom generation reaches middle age.

Table 5-11 presents two sets of estimates of the average percentages of income spent on furnishings and automobiles over the period 1967–95. In each case the first set of estimates applies the percentages spent by each age group in 1972–73 to the income distribution for each year to calculate an overall average for that year. For the second set of estimates the percentage spent by each age group in 1972–73 was adjusted up or down to reflect the level of real income for the group in each year.[46]

Both sets of estimates show that the effect of age structure has been, and can be expected to be, very small at best. When the percentages

Households and Families: 1979 to 1995" [GPO, 1979], pp. 5–10.) Of the projections available from the Census Bureau, this set is thus closest in spirit to the assumption made for the housing calculations—that incidence rates would not change at all after 1980. Average household income is assumed to grow 1 percent a year in real terms throughout the projection period; the growth rate chosen makes no difference to the distribution of income across age groups so long as the rate is the same for all groups, as it is in these projections.

The projections are for total money income before taxes, and thus the historical data also refer to before-tax income in order to be consistent. Before-tax income involves some double-counting, since social security pension and disability payments, for example, are counted as income for households that receive these payments, while the taxes that must be paid to finance them have not been subtracted from the incomes of other households.

46. The adjustment procedure was based on linear regressions relating expenditures on furnishings and automobiles to before-tax income. Separate regressions were estimated for each age group by using the average expenditures and income in 1972–73 for eleven income groups in BLS, *Consumer Expenditure Survey Series: Interview Survey 1972–73,* Bulletin 1985, table 12. The lowest income group was omitted because the data reported for it were sometimes peculiar. The 1972–73 data were chosen over those for 1960–61

Table 5-11. Average Percentages of Total Money Income Spent on Household Furnishings and Automobiles, Selected Years, 1967–95

Year	Household Furnishings		Automobiles	
	I	II	I	II
1967	3.18	3.28	6.47	6.74
1970	3.18	3.23	6.51	6.63
1975	3.21	3.25	6.52	6.68
1980	3.23	3.22	6.54	6.53
1985	3.25	3.21	6.52	6.40
1990	3.26	3.19	6.48	6.28
1995	3.22	3.12	6.44	6.15

Source: Author's calculations. Series I uses the 1972–73 percentages spent by each age group in calculating the overall average. Series II adjusts the 1972–73 percentages to reflect real incomes in each year (see note 45 for a detailed explanation of the adjustment procedure).

spent by each age group are held constant at the levels of 1972–73, the overall percentage spent on furnishings rises only slightly, from 3.18 percent in 1967 and 1970 to a high of 3.26 percent in 1990, before declining. The average percentage spent on automobiles peaks somewhat earlier, rising from 6.47 in 1967 to 6.54 in 1980, and falling thereafter. When the percentages spent by each age group are not held constant, but are more realistically allowed to rise or fall in response to real income, any effect of age structure is completely obscured and the average percentages decline throughout the period, except for the years 1970–75.

Conclusions

The baby boom generation began to swell the ranks of young households in the late 1960s and 1970s. Together with the growing number of old people, and the trend toward more and smaller households—particularly at the extremes of the age distribution—it helped to produce a population of households increasingly skewed toward the young and

because it was thought that the conditions affecting each age group in 1972–73—average tax rates, household size, and so on—were more likely to approximate future conditions.

The adjustment procedure for a given year t consisted of adding to 1972–73 dollar expenditure the amount $b\Delta Y$, where b is the regression coefficient for the age group and expenditure in question, and ΔY is the difference between the age group's average income in year t (expressed in 1972–73 dollars) and its income in 1972–73. The adjusted expenditure was then divided by the age group's income in year t to yield the adjusted percentage spent.

the old. Between 1970 and 1980 the number of households headed by someone under 35 jumped from 16,231,000 to 24,255,000, and accounted for 31 percent of all households in the later year (table 5-1). Households headed by someone 65 or over increased from 12,242,000 to 16,149,000, and accounted for 20 percent of all households in 1980.

The effect of these events on consumption and saving in the aggregate is unclear from the available studies. To a greater or lesser degree, research on the subject fails to address the issues in terms appropriate to macroeconomic policy—current consumption expenditures in relation to current income. The source of the difficulty is modern consumption theory, which stipulates that flows of services are consumers' primary concern, not the flows of expenditures that precede them, and that consumers make decisions in response to their longer-term income prospects, not to the income of a single year. Two studies of saving that take a more rough-cut approach, and essentially ignore some of these intricacies, conclude that changes in age structure have had little effect on the overall saving rate (including net investment in housing). Aggregate saving flows point to the same conclusion. They do not show the shifts between types of saving—particularly, a shift from saving in the form of financial assets to saving in the form of investment in housing—that would be expected when the number of young households increases.

Because of the difficulties of addressing the larger issues of total consumption and saving, and the mixed results produced by other studies, most of this chapter has been devoted to an investigation of the effect of age structure—and in particular the baby boom generation—on housing and durable goods. These are the areas in which a large increase in young households should have its greatest effect. If an effect is not clearly apparent here, it is unlikely that one can be discerned in other areas.

The analysis indicates that the effect of age structure on the consumption of durable goods is very small. Manufacturers, looking at the dollar amounts spent by certain age groups, anticipate that the 1980s will be a particularly good time for makers of furniture and home appliances.[47] But dollar averages exaggerate the apparent potential of age structure. Although people in their thirties and forties spend more on furniture and appliances than younger people, their incomes are so much greater that

47. "Why Furniture Makers Feel So Comfortable," *Business Week*, July 30, 1979, pp. 75–76; "Changing Population Patterns: What They Mean for the Investor," Standard and Poor's *Outlook*, March 26, 1979, p. 851.

the expenditures represent a smaller percentage of income. Thus the percentage of each dollar of income spent on furniture and appliances changes very little as the age distribution of households—hence of household income—changes. It appears that age structure can be expected to raise the percentage spent on furniture and appliances by less than one-tenth of a point between 1970 and 1990 (table 5-11), and even this effect disappears when changes in income per household are taken into account. Much the same is true for expenditures on automobiles, for which the effect of age structure has already peaked.

The analysis of housing separated housing starts (plus mobile homes) into those that replaced existing housing or accommodated migration and those that were demographically induced. Demographically induced starts were further distinguished by whether they were attributable to changes in population or in household incidence rates.[48] The results show that during the 1970s the baby boom generation proper (the cohorts born between 1946 and 1964) accounted for 40 to 45 percent of all demographically induced starts, or about 30 percent of total starts plus mobile homes. The rest were accounted for by young people born before the baby boom, during the war years, and by the rapidly growing number of older households.

Housing starts should remain high during the 1980s, and with smaller cohorts entering the market behind it as well as aging in front, the baby boom generation will probably be a much larger source of demographically induced demand than during the 1970s. Its share of this demand should rise to about two-thirds of the total. During the 1990s the age structure of the population will contribute to a lower level of housing starts as the small cohorts born during the late 1960s and the 1970s grow up.

The baby boom generation moved into the housing market during a decade when house prices were rising faster than other prices and mortgage interest rates were much higher than during the 1950s or 1960s. Concern was frequently expressed that many households, young ones in particular, were being priced out of the housing market and would never be able to realize the American dream of owning their own homes. But the facts show that homeownership increased rapidly among married couples, the traditional home buyers, during the 1970s and that the increases in rates of homeownership were particularly rapid for young

48. Demographically induced housing starts are labeled "actual additions" to the occupied housing stock in tables 5-4 and 5-5.

couples. The rise in homeownership among all households was less rapid, because of the shift toward types of households—especially one-person households—that have traditionally been less likely to buy a home.

The increase in homeownership occurred in part because incomes rose as fast as house prices, and in part because potential buyers recognized that the combination of fixed monthly payments in a period of rapid inflation, favorable tax treatment of homeowners, and the investment value of housing—precisely because its price was rising faster than other prices—meant that the true cost of owning a house was much less than it appeared at first glance. The obstacle that remained to trouble some new buyers—the heavy drain on income during the first few years—was relieved in a few cases by graduated-payment mortgage loans.[49] If these become available more widely, the particular handicap of new buyers will be largely removed. There were, however, signs in the late 1970s that the situation might be changing, that the true cost of owning a house was rising, as interest rates rose sharply higher and incomes began to lag behind house prices.

The overall impression left by the studies reviewed or undertaken in this chapter is that age structure in general, and the baby boom generation in particular, has had little effect on several broad categories of expenditure—total consumption, total saving, the percentage of consumer income spent on durables. Other conditions have changed so much that age structure has been only one factor among many, and not the most important.

The exception is housing. Here both age structure in general and the baby boom generation in particular have been important. This generation was not, however, the main force driving the housing market of the 1970s, as is often supposed. It has shared the stage with other age groups, rising rates of household incidence, and declining costs of homeownership.

Whether or not age structure affects the size of a broad category of expenditure, it may change the pattern of expenditure within the category. The analysis of housing, for example, indicated a decided shift toward owned housing in the residential construction market of the 1980s, and away from rental housing, as the baby boom generation becomes middle-aged and smaller cohorts move into the extremes of the

49. "Qualifying for a Better House," *Business Week*, January 29, 1979, p. 113.

age distribution. Shifts like this within major sectors such as housing and consumer durables may be more important in terms of the potential gains and losses, and the adjustments required of industry, than shifts between these sectors and other sectors. But here again, interest rates, energy prices, and other economic factors are likely to be at least as important as age structure in changing the character of demand.

chapter six Old Age

        People 65 and over made up 11 percent of the population in 1980. In 2030, when the last members of the baby boom turn 65, their share is projected to be about 18 percent. If the projections are right, almost one out of every five people will be in this age group.

        Both percentages reflect a trend that began more than a century ago. Throughout the Western world, as standards of living rose, sanitation improved, and medical care became more effective, increasing numbers of people survived to old age. In 1870 old people constituted only 3 percent of the population of the United States. That share rose steadily from decade to decade, to 4 percent in 1900, 8 percent in 1950, and the 11 percent just mentioned in 1980 (table 6-1). Impressive gains in life expectancy underlay the trend—a child born in 1900 could expect to live 47 years, while one born in 1977 could expect to live 73 years.[1]

        The projection of the trend is based on the assumption that death rates will continue to decline. Improvements in life expectancy have been unexpectedly rapid since 1970, especially for the very young and the middle-aged, and further improvements are clearly possible, since life expectancies are greater in several other countries than in the United States.[2] The Census Bureau has taken a conservative position in making its population estimates, and projects that death rates will decline steadily through 2050, but more slowly than in the recent past. If instead the rates decline more rapidly, the population of old people will be larger than predicted—considerably larger by a year as distant as 2030. If they decline more slowly, it will be smaller than predicted.

    1. Department of Health, Education, and Welfare, Public Health Service, National Center for Health Statistics, *Health, United States, 1979*, HEW publication (PHS) 80-1232 (HEW, 1980), p. 138.

    2. Bureau of the Census, *Current Population Reports,* series P-25, no. 704, "Projections of the Population of the United States: 1977 to 2050" (Government Printing Office, 1977), p. 15; and NCHS, *Health, United States, 1979*, pp. 134, 143.

Table 6-1. Older People in the Population of the United States, Selected Years, 1950–80, and Projections to 2050

Population in thousands

Year	Total population	Population 65 and over	Percent of total population		
			65 and over	75 and over	Under 15
1950	152,271	12,397	8.1	2.6	26.9
1960	180,671	16,675	9.2	3.1	31.0
1970	204,878	20,087	9.8	3.7	28.3
1980	226,505	25,544	11.3	4.4	22.6
1990	243,513	29,824	12.3	4.9	22.7
2000	260,378	31,822	12.2	5.5	21.9
2010	275,335	34,837	12.7	5.5	20.4
2020	290,115	45,102	15.6	5.9	20.7
2030	300,349	55,024	18.3	7.7	20.0
2040	308,400	54,925	17.8	9.0	20.0
2050	315,622	55,494	17.6	8.5	20.2

Sources: Bureau of the Census, *Current Population Reports*, series P-25: no. 311, "Estimates of the Population of the United States, by Single Years of Age, Color, and Sex, 1900 to 1950" (Government Printing Office, 1965); no. 519, "Estimates of the Population of the United States, by Age, Sex, and Race: April 1, 1960, to July 1, 1973" (GPO, 1974); no. 721, "Estimates of the Population by Age, Sex, and Race: 1970 to 1977" (GPO, 1978); no. 704, "Projections of the Population of the United States, 1977 to 2050" (GPO, 1977) (series II projections, which assume 2.1 births per woman); and Bureau of the Census, *Census of Population, 1980*. Supplementary Report PC 80-S1-1, "Age, Sex, Race, and Spanish Origin of the Population by Regions, Divisions, and States: 1980" (GPO, 1981)

Assumptions about future birth rates do not affect the estimated number of old people until 65 years after the projections begin, but because they change the estimates of total population they change the proportion old people represent of that total. High fertility means that the aged will be a smaller proportion, low fertility that they will be a larger proportion. The Census Bureau publishes projections based on three alternative assumptions about birth rates, which, it hopes, cover the range of likely possibilities. The projections given in table 6-1 are based on rates that imply 2.1 children per woman over a lifetime and are somewhat higher than the rates of the 1970s; under this assumption people 65 and over are 18 percent of the population in 2030. Under the alternative assumptions—1.7 and 2.7 children per woman—they are 22 and 14 percent of the total, respectively, in 2030.[3]

The baby boom generation and the small cohorts that precede and follow it imprint their characteristic pattern on all three sets of projections. For example, in the projections in table 6-1, the population share

3. Bureau of the Census, "Projections of the Population of the United States: 1977 to 2050," p. 14.

of the elderly remains the same between 1990 and 2000 as the people born during the 1920s and 1930s retire, and rises only slightly in the next decade. Then the baby boom generation begins to pass the 65-year mark, and the proportion of old people rises sharply to a peak in 2030. The smaller cohorts born in the later 1960s and the 1970s bring it down again after 2030.

The problems and opportunities this large population of old people will bring with them depends not only on their numbers but also on their personal characteristics. Here, as elsewhere, our ideas about the future are limited by our past experience. The only practicable approach is to assume that the old people of the next century will be similar to those of today in many ways, and that any differences will reflect the continuation of recent trends. But because the projections extend over such a long period of time, it is more important than usual to keep in mind that the past is not always a good guide to the future. The population 65 and over has changed rapidly over the last fifty years. The changes over the next fifty may be equally great, and they will not necessarily be further changes in the same direction.

If the mortality rates projected by the Census Bureau turn out to be correct, the population of old people will include a rising proportion of the very old. Those 75 and over will constitute more than 40 percent of that population in the next century—with some fluctuations because of the varying cohorts moving through these ages—as against just under 30 percent between 1900 and 1940, and 38 percent in 1980. Those 85 and over will account for more than 10 percent of the elderly; indeed, as the baby boom generation reaches very old age, their share will rise to 17 percent. The assumed trends in mortality also mean that old people will continue to be predominantly women, though the proportion of women is projected to hold steady at the level of 1980, about 60 percent. This is a recent development—until 1940 men were in the majority.

Clearly, the baby boom generation grown old will be better educated than earlier generations because it is better educated now (chapter 3). And barring a medical miracle, it also seems likely that old people will continue to suffer from poorer health than young people.

The future course of labor force participation by the elderly looks much less certain. The participation rates of men 65 and over have dropped sharply, from about 45 percent in the late 1940s and early 1950s to only 20 percent in the late 1970s. In the same age group, women's participation rates have remained at about 8 to 10 percent over the period. The scope for further decline is clearly limited, and there are even signs that labor force participation by the aged may increase in the future: the growing concern over the difficulties some people have adjusting to retirement, for example, a concern given concrete expression when Congress prohibited mandatory retirement before age 70; lengthening life expectancies; and the financial problems of public and private pension programs.

Similarly, so many old people now maintain separate households, rather than move in with children or other relatives, that this trend cannot continue much further (see chapter 5). Since the decision to live separately is sensitive to income, future trends in retirement income, as well as in the economy generally, will be important in determining whether the trend toward separate households for the aged continues, stops where it is, or reverses itself.

At this distance, it seems likely that the major concern about the aged population will be the same in fifty years as it is now—how to support them. Public and private programs to provide support for the elderly have grown enormously over the last few decades. Medicare and the social security retirement system are the largest and most obvious examples, but private pensions, and programs such as supplemental security income and medicaid, are also important sources of support. The costs of these programs have risen rapidly. With the prospect of still higher costs as the population of old people continues to grow, a wide-ranging debate has arisen over the future of these programs, and whether and how they should be changed.

But individual programs are only means for effecting a transfer of income that, without them, would be made through other programs or between individuals. It is important to state the larger issue before considering its components: what proportion of the gross national product is to be used to support the retired population? Whatever the mechanism for making the transfer, its size will depend on the size of the GNP and the nature of the competing claims on it, including those of the dependent young as well as of the dependent old (table 6-1). The decisions made will affect much more than the operation of current programs.

The rest of the chapter focuses on the implications of an aging baby boom generation for medical care and for programs of retirement income. The emphasis in the latter section is primarily on the social security program.

Medical Care

In 1978 expenditures on medical care for people 65 and over averaged $2,026 per person, compared with $764 per person for those between the ages of 19 and 64 and $286 for those under 19 (table 6-2). Although statistics are available only since the early 1960s, old people appear to have had higher expenditures than younger people for some years before that. The general pattern was well established by 1961, the first year for which data were published, and the first detailed data, for 1967, show the same relationships, overall and by type of care, as the data for 1978. More important for the purposes of this chapter, the pattern is likely to continue for many years because of the stability of the underlying health patterns and institutional arrangements.

Institutional care is far and away the major expense for the aged and is the main reason for their higher average expenditures. In 1978, $1,387 of the $2,026, or 68 percent, was spent on hospital and nursing home care, and some of the rest went to pay doctors for services rendered in these institutions. In comparison, about half the amount spent on the middle age group and less than 40 percent of the amount spent on young people went for institutional care. The differences were particularly marked for nursing home care—the average expense for the two younger groups was negligible, while the average for the older group was $518 per person.

Medicare and Medicaid

Congress created the medicare program in 1965 to help the aged pay these high medical expenses. Federally financed and federally run, the program has two parts: hospital insurance, supported by a payroll tax on workers; and supplementary medical insurance, financed by a combination of general tax revenues and the premiums paid by enrollees. Both parts are subject to various deductible and copayment provisions. At first everyone 65 and over was automatically entitled to hospital insurance, but entitlement has gradually been linked to coverage under the social security retirement program. Enrollment in the supplementary medical insurance part of the program has always been voluntary. In the late 1970s about 95 percent of the elderly were entitled to hospital

Table 6-2. Average per Person Expenditure on Medical Care, by Age, 1961, 1967, and 1978[a]

Dollars

Type of expenditure and age group	1961	1967	1978
Total			
1–18	} 128	92	286
19–64		228	764
65 and over	315	535	2,026
Hospital			
1–18	} 27	22	102
19–64		104	370
65 and over	76	224	869
Nursing home			
1–18	} *	*	1
19–64		1	24
65 and over	15	85	518

Sources: Dorothy P. Rice, "Estimated Expenditures for Medical Care of Aged Persons, 1961," *Social Security Bulletin*, vol. 26 (July 1963), pp. 23–24; Barbara S. Cooper, Nancy L. Worthington, and Mary F. McGee, *Compendium of National Health Expenditures Data*, Social Security Administration Publication (SSA) 76-11927 (Department of Health, Education, and Welfare, 1976), p. 100; and Charles R. Fisher, "Differences by Age Groups in Health Care Spending," *Health Care Financing Review*, vol. 1 (Spring 1980), p. 81.

* Less than $0.50.

a. The data for 1961 and 1978 are for calendar years; data for 1967 are for the fiscal year ending June 30.

benefits, and nearly as many had chosen to buy supplementary medical insurance.[4]

The importance of institutional care to the elderly is reflected in the expenditures as well as in the design of the medicare program. Almost three-quarters of the program's outlays go for hospital care.[5] The original plan was to pay for nursing home care whenever it could serve as a substitute for hospital care, but even this limited coverage was cut back as the costs of the program mounted. Currently medicare spends very little on nursing homes.

Partly as a result, the medicaid program picks up much of the cost of nursing home care for the aged. Also legislated in 1965, medicaid offers federal matching grants to the states to encourage them to expand the medical benefits available to people on welfare and, at the discretion of

4. These percentages were derived from data supplied by the Health Care Financing Administration. The percentage for hospital insurance is also given in the *1981 Annual Report of the Board of Trustees of the Federal Hospital Insurance Trust Fund*, p. 2.

5. Robert M. Gibson and Daniel R. Waldo, "National Health Expenditures, 1980," *Health Care Financing Review*, vol. 3 (September 1981), pp. 42–53.

the states, to people not on welfare who are nonetheless too poor to pay their medical bills. Medicaid has become the largest source of public funds for nursing home care. In 1978 it paid about 40 percent of the nursing home expenses of the elderly,[6] and nursing home payments accounted for 40 percent of the program's outlays in 1980—even more than hospitals.[7] Medicaid also pays some of the other medical expenses of the elderly poor—the deductibles and copayments charged by medicare, for example. Through these two programs combined, the federal and state governments accepted responsibility for about 60 percent of the medical expenses of the aged in the late 1970s.[8]

The costs of both programs have grown rapidly, as have total national expenditures on medical care. By 1980 medicare, which was expanded in 1973 to cover the disabled and those with chronic kidney disease, was spending $36 billion a year. Medicaid spent $14 billion in federal funds in 1980 and another $11 billion in state money. Total national expenditures rose from $42 billion in 1965, and 6 percent of GNP, to $247 billion and 9.4 percent of GNP in 1980. Expenditures on hospitals and nursing homes grew fastest.[9] The rapid growth of outlays and the prospect of further increases have created much concern, both about the future of these programs and about the medical care sector in general.

Changes in the age structure of the population were not an important factor in the growth of expenditures during the 1960s and 1970s. If they had been, total spending would have risen because of rapid growth in the high-cost age groups, while the averages within each group grew slowly, if at all. Instead, as table 6-2 shows, average expenditures have grown very rapidly in all three age groups and at similar rates—more than tripling between 1967 and 1978. Shifts in the age distribution have been modest by comparison—the proportion of people 65 and over grew from 9.5 percent to 11 percent over the same period.[10]

6. Charles R. Fisher, "Differences by Age Groups in Health Care Spending," *Health Care Financing Review,* vol. 1 (Spring 1980), p. 89.

7. Gibson and Waldo, "National Health Expenditures, 1980."

8. Fisher, "Differences by Age Groups in Health Care Spending," p. 89. As of 1978, the most recent year for which data are published, medicaid's percentage of the aged's expenses had declined for several years, but other sources, principally medicare, were stable or rising, so that the total supplied by government remained about 60 percent. With the recent attempts to cut federal expenditures, the government share may begin to decline.

9. Gibson and Waldo, "National Health Expenditures, 1980," pp. 18, 42.

10. Bureau of the Census, *Current Population Reports,* series P-25: no. 519, "Estimates of the Population of the United States, by Age, Sex, and Race: April 1, 1960 to July 1, 1973" (GPO, 1974); and no. 721, "Estimates of the Population of the United States by

Age structure will be a more important factor in the future—especially in the next century when the baby boom generation begins to retire. The size of the aged population is obviously important to medicare and medicaid, since they pay such a large part of its medical bills. In the present context—with both programs under pressure to restrain further growth in expenditures—it is useful to look ahead to some of the forces that will be working against them.

Institutional care is and will remain the primary concern. The effects of changes in the age distribution of the population can be estimated by applying current patterns of institutional use by age to projections of the population, also by age. Expenditures are not a good measure of current patterns for this purpose, because the age groups for which data are available are so broad. Important differences between people only a few years apart are submerged in the averages. Data on the use of hospital and nursing home care are available in much more detail and have been used here to project the effects of future changes in the population through 2050. For comparison, the same data were applied to the actual population back to 1950 to show the effect of population changes in the past.

When rates of use by age and sex are held constant, and only the population changes, the estimates of total use reflect changes in three things—the size of the total population, its distribution by age, and its distribution by sex. Estimates of use per capita, or per 1,000 persons, isolate the effects of changes in the age and sex distribution of the population from changes in its size. These estimates will be discussed as though they reflected age structure alone, since the changes in the distribution of the population by sex are minor by comparison. Neither the total nor the per capita figures are predictions of actual future use. Rather, they show what would happen to institutional care if all that changed were the size and the age structure of the population served.

Hospitals

Except in the first year after birth, the use of hospitals is lowest for young people and rises with age. Of the two measures shown in table

---

Age, Sex, and Race: 1970 to 1977'' (GPO, 1978). For a study of the factors that have been important for hospital costs, see Louise B. Russell, *Technology in Hospitals: Medical Advances and Their Diffusion* (Brookings Institution, 1979).

Table 6-3. Days of Hospital Care and Number of Discharges per 1,000 Population, by Age and Sex, 1966 and 1976[a]

	Days		Discharges	
Age and sex	1966	1976	1966	1976
Female				
Under 1	866	1,092	117	176
1–4	323	304	72	79
5–14	221	217	54	50
15–24	1,121	862	238	200
25–34	1,527	1,217	275	242
35–44	1,396	1,194	192	182
45–54	1,639	1,527	174	192
55–64	1,864	2,012	169	210
65–74	2,835	3,025	224	274
75 and over	5,110	5,522	336	456
Male				
Under 1	1,151	1,384	168	233
1–4	421	399	93	102
5–14	302	243	64	59
15–24	525	469	85	80
25–34	674	598	96	92
35–44	923	889	113	122
45–54	1,333	1,339	142	161
55–64	2,153	2,088	194	225
65–74	3,120	3,604	251	332
75 and over	4,852	6,015	364	503

Sources: Department of Health, Education, and Welfare, National Center for Health Statistics, "Utilization of Short-Stay Hospitals, Summary of Non-medical Statistics, United States, 1966," Vital and Health Statistics, series 13, no. 8 (NCHS, 1971), pp. 10, 16; and "Utilization of Short-Stay Hospitals, Annual Summary for the United States, 1976," Vital and Health Statistics, series 13, no. 37 (NCHS, 1978), pp. 22, 24. Data for infants under one year in 1966 are from *Statistical Abstract of the United States, 1969* (GPO, 1969), p. 70.

a. Based on the civilian, noninstitutionalized population. Newborns are excluded.

6-3, days per 1,000 is the more important, because the number of hospital beds required by a given population depends on the days of hospital care it uses.[11] Numbers of discharges complement the statistics for days by showing the number of separate hospital stays they represent.[12] But by either measure, the low point for the entire age range occurs between the ages of 5 and 14. The rates for young adult women are sharply higher

11. The total requirement for beds can be calculated by dividing days by the desired occupancy rate, expressed as a proportion, times 365. Beds per 1,000 population, which gives a better idea of the economic burden of providing the beds, can be computed by dividing days per 1,000 population by the specified occupancy rate times 365.

12. Neither measure reflects a third dimension of use—the number of services received per day in the hospital, such as X-rays, laboratory tests, hours of nursing care, and so on.

because these are the childbearing years and almost all births take place in hospitals.[13] The rates for men rise more slowly, but steadily.

The potential impact of an aging population is clear from the rates of use for older adults. Hospital use by both sexes is higher at ages 55 through 64 than for any previous age group and rises sharply thereafter. Further, days and discharges rose for older people between 1966 and 1976. By contrast, days of care held steady or declined for people under 55, again with the exception of infants less than one year of age. (For women in the childbearing years the changes reflect the fall in the birth rate.) For the most part the declines were caused by shorter stays—rates of discharge in the two years were quite close for many groups and higher in 1976 for some. As a result of these divergent trends, older people have become an even larger component of hospital use.

Table 6-4 projects hospital use forward and backward on the assumption that rates of use by age and sex are the same in every year as they were in 1976. The estimates show that total days of care, which reflect all three characteristics of the population (size, age, and sex), grew faster between 1950 and 1975, and are projected to grow faster to 1990, than at any later time, despite the aging baby boom generation. The size of the population is the primary cause. Changes in age structure have played a minor part. Indeed, days per 1,000 persons were only slightly higher in 1965 than in 1950. Since 1965 age structure has contributed modestly, but persistently, to the increase in hospital use. The sudden surge in days per 1,000 between 1975 and 1980, and again between 1980 and 1985, represents the confluence of several special factors—the aging of the baby boom generation into the young adult groups, with their rising rates of use, the assumption that mortality rates will continue to improve, and especially the Census Bureau's assumption that birth rates will rise from the low levels of the 1970s and thus that the use of hospitals by young women will rise.

Age structure is much more important after the turn of the century. Days per 1,000 grow 2 to 3 percent every five years from 2000 to 2030 as the baby boom generation reaches 65 and subsequently ages into even higher rates of hospital use. At the same time, with birth rates level at

13. For the projections the rates of hospital use by women 15 through 24 and 25 through 34 were adjusted to be consistent with the actual or projected birth rates underlying the population data in each year. The adjustments were based on regressions relating hospital use to birth rates over the period 1966–76. These regressions are reported in Louise B. Russell, "An Aging Population and the Use of Medical Care," *Medical Care*, vol. 19 (June 1981), p. 643 (Brookings Reprint 370).

Table 6-4. Estimates of Hospital Use, Selected Years, 1950–2050[a]

	Days				Discharges	
Year	Total (thousands)	Percent change	Per 1,000 population	Percent change	Total (thousands)	Per 1,000 population
1950	183,973	. . .	1,208	. . .	24,867	163
1955	203,614	10.7	1,227	1.6	27,152	164
1960	221,853	9.0	1,228	0.1	29,378	163
1965	235,481	6.1	1,212	−1.3	31,144	160
1970	251,421	6.8	1,227	1.3	33,139	162
1975	265,006	5.4	1,241	1.1	34,825	163
1980	285,832	7.9	1,287	3.7	37,303	168
1985	307,437	7.6	1,320	2.6	39,783	171
1990	326,157	6.1	1,339	1.5	41,762	171
1995	342,124	4.9	1,354	1.1	43,340	171
2000	358,287	4.7	1,376	1.7	44,986	173
2005	375,943	4.9	1,405	2.1	46,870	175
2010	394,796	5.0	1,434	2.1	48,863	177
2015	414,831	5.1	1,465	2.2	50,825	179
2020	436,545	5.2	1,505	2.7	52,752	182
2025	460,864	5.6	1,553	3.2	54,897	185
2030	478,347	3.8	1,593	2.5	56,443	188
2035	491,827	2.8	1,615	1.4	57,776	190
2040	499,808	1.6	1,621	0.3	58,652	190
2045	501,891	0.4	1,608	−0.8	59,032	189
2050	505,452	0.7	1,601	−0.4	59,520	189

Sources: Author's calculations, based on data from sources listed in tables 6-1 and 6-3.

a. Based on the rates of use for 1976 shown in table 6-3 and on population by age and sex for the years 1950–2050. The population data are actual numbers for 1950–75 and projected numbers for 1980–2050. Hospital use rates for women 15–24 and 25–34 were adjusted in each year to be consistent with the actual or assumed birth rates underlying the population data. See text note 13.

the 2.1 lifetime births per woman assumed by the Census Bureau, the growth in the total population slows down and so does the growth in total days.

An increase of 2 to 3 percent in days per 1,000 every five years is a moderate rate of growth, and one that can be accommodated with no great difficulty. But the cumulative impact of continuous growth, even when moderate, is substantial. At their peak in 2040, days per 1,000 are 18 percent higher than in the year 2000, and 31 percent higher than in 1975, the last year for which the estimates are based on actual, rather than projected, population figures.

Even with the current age structure, medicare has experienced increases in costs well above those expected when it was created by

Congress, and, as mentioned before, the program is under growing pressure to restrain further cost increases. Scheduled taxes are believed to be sufficient for the 1980s, but in their 1981 annual report the trustees of the hospital insurance trust fund concluded that the fund will be exhausted well before the end of the twenty-five-year projection period in 2005. Projections are made for three sets of assumptions, of which the intermediate set is considered to be the best guess about future conditions. Under the intermediate assumptions the trustees expect expenditures by the hospital insurance program to be between 5 and 5.5 percent of taxable payroll by the year 2000, while scheduled taxes will be less than 3 percent. Under the more optimistic assumptions expenditures would be about 4 percent of taxable payroll; under the more pessimistic assumptions they would be almost 8 percent.[14]

These projections involve assumptions about how rapidly the costs of a hospital stay will rise in the future, a factor that has been far more important in the past than demographic shifts. Recognizing the difficulties of projecting cost trends even twenty-five years ahead, the trustees do not carry the projections beyond that point and thus are unable to outline the effects of the baby boom on the program. Some of these effects can be indicated, however, by pursuing a point made in an appendix to the report.[15] It is observed there that the hospital costs of the program can be projected in two stages—by first estimating the growth in total hospital costs, and then estimating the share of the total accounted for by the program's beneficiaries, principally the aged. This share can be estimated independently of total hospital costs because it depends primarily on population trends.

In the mid-1970s expenditures on behalf of the aged were 27 or 28 percent of total hospital costs. Medicare paid the bulk of these hospital expenses for the aged—about three-quarters—and the rest was paid by individuals, private insurance, medicaid, the Veterans Administration, and other sources.[16] The estimates in table 6-5 show that as of 1975 the elderly accounted for a somewhat smaller share of hospital discharges than of costs (24 percent) and a larger share of days (36 percent).

As old people's share of discharges and days changes in the future,

14. *1981 Annual Report of the Board of Trustees of the Federal Hospital Insurance Trust Fund*, pp. 35, 40, 59.

15. Ibid., p. 44.

16. Marjorie Smith Mueller and Robert M. Gibson, "Age Differences in Health Care Spending, Fiscal Year 1975," *Social Security Bulletin*, vol. 39 (June 1976), p. 2; and Fisher, "Differences by Age Groups in Health Care Spending."

Table 6-5 Percentage of Estimated Hospital Care Used by Population 65 and Over, Selected Years, 1950–2050

Year	Discharges	Days
1950	17.8	24.5
1955	19.2	29.2
1960	20.4	30.9
1965	21.5	32.5
1970	22.2	33.6
1975	23.5	35.5
1980	24.4	36.6
1985	25.2	37.6
1990	26.4	38.9
1995	27.0	39.4
2000	26.7	38.8
2005	26.3	38.0
2010	26.7	38.2
2015	28.5	40.2
2020	30.2	43.3
2025	34.1	46.7
2030	36.3	49.5
2035	36.8	50.1
2040	36.3	49.5
2045	35.5	48.6
2050	35.7	48.7

Sources: Same as table 6-4.

their share of costs will change. The estimates in table 6-5 show their share of discharges reaching a peak of 37 percent of total discharges in 2035, more than half again as large as in 1975. Days spent in the hospital by the aged are fully half the total by 2035. Thus if the Census Bureau's population projections turn out to be correct, and if hospital use by older people follows the same patterns relative to younger people as it did in 1976,[17] by 2035 something over 40 percent of all hospital expenditures will be incurred by the aged. If the medicare program maintains its current rate of coverage, it will be paying over 30 percent of the nation's total hospital bill, compared with about 20 percent today.

Nursing Homes

Nursing homes are used primarily by old people. Nursing home residents per 1,000 population, which represent the proportion of each

17. The absolute levels of use may change, but as long as the ratios between age groups remain the same, the aged's share of admissions and days will be as stated.

age-sex group that is in a nursing home on an average day, rise sharply with age within the population 65 and over and are negligible for younger people (table 6-6).[18] The size of the population 85 and older is particularly crucial: in 1973–74, 290 of every 1,000 women this age were in nursing homes on an average day, as were 179 of every 1,000 men. Altogether, 9 out of 10 nursing home residents were 65 or older in 1973–74, and 7 out of 10 were women.[19]

Table 6-7 shows the results of applying the 1973–74 residence rates to the population through 2050. The estimated number of residents grows rapidly throughout the period. The number in 2050—4,029,000 residents on an average day—is double the number for the year 2000 and more than three times the number in 1975. The trend in residents per 1,000 population shows that age structure is, as expected, a strong force behind the growth of nursing homes. But in contrast to hospital care, the effects of age structure are greater in this century than after 2000. On average, residents per 1,000 grow faster between 1950 and 2000 than between 2000 and 2050. The fastest growth occurred between 1950 and 1955 and between 1965 and 1975, in large part because of the improvements in the life expectancy of the old that occurred during those years.[20]

If one accepts the assumptions about mortality used by the Census Bureau in its population projections—that death rates will continue to decline, but more slowly than in the past—the most rapid growth in residents per 1,000 is over. Future growth, while sizable and continuous, will occur at a somewhat slower pace. Even the large increases that accompany the aging of the baby boom generation between 2025 and 2035 do not quite match those of 1965–75.

The cumulative impact of so many years of steady growth is impressive. Residents per 1,000 population, which reflect the changes in the age distribution of the population, are projected to be 12.8 in 2050, almost 2.5 times the level of 1975 and 1.7 times the level of 2000. Since resident counts represent the census of patients on a given day, they can be

18. The proportion who spend some time in a home during the course of a year is higher.

19. NCHS, *Utilization of Nursing Homes, United States: National Nursing Home Survey, August 1973–April 1974,* Vital and Health Statistics, series 13, no. 28 (NCHS, 1977), p. 5.

20. The greatest improvements occurred between 1965 and 1975, when life expectancy at age 65 rose from 12.9 to 13.7 years for men, and from 16.3 to 18.1 years for women. Bureau of the Census, *Statistical Abstract of the United States, 1979* (GPO, 1979), p. 70, and previous editions.

Table 6-6. Nursing Home Residents per 1,000 Population, by Age and Sex, 1963 and 1973–74[a]

Age and sex	1963	1973–74
Female		
Under 45	⎫	⎧ 0.2
45–54	⎬ 0.3	0.7 ⎨ 1.3
55–64	⎭	⎩ 3.5
65–74	7.8	13.1
75–84	43.8	71.0
85 and over	158.7	289.5
Male		
Under 45	⎫	⎧ 0.2
45–54	⎬ 0.3	0.6 ⎨ 1.1
55–64	⎭	⎩ 3.0
65–74	5.9	11.3
75–84	26.7	40.8
85 and over	98.4	179.4

Sources: "Characteristics of Residents in Institutions for the Aged and Chronically Ill, United States: April–June 1963," Vital and Health Statistics, series 12, no. 2 (NCHS, 1965), p. 19; and "Utilization of Nursing Homes, United States: National Nursing Home Survey, August 1973–April 1974," Vital and Health Statistics, series 13, no. 28 (NCHS, 1977), p. 24. Rates based on resident population from the Bureau of the Census, *Current Population Reports,* series P-25: no. 721, "Estimates of the Population of the United States by Age, Sex, and Race: 1970 to 1977" (GPO, 1978); and no. 519, "Estimates of the Population of the United States, by Age, Sex, and Race: April 1, 1960 to July 1, 1973" (GPO, 1974).

a. Nursing homes plus personal care homes with nursing.

translated directly into the numbers of beds required to maintain future populations at the residence rates of 1973–74: residents per 1,000 divided by the occupancy rate (expressed as a proportion) yields beds per 1,000.[21] The number of beds will be greater than the number of residents, because occupancy is less than 100 percent, but the rates of growth in the two series will be exactly the same and can be read from table 6-7. Thus the level of nursing home beds per 1,000 in 2050 will also, if residence rates remain constant, be 2.5 times the level of 1975.

The recent history of residence rates gives no reason to expect them to remain constant. Between 1963 and 1973–74 residents per 1,000 rose by at least 50 percent in every age group (table 6-6). If they continue to rise, actual use of nursing homes will be higher than the estimates in table 6-7. But whatever the residence rates of the future may be, the changing age structure of the population will be an important force for greater use of nursing homes—so important that a large *reduction* in residence rates would be required to offset it.

21. The occupancy rate—the average proportion of beds with patients in them—was 87 percent in 1972. Total beds can be derived by dividing total residents by the occupancy rate, expressed as a proportion. NCHS, *Utilization of Nursing Homes, United States: 1973–74,* p. 5.

Table 6-7. Estimates of Nursing Home Residents, Selected Years, 1950–2050

Year	Total residents (thousands)	Percent change	Residents per 1,000 population	Percent change
1950	519	. . .	3.4	. . .
1955	624	20.4	3.8	10.5
1960	734	17.5	4.1	7.9
1965	839	14.3	4.3	6.3
1970	989	17.9	4.8	11.8
1975	1,160	17.3	5.4	12.6
1980	1,323	14.1	6.0	9.6
1985	1,480	11.8	6.4	6.7
1990	1,632	10.3	6.7	5.5
1995	1,807	10.7	7.2	6.7
2000	1,965	8.7	7.5	5.5
2005	2,103	7.0	7.9	4.1
2010	2,234	6.2	8.1	3.2
2015	2,354	5.4	8.3	2.5
2020	2,498	6.1	8.6	3.6
2025	2,744	9.8	9.2	7.4
2030	3,075	12.1	10.2	10.7
2035	3,459	12.5	11.4	11.0
2040	3,764	8.8	12.2	7.4
2045	3,955	5.1	12.7	3.9
2050	4,029	1.9	12.8	0.7

Source: Author's calculations, based on nursing home residents per 1,000 population for 1973–74, from table 6-6.

Although it might well be difficult to reduce residence rates, the possibility serves as a reminder that the trends shown in tables 6-4 and 6-7 are not inevitable, even if the population projections prove to be entirely correct. Age structure may be offset (or reinforced) by other factors acting on future rates of use—changes in the practice of medicine, in financing arrangements, and in the availability of institutional facilities and alternatives to them. Some of these changes may come about because of policies undertaken in recognition of the aging of the population.

Retirement Income

The sources of income available to people in old age have changed dramatically during this century, and are still changing. The landmark in this process was the creation of the social security program in 1935.

As more and more of the aged have qualified for benefits with the passage of time, and as benefits have been increased, social security has become the major source of retirement income. By the late 1970s more than 90 percent of people 65 and over received payments from the program.[22] Since World War II private pensions have also grown rapidly in importance. Public and private pension income, and the mandatory retirement that often goes with it, has encouraged older people to leave the labor force. As a result, the share of their income that comes from earnings has declined.

Table 6-8 shows the changes that occurred just between 1962 and 1976 in the shares of income from different sources. Social security rose from 30 percent of the aged's money income in 1962 to 39 percent in 1976. Private pensions more than doubled their share, but were still only 7 percent in 1976, while other public pensions held steady. Earnings dropped substantially, from 32 to 23 percent of income.[23]

The economic position of old people improved over this period as their incomes rose faster than inflation.[24] But the improvement has been even greater than the statistics suggest because of programs of in-kind transfers and special tax provisions for the aged that are not reflected in money income. The most important of the in-kind programs are medicare and medicaid, which pay for medical expenses that were formerly the responsibility of the aged themselves, and the food stamp program. People 65 and over also retain more spendable income from a given number of dollars because they are allowed double exemptions under the federal income tax, because social security benefits are not taxed, and because of other special tax provisions in various states. By one

22. This percentage was derived from the number of people 65 and older receiving social security benefits as of December each year (*Social Security Bulletin*, vol. 42 [December 1979], p. 35), and the population 65 and older for July of the same year (Bureau of the Census, *Current Population Reports*, series P-25, no. 721, "Estimates of the Population of the United States by Age, Sex, and Race: 1970 to 1977" [GPO, 1978], and earlier issues, nos. 519 and 311). For greater accuracy, the population numbers for two consecutive years were averaged to get an estimate of the December population.

23. The numbers refer to the money income received by all people 65 and older and their spouses. There are, of course, important differences in sources of income between elderly people of different ages and between those who are married and those who are not. See Susan Grad and Karen Foster, *Income of the Population 55 and Over, 1976*, Staff Paper 35, SSA publication 13-11865 (Social Security Administration, Office of Research and Statistics, 1979).

24. See Susan Grad, *Income of the Population Aged 60 and Older, 1971*, Staff Paper 26, HEW publication (SSA) 77-11851 (SSA, Office of Research and Statistics, 1977), table 2; and Grad and Foster, *Income of the Population 55 and Over, 1976*, table 3.

Table 6-8. Percent Distribution of Aggregate Income of Aged Units 65 and Over, by Source, 1962 and 1976[a]

Source of income	1962	1976
Retirement pensions	40	55
Social security	30	39
Other public	7	7
Private	3	7
Earnings	32	23
Income from assets	15	18
Public assistance	5	2
Other	8	2
Total	100	100

Sources: Data for 1962 are derived from Lenore A. Epstein and Janet H. Murray, *The Aged Population of the United States: The 1963 Social Security Survey of the Aged,* Social Security Administration, Office of Research and Statistics, Research Report 19 (SSA, 1967), p. 291; and for 1976, from Susan Grad and Karen Foster, *Income of the Population 55 and Over, 1976,* Staff Paper 35, SSA publication 13-11865 (SSA, Office of Research and Statistics, 1979), p. 46.

a. An aged unit is an unmarried person 65 or over, or a married couple with at least one member 65 or over.

estimate, poverty has been all but eliminated among the aged when in-kind programs and special tax provisions are taken into account. In 1976 only 6 percent of the aged were poor.[25] In 1964, before the passage of medicare and medicaid, the roughly comparable figure was 31 percent.[26]

Future Trends

The record of the recent past suggests that the baby boom generation can expect to do at least as well when it retires, and perhaps better. Most of its members will receive social security benefits. The annual reports of the trustees of the social security system project further gradual increases in the proportion of the aged receiving benefits.[27] And as women continue to participate in the work force in large numbers, more of them will be entitled to benefits in their own right rather than as the wives of retired workers.

25. Congressional Budget Office, *Poverty Status of Families under Alternative Definitions of Income,* Background Paper 17, rev. (GPO, 1977), pp. 11, 12. In-kind programs made a substantial difference in the percentage of aged who were poor, but the effect of special tax treatment was negligible.

26. Mollie Orshansky, "Recounting the Poor—A Five-Year Review," *Social Security Bulletin,* vol. 29 (April 1966), p. 32. Although this does not take account of in-kind programs, it is comparable to the estimate for 1976, because the two most important in-kind programs, medicare and medicaid, did not exist in 1964 and a third, food stamps, was much smaller than it later became.

27. *1979 Annual Report of the Board of Trustees of the Federal Old-Age and Survivors Insurance and Disability Insurance Trust Funds,* pp. 58–60; *1980 Annual Report,* pp. 95–99; and *1981 Annual Report,* pp. 75–78.

Further, if the current benefit formulas are maintained until the baby boom generation retires—and cost estimates for the system are predicated on the assumption that they will be—that generation can look forward to the same replacement rates as today and to benefits that are guaranteed to keep pace with inflation.[28] The current formulas, enacted in 1977, adjust the worker's earnings history for increases in the average wage since the earnings were recorded, and ensure that the initial benefit, calculated when the worker turns 62, will replace the same fraction of those adjusted wages as it does now. After age 62 the benefit is adjusted for inflation but not for further increases in real wages.

Private pensions, and similar pension systems in the public sector for the employees of federal, state, and local governments, are likely to continue to expand at least somewhat more. The proportion of private sector employees covered by a pension plan doubled between 1950 and 1975, from 23 percent to 46 percent,[29] and the growing importance of private pensions as a source of retirement income has already been described.[30]

Unfortunately, it is not possible to compare the pension coverage of the baby boom generation with that of earlier cohorts of young workers. Data for 1979 show that 48 percent of those 25 through 34 were covered by an employment-related pension plan, either private or public (see table 6-9), but there are no comparable data on coverage by age for earlier years. The requirements for pension coverage usually include a minimum age and length of service with the employer, so that coverage rises with age in a given year. In 1979, 62 percent of 45- through 54-year-old workers were covered. The long-term trends in coverage, together with the pattern by age in 1979, suggest that by the time the baby boom generation reaches middle age, the proportion will be somewhat higher than 62 percent.[31]

Being covered by a pension plan does not guarantee that the worker

28. Tax rates will have to rise substantially after 2010 to finance these benefits. See table 6-10 for the current cost projections, and the next subsection for a discussion of the long-term financing problems of the social security system.

29. Martha Remy Yohalem, "Employee-Benefit Plans, 1975," *Social Security Bulletin,* vol. 40 (November 1977), p. 22.

30. For a thorough discussion of the role of private pensions, see Alicia H. Munnell, *The Economics of Private Pensions* (Brookings Institution, 1982).

31. Currently, coverage is much higher for men than for women of the same age—in 1979, 72 percent of the men 45 through 54 were covered, compared with 48 percent of the women. President's Commission on Pension Policy, *Preliminary Findings of a Nationwide Survey on Retirement Income Issues* (The Commission, 1980), table 2.

Table 6-9. Pension Coverage by Age, 1979[a]

Age	Percent covered	Percent with vested rights
Under 25	28	14
25–34	48	21
35–44	55	28
45–54	62	35
55–64	57	41
65 and over	28	21
All ages	48	26

Source: President's Commission on Pension Policy, *Preliminary Findings of a Nationwide Survey on Retirement Income Issues* (The Commission, 1980), tables 1 and 3b.

a. Includes both full-time and part-time employees, and pension plans of federal, state, and local governments, as well as of private employers. Excludes the self-employed.

will receive benefits when he or she retires. That depends on whether the right to benefits is vested, namely, whether—having met certain requirements—the employee has gained a right to receive a pension at retirement even if he or she is no longer with the employer at that time. Like coverage, vesting increases with age, and for the same reasons. In 1979, 41 percent of all employees aged 55 through 64—70 percent of those covered by a plan—had vested pension rights (table 6-9). Data for workers in the private sector in 1972 and 1979 suggest that the vesting requirements of the Employee Retirement Income Security Act of 1974 have had an important effect: while pension coverage changed very little, the percentage of workers with vested rights was substantially higher in 1979.[32]

It is difficult to say anything about future trends in income from assets or earnings. Saving for retirement has been encouraged by recent provisions permitting some of it to be sheltered from taxation. But many economists argue that both the expectation of future social security benefits and the taxes levied on workers to support current benefits discourage private saving. There is a lively controversy in the profession about the validity of this argument and about the likely size of the effect on saving if it is true.[33]

32. Ibid., p. 3 and table 3c. For more detail, see Gayle Thompson Rogers, "Pension Coverage and Vesting among Private Wage and Salary Workers, 1979: Preliminary Estimates from the 1979 Survey of Pension Plan Coverage," Working Paper 16 (SSA, Office of Research and Statistics, 1980).

33. Alicia H. Munnell, *The Future of Social Security* (Brookings Institution, 1977), chap. 6; and Louis Esposito, "Effect of Social Security on Saving: Review of Studies Using U.S. Time-Series Data," *Social Security Bulletin*, vol. 41 (May 1978), pp. 9–17.

Although the labor force participation rates of the elderly (the percentage who are in the labor force during an average month) have reached very low levels—about 20 percent for men 65 and over in the late 1970s and 8 percent for women—the proportions who work at least part of the year, and who thus have some income from earnings, are higher. In the late 1970s, 26 to 28 percent of the men 65 and older, and 12 percent of the women, worked at some time during the year. Further, the proportions are much higher for those just past 65 than for older people. About 40 percent of men 65 through 69 worked during the year, as opposed to 18 to 20 percent of men 70 and over. The corresponding percentages for women were 21 and 7 percent.[34] There is thus some room left for further declines in income from earnings, particularly among people in their late sixties.

Recent discussion and legislative action, however, have focused on reversing the trend. In 1978 Congress raised the age at which people can be forced to retire, from 65 to 70. The Social Security Amendments of 1972 introduced a late retirement credit for the first time, which was subsequently revised in the 1977 amendments. In its present form the credit cannot be expected to have much effect on retirement decisions, because the increase in benefits for each year retirement is delayed is not large enough to compensate for the years of lost benefits, but it establishes a potentially important principle. The possibilities of raising the usual retirement age under social security from 65 to 68, of repealing the limit on earnings after retirement, or of introducing additional measures to encourage the aged to stay in the labor force, have been discussed. If policy continues to move in this direction, earnings might well become a larger source of income for the aged of the future rather than a smaller one.

Financing Social Security

Whatever the trends in other sources of retirement income, social security will remain an important source, and probably the dominant one. The system has been beset with a series of short-term financial problems and the promise of more serious problems to come when the baby boom generation retires after the year 2000.

34. Work experience data for people 65 and older are from the Bureau of Labor Statistics and Anne McDougall Young, "Work Experience of the Population in 1977," *Monthly Labor Review*, vol. 102 (March 1979), p. 54. Data for those 65 through 69, and 70 and older, are from the *Employment and Training Report of the President, 1979*, p. 314.

The short-term problems first developed in the mid-1970s because of the combined effects of higher than expected unemployment, lower than expected growth in productivity, and a benefit formula that overadjusted for inflation—and whose faults were particularly pronounced in periods of high inflation. Congress corrected the last problem in 1977 with a new formula for the computation of benefits and scheduled new, higher tax rates that were projected to keep the program operating smoothly through the end of the century.[35]

But problems developed again almost immediately as the economy continued to perform poorly and revenues to the program fell short of projections. In their 1981 report the trustees of the old age and survivors insurance trust fund (the trust fund for the retirement program) projected that the fund would be exhausted by late 1982 under even the most optimistic assumptions, and that expenditures would exceed revenues at least through 1985.[36] Late in 1981 Congress passed legislation permitting the retirement program to borrow from the disability and hospital insurance trust funds, both of which are expected to be in better shape during the 1980s, and to repay the loans in later years. The legislation, which authorizes borrowing only until December 1982, is likely to be extended. But if the economy continues to perform poorly, extension will delay the day of reckoning by only a few years, and leave all three trust funds depleted at the end.

The long-term financing problems of the system stem from an entirely different source—the age structure of the population. The social security system is financed by taxing the wages of the working population to pay the benefits of the retired population.[37] Each generation earns its right to benefits by paying the benefits of preceding generations. As birth rates declined in the late 1960s, and remained low during the 1970s, it became clear that the large cohorts of the baby boom generation would be

35. More recently it has been recognized that the consumer price index, which is used to adjust benefits for inflation, overstates the rate of inflation, primarily because of the way it incorporates the cost of housing. See, for example, Alan S. Blinder, "The Consumer Price Index and the Measurement of Recent Inflation," *Brookings Papers on Economic Activity, 2:1980*, pp. 539–65. The CPI is so widely watched and used that this creates difficulties well beyond the social security program. The Bureau of Labor Statistics is currently revising the index to improve its accuracy.

36. *1981 Annual Report of the Board of Trustees of the Federal Old-Age and Survivors Insurance and Disability Insurance Trust Funds*, pp. 2, 3.

37. Half the tax is levied on the employee, the other half on the employer. Both halves are expressed as a percentage of the employee's wages. Many economists believe that the entire tax is effectively borne by the employee. See John A. Brittain, *The Payroll Tax for Social Security* (Brookings Institution, 1972).

Table 6-10. Estimated OASDI Expenditures as a Percent of Taxable Payroll under Varying Assumptions, and Scheduled Tax Rates, Selected Years and Periods, 1981–2055[a]

Year or period	Assumptions underlying expenditure estimates			Scheduled tax rate[c]
	Optimistic	Intermediate[b]	Pessimistic	
1981	11.2	11.3	11.2	10.7
1985	10.9	11.6	12.0	11.4
1990	10.1	11.9	12.6	12.4
1995	9.8	11.7	13.0	12.4
2000	9.3	11.2	12.8	12.4
2005	9.1	11.1	13.1	12.4
2010	9.5	11.6	14.0	12.4
2015	10.4	12.9	15.8	12.4
2020	11.6	14.4	18.2	12.4
2025	12.5	15.9	20.7	12.4
2030	12.8	16.8	22.7	12.4
2035	12.6	17.0	24.0	12.4
2040	12.1	16.8	24.8	12.4
2045	11.6	16.7	25.8	12.4
2050	11.4	16.7	26.9	12.4
2055	11.3	16.8	27.8	12.4
25-year averages				
1981–2005	10.0	11.5	12.6	11.9
2006–30	11.1	13.9	17.5	12.4
2031–55	11.9	16.8	25.4	12.4

Source: *1981 Annual Report of the Board of Trustees of the Federal Old-Age and Survivors Insurance and Disability Insurance Trust Funds*, pp. 59, 63, 66.

a. Estimated expenditures include disability and survivors benefits as well as retirement benefits. Disability payments, which are larger than survivors benefits, and the tax rate earmarked for them are as follows:

Period	Optimistic	Intermediate	Pessimistic	Tax rate
1981–2005	1.1	1.3	1.4	2.0
2006–30	1.3	1.7	2.1	2.2
2031–55	1.2	1.6	2.1	2.2

b. Assumptions II-B.
c. The combined employer-employee tax.

followed in the working population by smaller cohorts rather than larger ones. And it became increasingly reasonable to project that birth rates would be low for some time into the future, prolonging the decline in the taxpaying population.

The earliest projections of the problem, presented in the 1975 report of the quadrennial advisory council and the trustees' reports of 1974, 1975, and 1976, were compounded by the faulty benefit formula then in force. The 1976 report showed the costs of the system rising to almost

30 percent of taxable payroll by 2050.[38] The new formula legislated in 1977 eliminated that part of the problem. But by continuing to make benefit increases automatic, and by maintaining replacement rates at constant levels over time, the formula still withheld a degree of flexibility enjoyed by the system before 1972, when benefit increases were enacted at the discretion of Congress. With benefit levels set independently of demographic patterns, the full burden of adjustment falls on taxes.

Table 6-10 presents cost projections through 2055 from the 1981 trustees' report. Costs are expressed as a percentage of taxable payroll so that they can be compared with the scheduled tax rate. To make these projections, the trustees must choose reasonable assumptions about the future course of the economy (inflation, real wage growth, unemployment, labor force participation rates) and of birth and death rates. Following the precedent set by earlier reports, the 1981 report projects costs under three sets of assumptions. The optimistic assumptions are those for which costs rise by the smallest amount (high birth rates, high real wage growth, slower decline in mortality rates, and so on); the pessimistic assumptions, those for which costs rise by the largest amount. The intermediate assumptions, subdivided into two further alternatives in the 1981 report, are the trustees' best guess about future conditions; the other two sets serve to suggest the possible range of variation.[39]

The most important assumptions are those about demographic factors, especially birth rates. The rate of growth in real wages is the most important of the economic assumptions, or at least so it appears in the current economic context. The ultimate values for these two factors— that is, the levels at which they are assumed to settle by the year 2000— are as follows for the projections presented in the 1981 report:[40]

38. Munnell, *Future of Social Security*, p. 100.

39. Both versions of the intermediate projections use the same demographic assumptions, but the A set assumes a stronger economy than the B set, to emphasize the importance of economic performance for the financial status of the program. The B projections, which assume an economy more like that of the recent past, are presented in table 6-10. The 1981 report also presents a fifth alternative for the very short run (1981–86), which is labeled the "worst-case."

40. *1981 Annual Report of the Board of Trustees of the Federal Old-Age and Survivors Insurance and Disability Insurance Trust Funds*, pp. 29, 32. Assumptions about mortality rates are also important to the cost projections, though not as important as the total fertility rate. The 1981 report assumed that by 2055 the age-sex–adjusted death rate would be 22 percent, 36 percent, and 58 percent less than the rate in 1978 under the optimistic, intermediate, and pessimistic assumptions. The sensitivity of the projections to these alternatives is discussed on pp. 87–88 of the report.

Assumptions	Real wage growth (percent)	Total fertility rate[41]
Optimistic	2.5	2.4
Intermediate (II-B)	1.5	2.1
Pessimistic	1.0	1.7

Even the most pessimistic assumption about real wage growth predicts that it will return most of the way to the postwar average (1.7 percent in the 1951–79 period) and that the experience of the 1970s is not the trend of the future.

Under all three sets of assumptions costs will rise sharply after 2010, when the baby boom generation begins to retire. The rise is steeper the more pessimistic the assumptions. Under the intermediate assumptions, costs are projected to average 16.8 percent of taxable payroll over the period 2031 to 2055, compared with a scheduled tax rate of 12.4 percent. The overwhelming importance of the demographic assumptions to these estimates is shown in table 6-11, which gives the number of beneficiaries per 100 covered workers for each set of assumptions through 2055. For the intermediate and pessimistic projections, the percentage increase in costs is close to the percentage increase in the ratio of beneficiaries to workers.

As the trustees have observed in each report, the long-term financing problem is far enough away to allow ample time to discuss solutions and introduce any changes slowly. One obvious solution, implicit in the cost estimates, is to raise the tax rate. This could be done either by setting taxes equal to expenditures in each year, or by raising the tax rate in advance of expenditures to the average level required over the period, and saving the extra revenues from the early years to meet the heavier expenses of the later years. Other proposed changes would reduce expenditures by delaying retirement to age 68 or by adjusting the benefit formula in ways that would allow the replacement rate to decline over time.[42]

One factor to consider in choosing the best policy is the fairness with which the policy would treat different generations. For example, if the system remains as it is, each generation will enjoy the same replacement rates and the same guarantee that the purchasing power of benefits will be maintained during retirement. But in order to support the benefits of

41. The total fertility rate is the sum of the birth rates assumed at each year of age. It can be thought of as the number of children the average woman would have in her lifetime if she experienced the assumed age-specific birth rates.

42. Munnell, *Future of Social Security*, pp. 106–11.

Table 6-11. Projected Beneficiaries per 100 Covered Workers, under Varying Assumptions, Selected Years, 1981–2055[a]

Year	Assumptions underlying estimates		
	Optimistic	Intermediate[b]	Pessimistic
1981	31	31	31
1985	30	31	31
1990	30	31	32
1995	30	32	34
2000	30	32	35
2005	30	33	37
2010	32	35	40
2015	35	39	45
2020	38	43	51
2025	41	47	58
2030	42	50	63
2035	42	50	67
2040	41	50	69
2045	39	50	72
2050	39	50	75
2055	38	50	77

Source: *1981 Annual Report of the Board of Trustees of the Federal Old-Age and Survivors Insurance and Disability Insurance Trust Funds*, pp. 60, 61.
a. Includes beneficiaries of disability and survivors benefits as well as of retirement benefits.
b. Assumptions II-B.

preceding generations, each working generation will have to pay different amounts of taxes. As a result, each generation's return on its taxes will differ. Whether this is a serious problem depends in large part on the size of the differences.

Lifetime Rates of Return under Social Security

The social security system can be viewed as an investment made by the worker to provide income for his retirement, much as he might invest in stocks and bonds. If a worker's tax payments are treated as the investment, one can then ask what rate of return on that investment the subsequent benefits represent. The rate of return calculated in answer to this question is the rate such that, if the average worker were able to invest his tax payments to earn that rate, the payments plus accumulated interest would allow him to pay himself the expected benefits during retirement.

Several writers have shown that the rate of return under a pay-as-you-go retirement plan (one in which revenues just equal benefits and are paid out as soon as they are received) depends primarily on two factors—the rate of growth in the labor force and the rate of growth in real wages.[43] Under certain conditions, it is simply the sum of these two factors. Thus the rate of return under social security will decline when these growth rates decline. In light of the emerging age structure of the population—and the stagnation of real wages during the 1970s—the rates of return for cohorts spanning the baby boom and succeeding generations can be expected to differ. If large, the differences may be the source of some dissatisfaction with the social security system.

This subsection presents average rates of return for cohorts entering the labor force in the years 1960, 1970, 1980, 1990, and 2000. Since it is assumed throughout that the age of entry is 22, these correspond to the cohorts born in 1938, before the baby boom; in 1948 and 1958, at the beginning and height of the baby boom; and in 1968 and 1978, after the baby boom.

The calculations are based on formulas closely related to those developed by John Brittain in *The Payroll Tax for Social Security*.[44] Like Brittain's, the formulas used here include only pension benefits and the taxes required to support them, and are based on the assumption that the system is operated on the pay-as-you-go principle. The employer tax is assumed to be borne by labor so that the average worker pays the average total tax.[45] The formulas differ from Brittain's in that they incorporate the most important characteristics of the benefit provisions enacted in 1977—the adjustment of the worker's earnings history for increases in the average wage and the adjustment of benefits for inflation.

The calculations are made for a worker who begins work at 22, as noted, and retires at 65. Since Brittain's study has shown that the older a person is when he or she starts work, the higher the rate of return, these calculations may produce rates of return that are a bit high for cohorts with an average age of entry less than 22.[46] This effect is, however, at least partly offset by the rather late age of retirement assumed. Many retirees claim social security benefits before age 65—62 is the earliest age permitted by law.

43. For a brief discussion of this literature, see ibid., pp. 127–28.

44. For the details of the formulas, see appendix B.

45. This implies that the worker earns the average taxable wage each year, although no such assumption is made explicitly. Ideally, the tax should be adjusted to follow an age-earnings profile. But it is not clear what age-earnings profile should be used, or whether the profile is the same for different cohorts. See chapter 4.

46. Brittain, *Payroll Tax for Social Security*, chap. 6.

The data for the variables required by the formulas were taken from the published experience of the social security program for past years. Projections of future numbers of retired beneficiaries, numbers of taxpaying workers, and mortality rates were taken from the 1979 trustees' report, the latest available at the time the calculations were made.[47] As before, the trustees' projections are referred to by the shorthand titles of the underlying assumptions—optimistic, intermediate, and pessimistic.

The trustees' projections primarily reflect their assumptions about the demographic factors that influence the growth of the population and the labor force, and are less affected by their assumptions about the second factor of particular importance for the rate of return—the rate of growth in real wages. The future values of this variable were set independently at zero, 1.0 percent, and 2.0 percent annually. The higher values bracket the historic average of 1.7 percent since 1951, and the zero value permits investigation of the consequences of continued stagnation.[48]

The rate of inflation was set at zero for future years. The result is that the rates of return calculated for the 1980, 1990, and 2000 cohorts are real rates of return. Since the benefit formula guarantees that benefits will keep pace with inflation, the nominal rate of return for any given level of inflation can be derived simply by adding the selected level to the real rate of return (see appendix B for details). The results for the 1960 and 1970 cohorts are not quite real rates, since the work experience of these cohorts includes past years, in which there was invariably some rise in the price level. The rates for these two cohorts are not, however, much different from real rates—the difference may be half a point for

47. The cost estimates presented in table 6-10 are from the 1981 report, which uses assumptions that differ in several respects from those in the 1979 report. The combined effect of the differences in assumptions is that the 1981 report projects lower costs after 1990 under its optimistic assumptions than the 1979 report does, and higher costs in all years under the other two sets of assumptions. In all three cases the differences are largest in the short run and small by the peak year of 2035. The assumptions can be compared in detail by referring to pp. 22 and 23 of the 1979 report and pp. 29 and 32 of the 1981 report. The 1979 cost projections are shown on p. 46 of the report.

48. The historic average is from the *1979 Annual Report of the Board of Trustees of the Federal Old-Age and Survivors Insurance and Disability Insurance Trust Funds*, pp. 64–65. The rate of growth in average real wages is not the same as the rate of growth in output per man-hour (productivity). The latter has averaged 2.4 percent annually since 1951. The difference is due to changes in the number of hours worked and the fact that an increasing portion of employee compensation has been given in the form of fringe benefits rather than wages.

the 1960 cohort, less for the 1970 cohort—and no great harm is done if they are treated as real rates.

The calculated rates of return are shown in table 6-12. It is important to keep in mind that these are average rates of return for the cohort. Some members of a cohort will fare better than the average, some worse. For example, the current benefit system gives low earners a better rate of return than high earners in the same cohort.[49] But the purpose of these calculations is to compare different generations with one another, not to compare individuals in the same generation, and for this purpose average rates are best.

For any given set of assumptions and rate of growth in real wages, the real rate of return under social security is, as expected, lower for later cohorts. With 1 percent growth in real wages, for example, the 1960 cohort has a real rate of return of 4.80 percent under the optimistic assumptions, the 1980 cohort has a 3.38 percent rate of return, and the 2000 cohort a 2.88 percent rate. For a zero rate of growth in real wages and the pessimistic assumptions, the rates of return for the same cohorts are 4.22 percent, 2.32 percent, and 1.07 percent, respectively.

For the cohorts of 1980, 1990, and 2000, the real rate of return declines as one moves from the optimistic to the pessimistic assumptions for a given rate of growth in real wages. The differences are larger for each succeeding cohort, but even for the 2000 cohort the optimistic and pessimistic assumptions differ by less than 1 percentage point.

This pattern does not hold for the 1960 and 1970 cohorts. Indeed, in 1960 the pessimistic assumptions produce the highest rates of return. The reason for this apparent anomaly is that the first twenty years of the taxpaying period are exactly the same under all three sets of assumptions for the 1960 cohort (the first ten years for the 1970 cohort) and the remaining taxpaying years are those early in the projection period, when the differences between the three alternatives are smallest. At the same time, mortality rates decline faster under the pessimistic than under the intermediate assumptions, and faster under the intermediate than the optimistic assumptions. As a result, the average worker lives longer and collects more benefits the more pessimistic the assumptions. For the 1960 cohort the longer life expectancy is enough to offset the higher taxes toward the end of the person's work life. For the 1970 cohort the

49. See Brittain, *Payroll Tax for Social Security,* chap. 6; and Advisory Council on Social Security, *Social Security Financing and Benefits, Report of the 1979 Advisory Council* (GPO, 1980), especially chap. 3.

Table 6-12. Lifetime Rates of Return under Social Security for Five Cohorts, by Year of Entry into the Labor Force
Percent

Year of entry[a]	Rate of growth in real wages	Rate of return[b]		
		Optimistic assumptions	Intermediate assumptions	Pessimistic assumptions
1960	0	4.13	4.20	4.22
	1.0	4.80	4.86	4.89
	2.0	5.46	5.52	5.56
1970	0	2.97	3.00	3.00
	1.0	3.80	3.82	3.81
	2.0	4.62	4.65	4.62
1980	0	2.45	2.43	2.32
	1.0	3.38	3.35	3.24
	2.0	4.30	4.27	4.15
1990	0	2.13	2.00	1.72
	1.0	3.12	2.98	2.69
	2.0	4.09	3.95	3.65
2000	0	1.87	1.60	1.07
	1.0	2.88	2.61	2.05
	2.0	3.88	3.59	3.04

a. At age 22.
b. Real rates of return, that is, rates calculated on the assumption that there is no inflation over the projection period. Nominal rates for any given rate of inflation can be calculated by adding the assumed rate of inflation to the rates of return shown in the table. Assumptions are those used in the *1979 Annual Report of the Board of Trustees of the Federal Old-Age and Survivors Insurance and Disability Insurance Trust Funds*, pp. 21–25.

two effects just balance each other. For 1980 and beyond, when the assumptions affect the entire period of taxpaying, higher taxes more than offset the longer life in retirement and the rates of return decline as the assumptions grow more pessimistic.

The importance of the future trend in real wage growth is clearly demonstrated by the table. For the cohorts of 1980, 1990, and 2000—for which the assumed conditions unfold smoothly into the future, uncomplicated by the vagaries of historical experience—an additional point of real wage growth adds almost a full point to the rate of return. Thus, under the intermediate assumptions, the 1990 cohort receives a real rate of return of 2 percent if there is no growth in real wages, but the return is almost 4 percent when real wage growth averages 2 percent.

Two points are worth considering when trying to decide whether the differences between cohorts are large enough to require changes in the financing and benefit structure of the system. The first is that the average rate of return is positive for each of the cohorts shown under even the most pessimistic assumptions, indicating that the automatic adjustments in earnings records and benefits manage to ensure that each cohort comes out at least a little ahead. This may not continue to be true for cohorts entering after the year 2000, but the possibility of negative rates of return for entire cohorts is in any event not an immediate problem under the current system.

The second point is that the rates have been calculated on the assumption that there will be no inflation in the future. Clearly, this will not be the case, and when a reasonable rate of inflation is added to the real rates of return, to yield nominal rates, the differences between cohorts become relatively less important. Suppose, for example, that inflation averages 5 percent annually in the future. Then, under the intermediate assumptions with 1 percent annual growth in real wages, the nominal rate of return is 9.86 percent for the 1960 cohort (approximately), 8.35 percent for the 1980 cohort, and 7.61 percent for the 2000 cohort. After a decade when rates of return on a wide variety of assets were not able to stay even with inflation, returns like these look rather good and the differences between them rather small.

Conclusions

Over the course of this century a variety of new arrangements have been devised for supporting the aged, arrangements that relieve elderly people and their families of sole responsibility. Private pension plans enable people to join together in relatively small, private groups to provide for retirement. Through programs like social security and medicare the nation as a whole has accepted responsibility for a large share of the support of the aged. These programs have developed partly in response to the growing number of the aged, and partly in response to changes in other social and economic conditions, such as the declining importance of farming as a source of employment and the rising national wealth.

Social security and medicare operate by transferring income from the working population to the retired population. A steadily growing labor force and rising productivity (and for many years the immaturity of the social security program) have made these transfers relatively easy to bear. But the emerging age structure of the population and the recent drop in productivity growth bring out the risks inherent in the financing of these programs, risks that are currently borne by the working population.

These programs have evolved continuously in the past and will continue to change in the future as the older population grows larger. Further, they will have to deal with the aging baby boom generation, which considerably exaggerates for a time in the next century the long-term trend in the population share of the elderly. This chapter has projected some of the forces that will condition the future evolution of programs for the aged.

Changes in age structure will be a persistent force pushing up the use of hospital and nursing home care, particularly once the baby boom generation begins to retire. If rates of use by age and sex remain at the levels of the mid-1970s, hospital days per 1,000 total population will be 31 percent higher at their peak in 2040 than they were in 1975, and the aged will account for more than 40 percent of all hospital expenditures, compared with 27 or 28 percent in the mid-1970s. Nursing homes are used almost exclusively by the aged, and the number of residents in nursing homes per 1,000 population in 2050 will be almost two-and-one-half times the level of 1975, again simply because of changes in age structure. About half the costs of nursing home care are currently paid by the government, largely through the medicaid program.

The trustees of the social security program project that expenditures will rise to almost 17 percent of taxable payroll by 2030 and remain at that level at least through 2055.[50] Because of the rising tax rates that will be required, real rates of return from the program will decline for succeeding cohorts of workers, but they are projected to remain positive, at least for cohorts entering the labor force by the year 2000.

All the projections show that the major changes will not occur for decades. The growth in the aged's share of the population will be small and gradual until about 2010, leaving ample time to consider how to respond. And all the projections assume that factors other than age structure—rates of medical care use by age, social security benefits, and the method of financing the program—will remain constant or change in accordance with current formulas. But the choices about how to respond to changes in age structure are precisely choices about whether and how to alter these other factors.

One alternative is to stay with present arrangements and absorb the

50. These estimates include disability and survivors benefits. See table 6-10.

higher costs when they arise. These costs will include the projected 17 percent of taxable payroll for social security, and something more than an additional 5 percent of payroll to support medicare's hospital insurance.[51] General revenues would continue to pay for physicians' services under medicare, for federal and state commitments to medicaid, and for other government programs with responsibilities for the aged. It is not possible to quantify all the costs, but the public costs of supporting the aged will clearly be much higher after 2000 than they are now if these programs continue to operate in the same way. It does not follow that the costs will be impossible to bear—the tax rates to support similar programs in a number of European countries are already well above the rate paid in the United States.[52]

The remaining alternatives would change current arrangements in order to moderate the rise in costs. Other factors have been more important than age structure in the past, and they can reinforce or offset age structure in the future. Certainly the effects of age structure on medical care were overwhelmed by other influences that caused rates of use and costs to rise rapidly for all age groups in the United States during the 1950s, 1960s, and 1970s. Future trends in medical care will depend in part on whether amounts and standards of care will be allowed to rise further at the same time that age structure is creating independent pressure for more care. Questions of this sort are already being asked because of the rapid increases in medical expenditures during the 1960s and 1970s, and in choosing answers the nation will set the stage for its response to future changes in age structure.[53]

For the social security program, the revision in 1977 of the formula for indexing benefits, and the decision to index benefits by prices rather than wages during retirement, will help keep future costs lower than they would have been otherwise.[54] Costs could be further reduced by raising the age of retirement or revising the benefit formula to allow replacement rates to decline. Any of these changes could be designed to be the same for all future generations, or to vary with the size of

51. In their 1981 annual report, the trustees of the hospital insurance trust fund project costs at between 5 and 5.5 percent in the year 2000; estimates have not been made for this program in later years.

52. Munnell, *Future of Social Security*, p. 108.

53. See, for example, Richard A. Knox, "Heart Transplants: To Pay or Not to Pay," *Science*, vol. 209, August 1, 1980, pp. 570–75.

54. At least this was the expectation at the time, based on historical experience. Since the revisions were passed, however, prices have risen faster than wages.

generations in a way that would maintain more nearly equal rates of return. For example, the tax loads of different generations could be made more equal by raising taxes in advance of expenditures; this would allow the trust funds to build up and tax rates to be kept somewhat below the peak values that would be required by a strict pay-as-you-go system.

The choice among these alternatives involves three larger issues about the effect of age structure and the desirability of different responses to it. In the first place, the problem is in large part one of sharing the risks of change in population trends. Richard Musgrave has dealt with this issue in some detail in a paper considering the effects of population and productivity trends on the social security program.[55] He analyzes the case of fixed replacement rates, in which the risk is borne by the working population in the form of higher taxes; and the case of a fixed tax rate, in which the risk is borne by the retired population in the form of lower benefits when their numbers increase. He then proposes a third possibility that would allow benefits per retiree and wages per worker (net of social security taxes) to rise and fall together, thus dividing the risk between the two groups. The question is an essential one in many areas affected by changes in age structure (or by changes in a number of other factors, for that matter). Who should bear the risk and under what conditions should the losers be compensated?

The second point is related to the first. When different generations are compared to determine whether they are treated with reasonable equality, the comparison should span the lifetime of each generation and the accumulation of inequalities over that lifetime. For example, the small cohorts following the baby boom generation will receive somewhat lower rates of return from social security than will the baby boom. On the other hand, if small cohorts really do earn higher wages than large ones (see chapter 4), their loss under social security is balanced by a gain in the labor market. If the nation does not compensate the baby boom generation for its lower wages, should it compensate later cohorts for their lower rates of return under social security? Indeed, the higher social security taxes paid by a small cohort could be viewed as one way of compensating the large cohort for its lower wages. The example points up the difficulty of trying to achieve equality between generations. If some things are adjusted for age structure and others are not, the overall result could be less fair than if nothing were done. The best course may

55. Richard A. Musgrave, "Financing Social Security: A Reappraisal," Harvard Institute of Economic Research Discussion Paper 753 (April 1980).

be to ignore differences between generations unless they are really huge.

Finally, rising costs for particular programs because of changes in age structure should be viewed from the perspective of the allocation of total national resources. That allocation will necessarily change as age structure changes. If the costs of social security and medicare rise because the proportion of aged people rises, then it should be possible to cut back costs in other areas where the population is declining in relative terms. In table 6-1, for example, the same projections that show a rising proportion of those 65 and older produce a declining proportion of children, which would justify a reduction in spending for education. The task will be to maintain this long-term perspective and to ease resources out of areas the baby boom generation has left in order to make them available for the area in which it has just arrived.

chapter seven Conclusions and Policy Implications

This study has investigated some of the past and future effects of the baby boom generation on the economy, and of the economy on the baby boom generation. Each chapter looked into a part of the generation's experience—birth (chapter 2), schooling (chapter 3), work (chapter 4), spending (chapter 5), and, still to come, retirement (chapter 6). The three sections of this chapter summarize the results of the study by answering the questions set out in the introduction.

1. Has the baby boom generation had a harder time economically than earlier generations? And the subtler, but related, issue: has it had a harder time than a smaller generation would have had in the same circumstances?

2. What effects has the baby boom generation had on the economy and how large are they?

3. How much can the age structure of the population help in predicting the future?

How the Generation Has Fared Economically

In recent years the baby boom generation has become known as unlucky—always too crowded in schools, in the job market, in housing, and, as a result, never getting the breaks it expected or deserved. By a similar line of reasoning, the small generation born in the 1930s has earned a reputation for being particularly lucky—good incomes, less crowded markets, and so on. Before the case can be fairly judged, the evidence should be reviewed, and, ideally, the review should span the lifetime of each generation. How serious the inequality between generations is in one area of life depends not only on the magnitude of the inequality, and its causes, but also on the larger pattern of inequalities—whether the record is one of straight wins or losses, or mixed.

163

For the baby boom only part of the record can be examined, since even the oldest members of the generation are still only in their thirties. The known facts about the generation include its schooling and its early experience with jobs and housing.

A higher proportion of the baby boom attended school—from kindergarten to college and graduate school—and more resources were devoted to the education of each student than in any previous generation. In the elementary and secondary schools each new class of students was better provided for than the previous one as real expenditure per student rose steadily during the postwar period. In higher education expenditure per student leveled off in the 1970s after rising substantially during the two preceding decades; the younger half of the generation was thus as well off as the older half, but not better off. Enrollment rates for men in higher education slipped from the peak levels attained in the late 1960s, although they were still above those of earlier generations. Enrollment rates for women continued to rise.

When they first entered the labor force, the members of the baby boom generation had more difficulty finding jobs than the young people who had started work earlier in the post–World War II period.[1] The unemployment rate for teenagers fluctuated between 15 and 20 percent during the later 1960s and the 1970s, as opposed to rates not much above 10 percent in the 1950s. The rates for people in their early twenties were several percentage points above the levels of the 1950s, often exceeding 10 percent. Some part of the higher rates may have been a direct result of the large numbers of young workers—too many inexperienced workers chasing too few jobs for inexperienced workers—but the evidence on the point is plausible rather than persuasive.

As young adults, the baby boom generation has earned higher real incomes than any previous generation. But its experience has differed in several ways from that of its predecessors. Perhaps most important, the real earnings of successive cohorts of young adults did not grow during the 1970s as they had during the 1950s and 1960s; instead, they were almost the same at the end of the decade as at the beginning. Thus the members of the baby boom generation who began full-time work at the end of the 1970s found themselves earning no more than the new workers of several years before had earned when they began, a disap-

1. Comparable statistics are not available for the period before World War II. But unemployment rates for young people, as for everyone else, must have been higher during the 1930s than they were after the war.

pointment considering the expectations created by the trends of the earlier decades. (The disappointment was not confined to young adults, of course; real incomes were stagnant for every age group in the 1970s.) Further, the premium earned by college graduates over high school graduates was no longer as great as it had been.

Some analysts found that the gap between the earnings of young men and older men widened during the 1970s, and concluded that the baby boom generation was suffering from its size in relative, if not absolute, terms. But the gap between the earnings of younger and older women did not change, although the number of young women in the labor force grew especially rapidly because of their rising participation rates. The different experiences of men and women suggest that trends in employment may be part of the explanation—employment in professional and managerial jobs grew faster for young women than for young men during the 1970s.

On the surface it appeared that the baby boom generation must be having a difficult time in the housing market of the 1970s, since house prices rose faster than other prices and nominal interest rates reached unprecedented levels.[2] The facts were otherwise. Neither prices nor interest rates were high enough to offset the advantages of fixed mortgage payments in a period of rapid inflation and tax-deductible interest. As the true cost of owning a house declined during the 1970s young adults were quick to seize the opportunity. Homeownership rose rapidly among young married couples, the traditional home buyers, and, for that matter, among non-couple households as well. The rise in homeownership among all young households taken together was less pronounced than the trends for each type separately because of the rapid growth of non-couple households, who are less likely than married couples to own their homes. The younger members of the generation may not, however, continue the trend. Since 1979 the cost of owning a house has risen sharply, even after adjustment for inflation and tax deductions.

How the baby boom generation will fare when it retires remains to be seen, but at this distance it looks as though it can expect to do reasonably well. If the benefit formulas currently used by the social security program remain in effect, it will enjoy a positive real rate of return on its tax payments. So will the smaller generations born in the late 1960s and the 1970s. Indeed, the likely differences in real rates of return because of differences in the size of each generation are rather small, and other

2. Rents rose more slowly than other prices.

factors, such as future trends in productivity, are potentially more important to the final outcome. These results run counter to the frequent charge that young people will lose money on the social security program.

It is perhaps worthwhile to make explicit some of the facts about the generation born during the 1930s that have been implicit in many of the statements about the baby boom. The members of this small generation grew up during the depression and attended school then and during World War II, when real expenditure per student dropped below the levels of the 1930s. They too attended college in greater numbers than any preceding generation, but not in the record proportions of the baby boom generation. They were fortunate in having lower unemployment rates when young. At the same time, their real earnings were considerably less, a fact that has been obscured by studies showing that young men's earnings were somewhat higher compared with those of older men than has been the case in recent years. They formed fewer separate households as young adults than the baby boom generation and proportionately more of those households were married couples with children. Yet fewer of the young couples of the 1930s generation owned their own homes.

To date, then, the baby boom generation has not had a harder time economically than other generations. There have been rough spots—the higher unemployment rates in particular. Established relationships have failed to hold for this generation, and it has had to adjust to the end (whether temporary or permanent remains to be seen) of the steady growth in educational expenditures, in earnings, and in many other aspects of life, which had come to be accepted as an economic birthright. Nonetheless it seems fair to say that, on balance, the baby boom has done better than earlier generations.

Might it have fared even better had it been smaller? Studies have found that the large size of the generation may have raised its unemployment rates during adolescence and early adulthood and depressed the earnings of young men relative to those of older men. But closer examination shows that the evidence is weak and contradictory, hardly enough to support the idea that demography is destiny. At most, it offers marginal qualifications to the conclusion that the baby boom generation has not been unlucky because of its size.

Effects on the Economy

The preceding chapters investigated a number of possible links between the age structure of the population and the economy. Although the large baby boom generation is the dominant feature of the current age structure, it is by no means the only important one. The small generations that surround and define the baby boom are a related feature, but distinguishable for some purposes; and the growing proportion of elderly people is a separate element altogether. The various assessments of the effects of age structure combined all these elements. In some instances it was possible to show the effects of the baby boom generation alone, in others not.

Most of the effect of age structure on the unemployment rate can be safely attributed to the baby boom generation—the elderly account for only a very small share of the labor force. Teenagers and young adults have historically had high unemployment rates, and as they poured into the labor force after 1965 the overall unemployment rate rose. By the mid-1970s the changes in the makeup of the labor force were adding between 0.5 and 1.0 percentage point to the overall rate. This was unquestionably an important addition, but it was not the largest part of the story during many of those years, when unemployment exceeded the 4 percent target by 2, 3, and even 4 percentage points.

There are also good reasons to suspect that age structure can influence the division of income between consumption and saving—for example, surveys show that young households save less and take on more debt than older households. Through the marginal propensity to consume, it could even influence the demand response to fiscal policies. Important as these possibilities are, economists have had considerable difficulty exploring them, for a variety of reasons outlined in chapter 5. As a result, the available studies often fail to address the issues.

The evidence to date suggests that age structure has had little or no effect on consumption and saving in the aggregate. Two studies of saving found that the proportion of income saved has changed only slightly in response to age structure, even with the growing number of old households—who also save less than middle-aged households—to reinforce the large number of young ones. The distribution of saving by type, particularly net investment in housing and in financial assets, shows no sign of having been altered by age structure. Similarly, the analysis of spending on durable goods presented in chapter 5 indicates that age structure has had, and is likely to have, little effect on the overall percentage of income consumers spend on automobiles or household furnishings.

The baby boom generation was an important factor, although not the dominant one, in the housing market of the 1970s. Between 1970 and

1975 *all* demographically induced additions to the housing stock accounted for two-thirds of housing starts and new mobile homes, a percentage that is close to the postwar average. Between 1975 and 1980 their share rose to 80 percent. Demographically induced additions include the effects of changing population numbers at all ages (the growing number of elderly people has consistently been an important factor) and the effects of rising rates of household incidence (another consistently important source of additions in the postwar period).[3] When the effects of numbers and household incidence are combined, the baby boom generation accounted for less than half of the demographically induced starts during the decade. The cohorts born just ahead of the baby boom were responsible for another 20 percent, and households headed by people over 50 for the rest.

If household incidence rates level off in the 1980s, the baby boom generation will be a larger source of demographically induced demand for housing in the next decade—and perhaps, for the first time, the dominant influence on the market. With smaller cohorts entering the market behind the baby boom as well as aging in front, its share of this demand may rise to two-thirds of the total.

The baby boom generation has influenced the allocation of resources to other sectors of the economy as well, but, once again, the link between numbers and spending is not mechanical. The schools are a good example. Several alternatives were open:

—spending per student could have been cut back to keep total spending on education constant;

—spending could have been increased in line with inflation, but not faster, to keep real resources per student at the levels provided earlier generations and allow total spending to grow; or

—spending per student could have been increased faster than inflation, in which case total spending would have grown even more.

The historical trends show that the third alternative was chosen for elementary and secondary schools. Spending per elementary and secondary student grew roughly in line with the gross national product, so that as the number of students rose, the share of GNP devoted to elementary and secondary education also rose, finally peaking at about 4 percent in the 1970s. Whether the choice was entirely deliberate or not, the result was to allow each student to share proportionately in the

3. The rate of household incidence is the number of households headed by someone in a specified age group per 1,000 persons in that age group.

growing affluence of the country. The same principle in a stagnant or declining economy would have meant stagnant or declining expenditures per student.

The projections presented in chapter 6 suggest the reallocations of resources that may occur in the future as the baby boom generation reaches retirement age. If patterns of medical care by age are like those of today, use of hospitals and nursing homes will greatly increase in the next century. The proportion of taxable payroll required to pay the social security retirement benefits promised by current law is projected to rise from 11 or 12 percent—the rate that should be sufficient from now through the year 2010—to an average of 17 percent between 2031 and 2055.

It is important to keep in mind that here again there is no reason to expect a mechanical reaction to the population numbers. The same choice that confronted society in education will present itself repeatedly—to cut resources per person, hold them constant, or let them grow. The general state of the economy at the time will have a crucial influence on the outcome, as it has had in the past. Projecting the consequences of current habits and practices sets the terms of the debate, but the decisions will inevitably be reconsidered and reshaped as the time approaches.

The answer to the second question, then, is that the baby boom generation has had a number of important effects on the economy. But even when important, it has not been the dominant factor, and in some cases it has apparently had little or no effect, contrary to the most reasonable expectations. In the growing, changing postwar economy other factors have played a more important part.

Predicting the Future

Much of the interest in age structure and its links with the economy stems from the hope that the links are strong enough, and important enough, to serve as a useful base for prediction. Age structure is an appealing base because it is itself relatively predictable. Projections of the population by age depend, except for the youngest age groups, on people already born and on mortality rates, which are low at most ages. Thus they can be made for one or two decades ahead with reasonable confidence. Then, if age structure is a major determinant of the course of the economy, the economy too can be projected with reasonable confidence.

The stability, or predictability, of age-related behavior is critical to the success of predictions based on age structure. At times in our national history that behavior has been relatively stable—as noted in chapter 5, Burnham Campbell showed that additions to the housing stock followed changes in the population rather closely for decades before 1940. But the postwar period has not been one of those times. The behavior of people at given ages, such as birth rates, college enrollment rates, and rates of household incidence, has changed so much that age structure has been a poor guide to events. The answer to the second question is pertinent: age structure has sometimes been important, but, in the postwar years, never dominant.

Predictions of births in the late 1940s and again in the 1960s were based in large part on age structure. In the late 1940s demographers expected the birth rate to return to the low levels indicated by the trends of the previous century. Total births should have declined as small cohorts reached childbearing age during the 1950s. They rose instead. In the 1960s birth rates finally fell, but demographers had every reason to expect total births to rise as the first cohorts of the baby boom generation reached adulthood. Instead, birth rates continued to decline, more than offsetting the large numbers of young adults, and total births dropped.

Predictions about the 1980s may prove equally wrong. Recent history suggests that the overall unemployment rate should drop as the share of teenagers and young adults in the labor force drops. The baby boom generation should remain an important force in the housing market, and may become the dominant force if rates of household incidence level off. But either or both of these predictions could be undone by further changes in behavior. Or the effect of age structure could be overwhelmed by other events—rising unemployment in response to further increases in energy prices, for example.

Like the short-run predictions, the speculation presented in chapter 6 about the baby boom generation in retirement rests on specific assumptions about behavior and policy. The projections show how important age structure would be under those conditions. How important age structure actually turns out to be will depend on whether behavior or policies change. A trend toward less institutionalization of the elderly, perhaps made possible by new discoveries in biomedical research, could offset the effects of the growing number of elderly people on the use of hospitals and nursing homes. Fluctuations in the growth of real wages, or changes in the current benefit formula, could cancel out the modest differences between generations in lifetime rates of return from social security.

The answer to the third question is that age structure is a useful but limited guide to the future. Its greatest value is perhaps that of alerting us to the possibility of a repeating pattern of decline-growth-decline in the commitment of resources—in schools, in housing, in medical care and social security—as the population ages. But the pattern will not always materialize—it did not in births (at least not with the expected timing!). Because of changes in age-related behavior, age structure has seldom been the most important factor even in those areas of the economy where it has played a major part.

appendix A **Did Other Countries Have Baby Booms?**

There have been fluctuations in the number of births in industrial countries other than the United States in this century, and thus fluctuations in the age structures of their populations. Table A-1 shows annual births since 1932, the earliest year available from UN documents, for six countries—Australia, Canada, England and Wales, France, Sweden, and West Germany.[1]

Although the exact pattern of births differs among the countries, there are some common elements. Births in every country were lower during the depression and the first year or two of the Second World War than at any time since (except briefly in England and Wales, where births dipped below depression levels in 1976 and 1977). After the war, all but one of the countries participated in the baby boom of the late 1940s; the exception was Sweden, neutral during the war, where births reached record levels during the early 1940s. The patterns diverged during the 1950s and 1960s. There was a sustained rise in births in Canada and Australia that peaked about 1960; births then declined in Canada, while they dipped and went on to a second, higher peak about 1970 in Australia. Births were below the postwar boom levels in England and Wales and Sweden during the 1950s, and in West Germany during the early 1950s, and then rose again during the 1960s. They maintained a fairly steady level, below the levels of the late 1940s, in France. In the late 1960s and the 1970s the various patterns converged again and total births declined in every country.

Numbers of births per 1,000 women aged 15 through 44, also shown in the table for the years 1940–70, indicate that the fluctuations in total

1. Data are available for West Germany since 1946. Japan was left out of the table because of inconsistencies between the data on births and those on the population by age.

births were usually determined by the rate at which women had children rather than by the number of women of childbearing age. By and large, births per 1,000 women and total births rose and fell together—rising after World War II, remaining high in Canada and Australia and declining in the other countries during the 1950s, rising again during the early 1960s in several countries, and then declining everywhere. In Europe the variations in births per 1,000 women reflect variations in the timing of marriage and children more than in the size of completed families. Interestingly, the trends in Europe have been similar to those in the United States—more people have married, they have married younger, and women have increasingly concentrated their childbearing between the ages of twenty and thirty.[2]

Canada is the only one of the six countries, however, that experienced a baby boom like the one in the United States, with the same pattern of births, and the same factors underlying that pattern.[3] As in the United States, births per 1,000 women declined briefly from the levels of the immediate postwar years, rose to a peak in the late 1950s, and then began to drop again, quite rapidly after the early 1960s. Total births followed a similar path, averaging 470,000 a year during the late 1950s and early 1960s. By the middle 1970s they had declined to about 350,000 a year.

More generally, however, several of the six countries have experienced significant variations in age structure, and to the extent that age structure affects economic activity, their economies may exhibit some of the symptoms. The possibilities for research are not pursued in this study. But it should be pointed out that, in Europe especially, the age structure of the native population, and thus its economic effects, may have been modified in several ways by immigration. First, the variation in births often occurred at different times in different countries, and immigration between countries, which has intentionally been made easy within the European Community, can even out the irregularities that each would experience alone. Second, temporary flows of "guest workers" are important in several countries—West Germany and France, for example—and these flows can be manipulated to offset any effects of the age structure of the native population on the labor market. Finally,

2. United Nations, Secretariat of the Economic Commission for Europe, *Economic Survey of Europe in 1974*, pt. 2: *Post-War Demographic Trends in Europe and the Outlook until the Year 2000* (New York: UN, 1975), chap. 5.

3. See Carl F. Grindstaff, "The Baby Bust: Changes in Fertility Patterns in Canada," *Canadian Studies in Population*, vol. 2 (1975), pp. 15–22.

Table A-1. Live Births and Births per 1,000 Women Aged 15 through 44 in Six Industrial Countries, 1932–77

Year	Australia		Canada		England and Wales		France		Sweden		West Germany	
	Live births	Births per 1,000 women	Live births	Births per 1,000 women	Live births	Births per 1,000 women	Live births	Births per 1,000 women	Live births	Births per 1,000 women	Live births	Births per 1,000 women
1932	110,933	n.a.	235,905	n.a.	613,972	n.a.	722,371	n.a.	89,779	n.a.	...	...
1933	111,269	n.a.	223,105	n.a.	580,413	n.a.	678,700	n.a.	85,020	n.a.	...	...
1934	109,475	n.a.	221,550	n.a.	597,642	n.a.	677,878	n.a.	85,092	n.a.	...	...
1935	111,325	n.a.	221,740	n.a.	598,756	n.a.	640,527	n.a.	85,906	n.a.	...	...
1936	116,073	n.a.	220,638	n.a.	605,292	n.a.	630,818	n.a.	88,938	n.a.	...	...
1937	119,131	n.a.	220,529	n.a.	610,557	n.a.	618,071	n.a.	90,373	n.a.	...	...
1938	120,415	n.a.	229,748	n.a.	621,204	n.a.	612,248	n.a.	93,946	n.a.	...	...
1939	122,891	n.a.	229,765	n.a.	614,479	n.a.	612,395	n.a.	97,380	n.a.	...	...
1940	126,347	76.9	244,640	93.4	590,120	58.7	559,100	64.9	95,778	62.2	...	...
1941	134,525	81.0	255,705	92.9	579,091	57.9	519,600	60.7	99,727	64.8	...	...
1942	136,708	81.6	272,778	101.6	651,503	65.2	573,000	67.0	113,961	74.2	...	...
1943	149,295	88.5	284,082	104.6	684,334	68.6	613,100	71.7	125,392	81.8	...	...
1944	153,344	90.3	284,672	103.4	751,478	75.7	626,500	73.5	134,991	88.2	...	...
1945	160,560	94.4	289,347	103.9	679,937	68.8	641,324	75.1	135,373	88.8	...	...
1946	176,379	103.6	343,504	121.4	820,719	83.3	843,904	95.5	132,597	87.0	718,551	64.9
1947	182,384	107.4	372,589	129.9	881,026	90.6	970,472	109.4	128,779	84.5	762,314	68.2
1948	177,976	103.2	359,860	123.9	775,306	80.2	870,836	98.4	126,683	83.4	785,986	70.3
1949	181,261	103.5	367,092	121.5	730,518	76.0	872,661	98.8	121,272	80.1	812,200	73.0
1950	190,591	106.5	372,009	121.6	697,097	73.0	862,310	97.9	115,414	76.7	791,221	71.2
1951	193,298	105.9	381,092	122.8	677,529	71.4	826,722	94.3	110,168	73.3	776,144	69.7
1952	201,650	109.1	403,559	127.2	673,735	71.7	822,204	94.2	110,192	73.6	781,029	70.1
1953	202,235	108.5	417,884	129.4	684,372	73.5	804,696	92.9	110,144	74.0	778,206	68.2
1954	202,256	107.6	436,198	132.5	673,651	72.9	810,754	94.3	105,096	71.0	798,479	69.6

Year												
1955	207,677	109.1	442,937	132.2	667,811	72.8	805,917	94.6	107,305	72.8	803,012	69.5
1956	212,133	109.9	450,739	132.4	700,335	77.0	806,916	94.6	107,960	73.4	838,401	72.8
1957	220,358	112.3	469,093	134.4	723,381	80.0	816,467	95.9	107,168	72.9	874,365	76.3
1958	222,504	111.5	470,118	132.1	740,715	82.2	812,215	95.4	105,502	71.4	885,659	77.4
1959	226,976	112.0	479,275	132.8	748,501	83.0	829,249	97.4	104,743	70.6	930,944	81.4
1960	230,326	111.7	478,551	130.6	785,005	86.8	819,819	95.6	102,219	68.1	947,124	83.2
1961	239,986	114.1	475,700	127.8	811,281	89.4	838,633	95.7	104,501	69.3	989,484	87.0
1962	237,081	109.7	469,693	124.3	838,736	90.5	832,353	90.9	107,284	70.6	994,425	86.1
1963	235,689	106.5	465,767	121.2	854,055	90.9	868,876	90.8	112,903	73.7	1,028,187	87.8
1964	229,149	101.0	452,915	115.4	875,972	92.6	877,704	89.4	122,664	79.5	1,038,788	87.8
1965	222,854	96.2	418,595	104.4	862,725	91.2	865,688	87.3	122,806	79.2	1,018,259	85.9
1966	222,626	94.1	387,710	93.5	849,823	90.1	863,527	86.4	123,354	79.5	1,024,261	86.2
1967	229,296	94.7	370,894	86.9	832,164	88.4	840,568	83.4	121,360	78.1	994,244	84.7
1968	240,906	97.3	364,310	83.2	819,272	87.0	835,796	82.6	113,087	72.7	946,325	80.9
1969	250,176	98.5	369,647	82.4	797,538	84.7	842,245	n.a.	107,622	68.8	903,458	n.a.
1970	257,516	n.a.	371,988	80.9	784,486	83.3	850,381	n.a.	110,150	n.a.	810,808	n.a.
1971	276,362	n.a.	362,187	n.a.	783,155	n.a.	881,284	n.a.	114,484	n.a.	778,526	n.a.
1972	265,124	n.a.	347,319	n.a.	725,440	n.a.	875,870	n.a.	112,273	n.a.	701,000	n.a.
1973	247,670	n.a.	343,373	n.a.	675,953	n.a.	857,186	n.a.	109,663	n.a.	635,633	n.a.
1974	245,177	n.a.	345,645	n.a.	639,885	n.a.	801,212	n.a.	109,874	n.a.	626,373	n.a.
1975	233,012	n.a.	358,621	n.a.	603,445	n.a.	742,200	n.a.	103,632	n.a.	600,512	n.a.
1976	227,645	n.a.	364,630	n.a.	584,270	n.a.	717,800	n.a.	98,345	n.a.	602,851	n.a.
1977	226,480	n.a.	360,340	n.a.	568,418	n.a.	744,830	n.a.	96,006	n.a.	582,944	n.a.

Sources: United Nations, Department of International Economic and Social Affairs, *Demographic Yearbook, 1977*, ST/ESA/STAT/SER. R/6, and previous issues.
n.a. Not available.

longer-term flows of population—such as those to England from her former colonies—also change the age structure of the population, although they will not necessarily fill in the gaps in the native population and may even exacerbate them.

appendix B Computation of Lifetime Rates of Return

The computation of the lifetime rates of return follows the general principles established by John Brittain.[1] The formulas have been revised, however, to incorporate the procedures for calculating and adjusting benefits established by the 1977 amendments to the Social Security Act.

The internal rate of return, i, is the rate at which the taxes paid by the worker until age 65, plus accumulated interest on those taxes, equal the benefits he can expect to receive, discounted to age 65. Interest is credited on the tax payments at the rate i, and the benefits are discounted at the same rate. Like Brittain's, the formulas used here focus on average taxes and benefits, ignoring differences between individuals in the same cohort. They also assume a strict pay-as-you-go system, with taxes equal to expenditures in each year. Only pension benefits and the taxes required to pay them are analyzed.

Consider a worker just entering the labor force and the benefits he can expect to receive under the present formula. Let the average initial benefit for 62-year-old workers in that year be represented by b_1. Then the initial benefit for the new worker when he or she reaches age 62 will be

$$b_1(1 + r + c)^{L_{62}},$$

where r is the rate of growth in real wages, c is the rate of inflation, and L_{62} is the number of working years until he or she reaches 62. This expression reflects the fact that the average initial benefit increases each year by the rate of growth in nominal wages, and that this growth is the sum of real growth and inflation.

After age 62 the worker's initial benefit is adjusted to keep pace with

1. John A. Brittain, *The Payroll Tax for Social Security* (Brookings Institution, 1972), chap. 6. See especially the technical note at the end of the chapter.

inflation. If the worker then retires at age 65, his or her discounted benefit stream during retirement is

$$b_1 \sum_{n=65}^{\infty} \frac{(1 + r + c)^{L_{62}}(1 + c)^{n-62}}{(1 + i)^{n-65}} (P_n),$$

where P_n is the probability of surviving to age n, given that the worker has reached age 65 (for $n = 65$, P_n is 1.0).

For historical years, the taxes the worker pays each year, $\overline{T}_t$, can be expressed as

$$\overline{T}_t = \frac{R_t \overline{b}_t}{N_t},$$

where R_t is the number of retired beneficiaries of the program, $\overline{b}_t$ is the average benefit paid in the year, and N_t is the number of taxpaying workers. Historic values for these variables are available from the *Social Security Bulletin*.

The calculation of taxes for years during the projection period is more complicated because the average benefit is not known and must be calculated from the averages for two groups of retirees whose benefits are adjusted in different ways. Those already on the beneficiary rolls from the previous year will have their average benefit increased by the rate of inflation. Those joining the beneficiary rolls for the first time will receive a benefit that has grown over the years in line with earnings (until age 62); hence it will include both real and inflationary increases. Thus the tax per worker in a year t during the projection period can be written as

$$\overline{T}_t = \frac{s_{t-1} R_{t-1} \overline{b}_{t-1}(1 + c) + A_t b_1 (1 + r + c)^{t-1}}{N_t},$$

where s_{t-1} is the proportion of retirees who survive from year $t - 1$ to year t, and A_t is the number of new retirees who enter the program in year t (sometimes called new awards).

Accumulated taxes for a worker who retires at 65, plus interest at rate i, are then computed as follows:

$$\sum_{t=1}^{L_{65}} \overline{T}_t (1 + i)^{L_{65}-(t-1)},$$

where L_{65} is the number of years the worker has spent in the labor force by the time he reaches age 65 and retires.

Finally, the internal rate of return is the rate that satisfies the condition that the accumulated taxes equal the discounted benefits:

$$b_1 \sum_{n=65}^{\infty} \frac{(1 + r + c)^{L_{62}} (1 + c)^{n-62}}{(1 + i)^{n-65}} (P_n) = \sum_{t=1}^{L_{65}} \overline{T}_t (1 + i)^{L_{65}-(t-1)}.$$

If c is zero, then i is the real rate of return. Since the nominal rate for any rate of inflation, c, can be calculated by simply adding c to the real internal rate of return, c was set at zero in the computations.

As noted, the historical data needed to calculate taxes for past years were taken from various issues of the *Social Security Bulletin;* the average benefits were those actually paid and in most years were not based on the adjustment procedures in the Social Security Amendments of 1977. For the projection period, the data needed to calculate taxes paid and benefits received (note that all the cohorts considered in the chapter retire during the projection period) were available in some cases from the Social Security Administration and had to be approximated in others by using data from the Social Security Administration and the Census Bureau. In particular, projections of numbers of retired beneficiaries and taxpaying workers were available for every fifth year through 2050, and probabilities of survival by sex and individual year of age were available for every year through 2085. These data, together with historical values for benefits, and population weights by age and sex derived from Census Bureau projections, permitted the approximation of all the other items needed for the computations.

Index